The New
Rainbow Bridge

The New Rainbow Bridge

HEAVEN ON EARTH

DEREKA DODSON

Quicksilver Publications

First published by Quicksilver Publications in the United Kingdom in 2012.

Copyright © Dereka Dodson 2012
This edition published 2012

ISBN 978-0-9557600-6-8

Typeset in Garamond 14 point. Transcripts in 13 point.
Scanning by Bookcraft Ltd, Stroud - www.bookcraft.co.uk
Printed by Henry Ling Limited, Dorchester, Dorset.

Dedication

*To Angus and the dolphins,
Jonathan and Sarah*

Contents

Acknowledgements

I should like to say a big thank you to my parents and all the friends and teachers who have helped me along my path. Especially to Bridget and Daphne, who introduced me to crop circles, Margaret W (Maggie) who sadly died in January 2011, Lisa, Margaret N, Marian and Sid, Tina and Nigel, Carroll and David. To all the healers who have helped me, with special thanks to Kate for all the home visits, to Francesca in Glastonbury, and Anne and Julia at the Crown Centre in Devizes.

An additional huge thank you to friend and healer Julia, who undertook the mammoth task of deciphering my handwriting in the purple ink, typing and editing my manuscript for *The New Rainbow Bridge*. Special thanks go to Trish who agreed to put the book together, without all her hard work and editing it would not have happened.

I should also like to say thank you to: Nanna, Beryl, Flordemayo, Simon, Roy and Peg, Dawn and Keith, Harold and Sally, Priscilla and Mike, Anne C and John, Anne G and Edryd, Chris and Vic, Stella, Kate and Chris, Stephen and Victoria, Simon Peter, Isabelle, Granville and Andy and Lyndon, to all the friends I made in the Wiltshire Crop

Circle Study Group (WCCSG) and all those involved in the Save Our Tree Campaign in Devizes.

An enormous thank you to Mavis and 'The Energies' for all the hours we have spent in conversation. It was the Energies who suggested I write this book and encouraged me along the way.

Finally, my undying gratitude to Captain Hugo E. Marxer, thc US Navy ship *Canopus* and her crew who saved my life in October 1980.

Dereka Dodson
Devizes

Chapter One
"Do you believe in aliens, Dad?"

Room 516, The Georgian Terrace Hotel, Atlanta, November 12, 2004.

Yesterday I returned to Atlanta, Georgia. It was to the British Consulate here that I came just over twenty-four years ago in order to be repatriated back to England. I had been found a few days earlier on October 28, 1980, drifting in a life raft alone in the Atlantic Ocean. I was 185 miles south east of Charleston, South Carolina.

The ship that found me was the US Navy Submarine Tender *Canopus*. Tonight I am meeting up again with the then Captain of that ship, Hugo Marxer and his wife, Jackie. We are to have dinner at the home of one of their daughters, Shawn, her husband David and baby son Max.

I will try to explain later how and by whom since 2003 I have been asked to write this book.

Shortly after my rescue I wrote a book entitled, *For Those in Peril*. This gave details of the storm that led to the capsize of the yacht *Demon of Hamble*, owned by my soulmate, on which he and I had been sailing. We were heading for Fort Lauderdale in Florida. The storm blew up on the morning of Thursday October 23. At around midnight, after a huge

1

wave had rolled us over through 180°, we waited for what seemed like an eternity before the boat completed the 360° roll. As she came back upright her stern was underwater, her bow up in the air. She sank within two minutes. Some twenty minutes later the ocean also claimed her skipper, Angus, and *Demon* had gone.

I was left alone in the water surrounded by mountainous waves, clinging to the boat's life raft which had inflated upside down.

In that earlier book I described how difficult I found it and how long it took, firstly to right the life raft and then to clamber into it. The raft was my home for five nights.

At daybreak on the Friday morning, as I tried to assess my situation, I was given a message. I was told that I would be rescued, but that I would have to wait for four days. I had no idea at the time how that message was sent to me or from whom it came. All I knew was that it was very clear and I believed it.

The message was true. At dawn four days later, on Tuesday October 28, looking east, I saw the silhouette of a ship on the horizon. That ship was *Canopus* – but she was heading east, away from me.

Would anyone see my tiny raft? I couldn't keep watching, but prayed very hard. When I first saw she had altered her course, she was so far away that for some time I couldn't tell whether she was sailing towards me or away from me.

Finally I was able to see her bow wave, it looked like a seagull skimming the water. I cried a lot and sent up some mega thank yous as she grew larger and larger until she stopped alongside, towering above my raft and me.

For Those in Peril was never published. At the time it was therapeutic to write about what had happened. Also, as the title implies, I wanted to try to make things easier for anyone who might find themselves in a similar situation.

To this end I brought the life raft back to England and worked with the manufacturers on a few modifications that I suggested. Their rafts are now less likely to inflate upside down, a boarding ramp is included in the standard design and the survival gear is secured so that it can no longer fall out should the raft be upside down.

While I was at their factory in Liverpool they demonstrated to me how to turn a raft the right way up. They did this in an indoor swimming pool which in no way compared to trying to do the same thing in an Atlantic storm! I was told that they were unable to obtain insurance to cover trials in storm conditions at sea. They were pleased to be able to inspect a raft that had survived a four-day storm.

I am glad now that the book was not published in the early 1980s. It was only in the year 2000 that I came to understand more about the communication that was received not only by me, but also by Hugo Marxer. I was told on the Friday morning that I had to wait for four days. Hugo was told the night before they spotted me to alter the ship's course.

He told me he had no idea why he had altered course that night. I jokingly said to him that I was afraid he had to because I was expecting to be picked up at dawn and they were the only ship in the area!

The messages we both received were, I now believe, sent by dolphins. I shall talk more of this later on.

It was not until I wrote about spending five nights in the life raft and being picked up early on the Tuesday, that I made the connection with having checked in to the Georgian Terrace Hotel on Thursday – for five nights! I am due to check out early on Tuesday and catch an 8.30 a.m. flight to Phoenix. There could hardly be a greater contrast.

I remembered staying near the Lennox Shopping Mall in Atlanta at the Terrace Garden Inn on Peachtree some fifteen years earlier. It turns out that hotel was on Peachtree Road and this one is on Peachtree Street, but with no tempting shops!

I find myself in a luxury suite in one of Atlanta's most historic hotels. Suite 516 has a fully fitted kitchen with a tall fridge-freezer, large electric cooker, microwave and washing up machine, in addition to the usual coffee/tea making machine. What I thought was a second wardrobe contains a huge washing machine and spin dryer.

Were I to sit my five-foot raft on top of the vast bed it would look very tiny. Add in the lack at sea of any food or water and the hotel wins every time!

There are two framed prints hanging in front of me on the wall above the desk in the bedroom. The one on the left shows a lady dressed in a 1920s-style evening dress. The dress is terracotta, and has a gold-coloured train which she drapes elegantly over her right arm. The background colour of both prints is black.

Just to the right of the lady in the left-hand picture is a square grid pattern made up of 25 gold hearts. The other lady is standing in front of a similar grid of golden hearts, this time to the left of the picture, and rectangular in shape. Some of the hearts are obscured by her right arm and shoulder. When I counted the hearts I found that there are 34 showing.

To me the significance of these two pictures was enormous and made me realise why I had been sent to this room in this particular hotel at this particular time.

Nobody was looking for me in the ocean in 1980. When our Mayday call was sent out we were upside down, so it probably went to the creatures of the sea.

My rescue gave me a second chance at life and I decided to celebrate two birthdays each year. So in 2004, on June 10 I reached the age of 60 and then on October 28, I became 24 years old in my 'second' life – putting me in to my twenty-fifth year.

As I counted the 25 hearts hanging on the wall I made an immediate connection and was stunned to find 34 in the other picture – that being *Canopus'* registration number.

Below the 25-heart grid the lady has two cords draped from her left wrist, each ending in a tassel. This to me emphasised the 'second chance'

Also, the two cords are wrapped twice around her left arm. Not trusting my hands to hold sufficiently tightly to the straps on the raft, I put my left arm down through one of them. That saved me.

I find it hard to begin writing about all the information that the picture on the right offers me.

When I leave here on Tuesday, as I said earlier, I am going to Phoenix in Arizona. My reason for being there is to attend a conference next weekend – Signs of Destiny 2004: Crop Circles and the Road to 2012.

I mention that before talking about the second picture because I see within it several references to crop circles (of which much more later!)

The colours are the same, a terracotta dress largely obscured by a voluminous golden wrap. From her right arm the lady drapes her wrap with much of it lying on the floor. On the other side she holds out a shorter length – it ends at hip level with three rows of seven tassels hanging down to calf level. On both sides the vertical sections of the wrap have printed on them a circular pattern, very similar to an English crop circle that came two years ago in Wiltshire in a field of wheat. There are three more circular patterns showing in the material lying on the floor.

On her head is a spectacular headdress. It has a frame, which looks like a crown or an upside down lampshade frame, from which protrude nine tall plumes fanning out in a circular shape. My description of the frame is exactly how I tried to describe another recent Wiltshire crop circle, also in wheat.

That shape, wider at the top than at the base, also describes the shape of the ancient towers at Sillustani, in Peru, the Chullpas. These shapes had interested me so much (having seen their design replicated in the crop circle) that when in Peru in 2003 I decided to leave my travelling companions and go to see the towers for myself. It was a magical experience. When I rejoined the group back in Cusco I was told that the experience showed in my face.

I am not a numerologist but I understand from a friend that the number 9 represents completion. Issuing from the crown are the nine plumes. In 2004 a crop circle contained a square divided into nine equal squares. The three rows of tassels give a total of 21. By tradition when one reaches that age, one is given the key to the door. Many people are looking for a key to unlock the mystery of the crop circles.

The 21 tassels reminded me of Saturday August 21 2004. That was the date when I finally plucked up the courage to visit one of that summer's most amazing crop circles. The design of this formation looked to me like two dolphins encircling four baby whales. Sadly, the farmer was persuaded that the formation had been man-made and was very angry.

I understand that he armed himself with a gun to dissuade any visitors and also asked police to prevent people trying to enter from the car park on the hill above the field.

The formation had been there for four weeks before I tried to visit it. On the Saturday I waited until I thought I saw the farmer going to lunch, then tried to hide my car down a track behind a hedge. This was at the opposite side of the field to the car park.

From there it was a long walk up one of the tramlines (tractor tracks) to reach my destination. I kept saying to myself "think invisible" – not only did I not want the farmer to see me, I didn't want anyone deciding to follow me and increase the risk of being spotted.

The tramline up which I had chosen to walk led me into the formation at the tip of a fin of one of the two dolphins. It felt as if I was entering the most sacred of spaces – I found that I had taken off my shoes before treading on the downed wheat without even thinking about it. I can only describe that feeling as 'Heaven on Earth'. It gave me part of the title for this book.

I had with me a video camera and a still 35mm camera (both non-digital). I had taken three pictures as I approached the formation. I took picture number 4 on that film (see photo 150 in colour plate section) as soon as I had both feet on the tip of the fin. Later that afternoon I took my film to a one-hour development service.

Photo 4 confirmed my first feeling on entering the formation. Some of us believe there is a rainbow bridge that connects heaven and earth. On photo 4 that bridge is shown like a bar code lying horizontally on the wheat within the formation. I didn't see the rainbow when I took the photo but it was gifted to me on the film.

I will elaborate on this later – I often find on my photographs evidence of 'energy' that I was unable to see with my eyes, but which on occasions I have felt.

Back to the number 21 . . . I'm talking now of photo number 21 on the same 35mm film (photo 151 in colour plate section). I walked all round the outside of the circle, the dolphin element, before entering the inner whale section. Half way round the whales, I was standing roughly in the heart region of one of them, using my video camera. Through the view-finder I saw with my right eye a rush of pink energy spiralling in towards me. I could feel that rush of beautiful energy and hoped that there would be something amazing on my video film.

It wasn't until the next day that I got to watch what I had filmed – nothing out of the ordinary did I see! That didn't really bother me because the energy I'd seen coming in presented on the still photo I took standing in the same heart space. Photo 21 has on it a UFO or, as they say, a flying saucer. Once again, I will try to explain later what I mean by 'they'.

All the above was written over the space of several days in Atlanta. I smiled to myself at the airport when I was told that the flight to Phoenix would be boarding at Gate 34, *Canopus'* ship's number again.

Shortly after returning to England in 1980 I went back to work at the dental practice in Surrey that I had joined in 1969. Any National Health Service Dental Surgeon who exceeds the holiday time they planned to take is kept pretty busy trying to catch up with their patients when they finally report back for duty. So it was for me.

I think that probably everyone who survives an incident – where others do not – has a feeling of guilt. 'Why me?' is the question you ask yourself. For me it was a question I answered by deciding that it had not been my time 'to go'. In that case, what was I supposed to do with the rest of my current life, until it *is* time for me to go?

No answer came to that question, and I felt as if I was just plodding along in a kind of limbo – waiting to be told my reason for surviving. It wasn't until the month of May in 1998 that I got my first clue.

My mother and I used to drive regularly to Wiltshire to visit my godmother, Beryl Townsend. We used to stay with her at her flat at The Ark in Devizes. When she moved into residential accommodation we would book into the nearby Bear Hotel for the weekend. On the Friday afternoon two of her friends would join us at the hotel for tea. We would drive on the Saturday to visit her at Derry Hill, some 8 miles out of Devizes and return home to Surrey on the Sunday.

It was on one of these Friday drives that a strange thing happened. Looking back it was almost as if a switch in my brain had been turned on. We had just driven past the military base at Upavon when I found myself saying to my mother, "Of course you realise we are now entering crop circle country?" She seemed unimpressed and I carried on driving, wondering from where on earth the thought had come.

At tea-time one of the friends, Daphne, arrived on time while the other, Bridget, arrived late, apologising and saying she had been at a meeting. I asked her about the meeting – thinking in terms of the Women's Institute or something similar. She seemed reluctant to answer, turning her head away as she muttered very quickly that it had been a Crop Circle meeting.

"I beg your pardon?" I said, as I felt the switch in my brain re-activated. Poor Bridget once again tried to gloss over the answer as she repeated it.

I then realised that she half expected me to ridicule the subject of crop circles. As soon as she saw that I was more than a little interested, she opened her handbag and gave me a photograph. It was an aerial picture taken of a recent formation in oilseed rape that was about two weeks old. I couldn't believe my eyes. All I knew about crop circles was that they were round and in wheat, found mainly in Wiltshire, with all the crop within the circle lying flat on the ground. I had seen a black and white picture in a newspaper some years earlier, showing just that.

The photograph I now held was so different. The colour of the crop was bright yellow. Where the plants had been laid down in the design of the formation it showed the green of the stalks. It wasn't a solid green circle in a yellow field. The central crop was standing, solid yellow. The perimeter or circumference was depicted by 33 tongues of flame, each of which looked to be many yards long.

I was in awe. Sensing this, Daphne then opened her handbag and handed me a set of photographs that she had taken on the ground when she had visited the formation a few days earlier.

I decided that I had to go the very next day and see it for myself. Bridget and Daphne gave me instructions telling me where to find it, across the A4 road opposite Silbury Hill in the field to the right of and just below the West Kennet Long Barrow.

What I hadn't been told was that the field was on quite a slope up towards the Barrow. This meant that you could get a very good view of the formation from the road.

I abandoned my mother in the car and left her reading the paper. As I walked up the track towards the field I passed people returning – either from the Barrow or the formation

– maybe both. I shall always remember a young boy aged around eight saying to his father as they went by, "Do you believe in aliens, Dad?" I couldn't hear his reply. For me the question was, did I? I'd never really thought much about it.

As I walked up one of the tramlines towards the circle, I was surprised at how tall the crop was. I'm 5'7" and some of the flowers were above my head. They had a sweet perfume which, whenever I smell it now, reminds me of that day. When the crop gets a little older, it smells more akin to stale cabbage – hardly a perfume!

Quite why I had not only a camera but also a video camera with me that weekend I have no idea. Both were put to great use. I must have spent well over two hours inside that crop circle. It's very difficult to describe what it feels like to enter such a formation. They all have their own energy and I believe that no two people experience that energy in the same way. You just have to go in and see what you feel, if anything. It's no good listening to the experience of anyone else, and relying on that, without going in yourself.

Also, you don't necessarily have to feel that energy for it to impact on your body. Samples of water left in crop circles show changes in energy when photographed at biophoton level. Human beings have a very high water content – over 70%. Needless to say the 'switch in my brain' was fully turned on that weekend – I was totally hooked from day one.

I started to awaken and was given a helping hand on to my spiritual path. My desire to learn and experience more was so great that I worked ever shorter weeks. Within a year I had sold my flat near the surgery and bought a tiny cottage in Devizes. I would drive there after work on a Wednesday evening, and stay until 5 a.m. on Monday, arriving back at the Surgery in time for my 8.30 a.m. patient.

This arrangement proved unsatisfactory for everyone. In October 2000 I stopped working as a dentist and moved my mother down to Wiltshire, having sold what had been the family home for some fifty years. I was already busy in Wiltshire helping as a volunteer with the administration of a locally-based group studying the crop circle phenomenon.

I think my own personal research into the subject was probably sparked by that young boy asking his father about aliens.

Initially, I was fascinated by the energy, the beauty of the designs, the physical changes in the crops and the soil within the formations. However, I wanted to know who was responsible for what was happening, why it was happening and how to establish communication with 'the manufacturers'. Who had turned on that switch in my brain?

I worked at trying to develop a telepathic link with these beings or energies. By the year 2000 it felt as if there was a connection. Things I had been told would happen, began to do so.

In July 2002 I had my first reading with a Psychic Counsellor, Mavis Meaker. She had been highly recommended to me. I had been warned though, that I would have to be prepared to hear and accept the truth, the whole truth and nothing but the truth!

By the time her team of spirit guides had combined with mine in order to tell me, through her, exactly what was what, I felt pretty stunned. Between them they knew everything about my whole life.

Then came my chance to ask questions – I didn't seem to be able to think, let alone ask. They prompted me by asking if I wanted to ask about another relationship. Another human relationship didn't interest me, but I suddenly thought I could ask about the connection I had been trying to develop with those putting the 'information' in the fields.

To my amazement a 'direct line' was opened and I was given answers to all my questions. I shall write more about this later. When she finished, Mavis said she couldn't believe what she had just been saying!

In February 2003 I had the second of many such readings. Once again I was able to ask about some of the crop circles. They asked if I wanted to have a greater communication with them.

"Yes," I replied.

"Well, we cannot communicate with sadness, anger or fear, Dereka," I heard Mavis say. I was then told that I needed to replace the sadness with joy, the anger with boundaries and the fear with love. I realised then it was time to do some inner work on myself in order to achieve anything.

During the last three years I have become aware of formations in clouds in the sky, as well as in crops. I have tried to photograph most of them.

Last year, as I opened my eyes after a meditation one morning, and looked out of my bedroom window, there in an otherwise clear blue sky, was a white cloud that looked just like a signpost. A vertical line, with a shorter line at the top pointing to the right, slightly above the horizontal. It was so striking I went down into the garden to take a picture.

When I looked at the photograph later, the shape looked quite different – there were four sides to it, with an addition on the second vertical line. I knew what I thought it represented but waited to ask through Mavis.

"It is the start of your book," I was told. This confirmed my thought that it looked like a hand holding a pen, writing on a note-pad. They instructed me to take the pad with me everywhere I went, and to write down my feelings.

My task, I was told, is to write about my experiences, going way back to my teens. They told me this was when I first started dealing with their dimension. Their idea was that I should try to explain to those who find it hard to understand there is more than what we can actually see and touch in our three dimensional world.

To help illustrate this, they have shown on some of my photographs, energies that I couldn't see at the time of taking the pictures.

Not long after being told about writing this book, I asked if it was time to begin.

"You are a most impatient lady," was the reply! The next time I asked I was told, "Yes, most definitely."

I couldn't think how to start and it got to the point where they were saying to me, "What is the problem with starting your book? You already have the scribblings." I think they were referring to a few articles I had written for a crop circle newsletter.

They really have been very helpful in nudging me into action and going through events in a chronological fashion.

Going back to Atlanta was my way of making myself get started. The help that was so lovingly given to me when I looked at the two pictures above the writing desk made me cry.

When Hugo and Jackie picked me up on the Friday evening, he handed me an envelope containing photographs. These had been taken by the ship's photographer as I was being rescued. They certainly brought back the feelings I experienced at the time.

Some of the names in this book will be real, some I shall change. A few weeks ago I was thinking that, because this has to be written in the first person, the ninth letter of the alphabet is going to be peppered all over the pages. To break this up a little I propose to call some people by initials – probably not their own!

I was sitting in a café writing notes in my notepad. At the very moment I thought about using initials instead of names, a wee spider let itself down from my fringe past my nose.

As I understand it, Native Americans credit the spider, amongst other things, with having given us in her web the letters of the alphabet.

I was very grateful for the vote of confidence, as I perceived it, from the spider. I am under strict instructions not to write from my head – but from my heart.

CHAPTER TWO
Learning to heed my premonitions

The energies from beyond this dimension that are encouraging and helping me to write this book, suggested I might start by saying I grew up in a family who could be said to be 'unconscious'. They believed in what they could see and touch: so when I started to have premonitions or hear voices it was just thought I had become a bit wacky.

I had no idea where the information I was receiving had come from. It seems to me now that I have always been protected and often forewarned of events.

During the summer holidays we used to stay for two weeks at Pagham on the south coast of England. We always stayed at the same bungalow which belonged to friends of my grandmother. All the bungalows in the road were built on the sea side of the road, actually on the beach. You walked out of the back directly onto the pebbles which sloped down to the sea. At high tide the waves were only a few yards away; sitting at the dining table and looking out was like being on the ocean on board ship. The building was in actual fact a modified railway carriage. To open some of the doors it was necessary to lower the window using the wide leather straps to unhook it and lean through to turn the door handle on the outside of the carriage.

We used to watch the liners as they sailed in and out of Southampton, silhouettes on the horizon, counting funnels to try to identify which 'Queen' was sailing by – 'Mary' or 'Elizabeth'.

A few hundred yards off shore was a Mulberry Harbour. It only became visible as the tide went out. A square concrete block, a reminder of the war – World War II.

Looking out to sea after dark, on the horizon the bright beam of a lightship flashed as it rotated. When I was about twelve years old, and for many years after, I enjoyed going down the shingle at night; sitting, watching and listening to the waves breaking on the pebbles, dragging some of them back down the beach. The bigger the waves the better.

Sitting there on my own I loved to look up at the stars and watch the reflection of the moon on the water. I became almost mesmerised watching the beams from the lightship sweeping round.

It was there alone on the beach at night that I started to do my first serious thinking. I am a war baby, having been born four days after D Day, on June 10 1944. I have no memories of the last months of World War II, being too young. My mother was twenty two years old when I was born and my father, twice her age, was in the RAF at the Ordnance Board, working with Barnes Wallace, designer of the bouncing Dambuster bombs.

I find it hard to imagine what it must have been like to be so young, with a new-born baby, listening as the engines of the Doodle Bug bombs cut out above, and then dropped to earth. I don't know how many times she had to crawl under the Morrison Shelter, otherwise known as a metal table, with me – not only on those occasions but also whenever the air raid siren sounded.

It was the Mulberry Harbour, built for the war, that started me thinking not only about the war, but also the sea. I began to wonder how people who had lost their loved ones to the sea, felt about it themselves. So many men and women from all of the Services, were claimed by the ocean one way or another, it is their grave. There were also many civilians. The sea claims fishermen, sailors, swimmers . . .

Why, at the age of twelve, did I start having such serious, some would say morbid, thoughts about the water? At that age the sea also meant sunshine, summer holidays, swimming, fish and excitement, seaweed, pebbles, shells and sand, rock pools – even the smell of the seaside. And I loved really big waves.

I remember, at the age of six, nearly drowning myself and my father. The family was staying with my grandmother on the Isle of Wight. She was the only grandparent my brother and I ever knew, my mother's mother. My father and his three brothers were orphaned young and my mother's father died of cancer during the war. Her mother joined the WRAF – Women's Royal Air Force – not long after being widowed. After the War she became a Borstal Matron. Her first Borstal was at Camp Hill, now a prison, on the Isle of Wight.

It was at Camp Hill that we were staying; my brother was only two at the time. We had been lent a car and my father was taking me swimming. I wanted huge waves and kept asking him to drive further on to the next beach. Looking down from the passenger seat, as we drove around the coast road, the waves didn't look big enough to me.

I selected my 'mega wave' beach – these days there would have been red warning flags flapping in the wind, forbidding swimmers to enter the water. I can remember being surprised as we walked into the sea by how much bigger the waves were than they had seemed from the safety of the car.

The very first one knocked us both over. I remember it so well, I kept my eyes open as we were swept under the water. My father was about four feet to my left, even now I can see the colour of his swimming trunks. We slid on our stomachs over chaos – sand, shells and pebbles were dragged with and below us until the next wave rolled in, picked us up and spat us back out on the beach. I had escaped unharmed but my father was bleeding from under his right arm. Back to Borstal I was taken!

What a lesson that was for a six year old. It taught me always to have the greatest respect for the sea, and for water in general. I had been too fearless until then.

My mother always had a fear of water. She was first taken to Pagham when she was six, my grandparents used to stay regularly with their friends. My grandmother was a very strong and stylish swimmer, so there was probably no great need for my mother to learn to swim as a child. It was as an adult and a mother of two that she took lessons. A friend had persuaded her, saying she would never forgive herself if my brother or I were in difficulties in the water and she was unable to save us.

It wasn't only in the summer that she was taken to Pagham. She was ten years old when the family went there for Christmas. One night, when everybody was in bed, a tidal wave swept over the bungalow, considerably rearranging the beach. The pebbles were no longer all at the back. Being woken by the sound of the wave going over would have done nothing to lessen her fear of water.

As I sat at night alone on the beach, despite what I knew about the power of large waves, they still fascinated me. The lack of fear had been replaced by respect.

Over the years, as a teenager, I spent many hours trying to imagine what it must be like to have a loved one lost at sea, a grave without limits – covering much of the planet. Could those left behind ever enjoy going to the seaside? Would they want to swim in the sea? Would they ever want to swim or play in any water for pleasure?

In 1980 it happened to me, as Angus my soulmate and I clung to the upturned life raft in the Atlantic. It was a huge wave that swept him away. I was then thirty-six years old but I now believe that Energies in the next dimension had been preparing me for twenty-four years. How loving is that? The sea and the darkness and my situation were somehow familiar territory, although I had *never* seen such monstrous waves.

A few years ago a friend told me she had heard that one's address is very important. I wondered how important Station Road might be as an address! For three periods in my life I have either lived or worked in a Station Road. The converted railway carriage on East Front Road, Pagham was No 80. Was I being prepared for the year 1980? My rescue ship *Canopus* came to me from out of the east.

Our first family home backed on to the fourth green of the golf course at Effingham in Surrey. On one side we were able to walk straight into a wood.

My parents bought part of a field in Station Road, but had to wait five years for building permission. My father used to bicycle there and back, and work really hard converting what was part of a ploughed field into an orchard and garden. When it was finally built the house was called Brookfield. This had been the name of the house of my great grandfather in Didsbury, Manchester where my father and his brothers spent part of their childhood. For us the name was quite apt as the remainder of the field was to one side and the garden extended back into a bluebell wood and ended there at the edge of what was then a brook or stream.

The method of preparing me for events in the future changed when I was nineteen. It was then that I had my first premonition. Four of my school friends, my brother and I had booked a cabin cruiser for a week's holiday on the River Thames.

The night before we were due to pick up the boat I had a very vivid dream. In my dream I was already on the boat, leaning out and using a little fishing net. I was trying to retrieve one of my fingers from the water. When I woke up I recalled the dream but didn't really take any notice of it.

Between school and university I had been working for six months as a dispensary assistant at a chemist shop in Cobham. The first day of the holiday was also my last day at work. My parents picked me up from work and took us to Thames Ditton. On the way there my mother twice asked me what was the matter. I said "Nothing." I felt fine.

However, she had sensed that I was very tense although I wasn't aware of any tension or sense of apprehension. I had forgotten my dream.

By the time we had all boarded the boat it was getting quite late. One of the men from the boatyard came with us to show us how to handle the boat and go through the locks. He took the boat through the first lock as we went up river. After a while we turned around to go back to the boatyard and drop him off. By the time we reached the lock again the lock keeper had gone off duty so our boatman operated the lock gates. We needed to stop and pick him up after he had let us through and closed the gates – not a manoeuvre we had been taught! The boat went out of control. Putting my hands behind me I leaned backwards to give the girl at the wheel a clearer view of what was happening.

There was a great crump as we hit a wooden post sticking up out of the water. We had been travelling sideways. I felt no pain but as I looked at my right hand I saw that my ring finger was only hanging on by a piece of skin. It had been split open down the inner surface so that the bones were bare and not quite as they should be.

I tried to put it back together again, scraping the skin back around the bones and held it all in place as best I could. Luckily we had hit a corner of the square post and only one finger was in the way – all four fingers could have been crushed had we collided with one of the flat surfaces. I remembered my dream – it wasn't quite right – my finger was still just attached. I didn't have to fish it out of the water, lucky me! Anyway, I had no net!

Some while later, lying on an operating table in the Accident and Emergency Department at a local hospital, the initial numbness and the local anaesthetic both started to wear off. As I watched the last few stitches being inserted I felt them. The Casualty Officer apologised but said he didn't want to use any more anaesthetic. I had watched the whole operation because I found it fascinating. At one point I decided it would be great if I was still in my dream. I literally pinched my left thigh to check it out. I was not dreaming. After my finger was put in plaster of Paris I was taken back on board the boat.

That night turned into the longest night of my life. For someone who was due, a few weeks later, to start training to be a dental surgeon, I was given some very practical lessons about pain. Pain can bring you out in a sweat, painkiller tablets only last so long, they take time to kick in. Earlier that evening I had learned what it feels like when local anaesthetic wears off too soon, and later how it feels when there is insufficient blood supply, and gangrene starts to set in. This was not actually a one-night experience but continued for several days.

At first light I saw that I had bled through my plaster – it was no longer white. My poor brother, who was only fifteen at the time, was wonderful and came with me as we caught a dawn bus back to the hospital. I tried to hide my scarlet plaster from the other passengers. All that happened at the hospital was that a second layer of plaster was applied over the first. At least it didn't look so gruesome. We went back to the boat and the holiday began.

As soon as my Godmother heard about the accident she contacted a Radionics practitioner in Ireland in whom she had great faith. When we got home I had to put a drop of blood on a piece of blotting paper and send it to him. He then wrote to say that it was a nasty fracture but he saw no need for amputation. He said which finger on which hand was involved – something my Godmother didn't know and we hadn't told him.

It took an hour for the technician to remove the double layer of plaster when I went to the Orthopaedic Clinic near home. When I saw my finger I had quite a shock. It was black and shrivelled and looked just like a stick removed from a fire. It had dry gangrene, the Consultant advised amputation.

Since I was just about to start my training at King's College Hospital I was referred to the Consultant there. Remembering the advice from Ireland, my GP, a family friend, suggested a visit to Harley Street to see someone described as *the* hand specialist.

I was sure that deep down I could feel a slight tingling sensation in my finger and told the Surgeon that. He wouldn't even touch my finger – he picked it up with a pair of forceps, scrunched it and told me that common sense should tell me my finger was dead.

Nobody wanted to touch my hand and I really began to feel like an untouchable, or leper.

Initially it was no better at King's. One option was to try to leave the top joint as a 'useful hook'. Another was to remove the whole finger and the bones above it in my hand, close the hand up and nobody would ever notice that I only had three fingers! Plastic surgery was ruled out and I felt very despondent as I went off for x-rays.

My mother had worked as a nurse during the war in the operating theatre at Leatherhead Hospital, an out-post for King's College Hospital. She had worked with the Consultant in the past and, while they waited for me to return, told him how much she had admired his work.

By the time I got back with my x-rays an appointment had been made for me to see the Consultant Plastic Surgeon the following Wednesday. He was based at the Queen Victoria Hospital at East Grinstead but came to King's one day a week. How true it seemed that it's not *what* you know but *who* you know.

As the nurse un-bandaged my finger on that Wednesday, I watched the Surgeon's face, he was my last hope. When he saw the 'black stick' he winced and my heart sank. But he took my hand in his and started to examine the damaged finger, gently squeezing it between his thumb and fingers – the first person to touch it since the night of the accident.

After a while he said "I can't be sure the nail bed is dead."

"The nail bed?" I said. "But that's near the end. I've been told the finger is dead and has to be amputated."

"Good gracious," he sounded shocked. "You can't just go chopping off a young girl's finger."

The tears started running down my face. For several weeks I had felt like an Untouchable, a very uncomfortable feeling. Here was a man who was not only happy to touch my dead finger but was also prepared to try and save it – which he did.

It was two years later when I was twenty-one, that I had my second premonition. I had completed my pre-clinical training at King's College in the Strand and was a clinical student at the Dental School at the hospital at Denmark Hill in south London. Roy, the technician who ran the laboratory in the Conservation Department, and his wife Peg, were very accomplished ice-skaters. They used to organise an annual coach trip from the hospital to the rink at Richmond. I couldn't skate but had enjoyed trying on several occasions. It used to take me most of a session on the ice to pluck up the courage to let go of the barrier! The remaining time I spent trying to get up after my falls. I thought it would be fun to go on the trip and booked my place.

The night before going I had a dream. In the dream I was lying on the ice, having fallen. Before I could pick myself up somebody accidentally skated over my outstretched left hand over all four fingers.

After waking up, this premonition was very different in that I couldn't get the dream out of my mind. It was with me all day. I started to feel a knot in my stomach. My solar plexus had kicked in. I tried to tell myself I was being stupid and should ignore these feelings of foreboding. As I sat in the coach on the way to the rink it got worse, the feeling in my solar plexus actually became a pain. If anybody had asked me what the matter was, on this occasion I could have told them.

Finally, I decided to remove the risk of my dream coming true. I wouldn't hire any skates, I wouldn't go on the ice. I'd sit at the side and enjoy watching everybody else. Within seconds all my feelings of apprehension and discomfort had vanished – and I thoroughly enjoyed the evening.

That had been a huge lesson. I decided in future I must listen to my body and heed my dreams.

CHAPTER THREE
Demon *sinks in my recurring dream*

There followed a period of some fourteen years with no such warning dreams. I didn't forget them though and was always aware I might have another at any time.

Angus and I used to talk about what we would do in the event of another of my premonitions. I once asked him what would happen if, the night before we were due to catch a plane, I had a dream about a plane crashing and felt as I had after the skating dream. He said we'd cancel the flight and go the next day.

"But what if nothing happens to the plane?" I asked.

"That's alright – you weren't on it," he said.

Whenever we discussed the paranormal he would talk about 'little wigglies' that are invisible to our eyes, like sound waves. We talked about life after death and communication with the next dimension. Not long after his father died, his mother wanted to visit a medium. He decided to go with her because he didn't want her to be taken for a ride and/or upset. He found he need not have worried, and was pleased to hear what his father had to say, through the medium.

In 1980 Angus raced *Demon* across the Atlantic and flew back to England, leaving her at Newport, Rhode Island.

He had decided to sell her in America and we flew over to sail her down to Florida and deliver her to the agent in charge of the sale.

Before we set off, I started having dreams again, a recurring dream in which *Demon* was sinking. Every time she went down bow first, followed by the stern. I didn't talk about it because I never got the bad feeling in my solar plexus. The first time I did feel it was just as we were about to step aboard after arriving from England.

I sensed that the boat was not happy – she didn't want to be sold. I always used to talk to her – in the same way that I say "Hi" to my car in the mornings and ask if it will start please. Over the years different cars have had their own personalities and little ways.

A knot started to develop in my stomach. I felt guilty about the fact that she was being sold and I didn't know what to say to her. I just put my hands on her wheel and silently said hello and congratulated her on crossing the Atlantic with Angus.

My problem was that I had to keep my dreams to myself; it wasn't as easy as cancelling a flight and taking a different plane. We had to take *Demon*, the agent was expecting her.

I suspect Angus picked up on my premonition without my ever talking about it. We were at Annapolis in Maryland during their Boat Show when he asked if I would mind if we didn't go down to Florida. His idea was that we could just spend a couple of weeks sailing around the Chesapeake Bay area.

That idea seemed like the perfect solution to my problem and I said I didn't mind where we spent the two weeks. He just needed to tell the lady agent. She was at the Show and I accompanied him when he went to ask how important it was that the boat be delivered to Fort Lauderdale. My heart sank as I heard her say it was vital *Demon* was there, magazine advertisements saying she was lying at Fort Lauderdale were already out.

So it was that we sailed, heading south. Two mishaps delayed us and prolonged *Demon*'s life.

The first happened in New York harbour. Sailing down between Long Island and Manhattan was like being in a dream. As a child I had always had an ambition to visit New York and thought the only way I could possibly do so would be to work there as a nanny, with my employers paying my fare. This was not my first visit, but looking up from *Demon* at the skyline along the East River was unreal.

Our problem in the harbour turned out to be a submerged wooden packing-case, which, when we hit it, bent the propeller shaft. We had to cut the engine to stop the severe vibrations, and set the sails. First though, Angus climbed overboard and dived underwater to assess the damage, the third time I had watched him do this.

The first time had been several years earlier, on the Norfolk Broads. A sheet of polythene, unseen in the water, had wrapped itself around the propeller of a cabin cruiser that had been loaned to us. Angus had been unable to remove it by hand and climbed back on board. The only gear he could engage was reverse. So it was that we spent the rest of the day motoring stern first. This did not go un-noticed; as we went into a pub for a meal that evening, a small boy was heard to say, "Dad, Dad, there's that man who's been going backwards all day."

The second time, a few years later, Angus had been able to sort out the problem. We were on one of the British boats that had been on exhibition at the Annapolis Boat Show.

It was a day trip in Chesapeake Bay with a host of people on board. A rope managed to find its way overboard and wrapped around the propeller. Holding his breath underwater, he managed to free the rope and was cheered by all as he climbed back on board.

Now we sailed down the coast, heading for Cape May in New Jersey for repairs.

Angus' daughter, Sally, had flown out to America to greet him and *Demon* when they reached Newport in the July. She had spent the summer there and joined us for the first part of the journey south.

CHAPTER FOUR

Five nights alone in the life raft

Our journey started in London on September 22, a Monday. Angus decided to spend an extra day there so it wasn't until the Wednesday that we set out for the States. We took the Tube to Heathrow and caught a British Airways flight to Boston. The in-flight movie was *Kramer vs Kramer*, which had us both in tears.

When we arrived in Boston we found there were no hotel rooms available. There was a mayoral conference in town so we hired a car and drove to Fall River where we spent the night. The next day we drove down to Newport, Rhode Island and went on board *Demon*. She was on a mooring at the Ida Lewis Yacht Club. It was the last day of yacht races in the America's Cup, and there was much ballyhoo as *Freedom* and *Australia* came in after their last race.

Angus went off and met up with Sally and we later moved *Demon* round to D Dock in Goat Island Marina. We spent five days at Newport. On the Saturday the skipper of *Captiva II* came on board for lunch. He invited us to go for a trip on *Captiva* on the Sunday. It was during this trip that I saw a map of all the wrecks off Cape Hatteras. I didn't like it, it gave me a very uneasy feeling.

What I did like was a large book entitled, *In Praise of Sailors*. All three of us were much impressed by one particular verse (taken from the poem 'The Triumph of Time'), written by Algernon Charles Swinburne.

> I will go back to the great sweet mother,
> Mother and lover of men, the sea.
> I will go down to her, I and none other,
> Close with her, kiss her and mix her with me;
> Cling to her, strive with her, hold her fast:
> O fair white mother, in days long past
> Born without sister, born without brother,
> Set free my soul as thy soul is free.

Something else that impressed me on that boat was her perfectly varnished woodwork. It looked so good I found myself wanting to bite into it, it put me in mind of toffee apples!

Another thing that upset me on board was that the chunky silver ring I always wore on my little finger, mysteriously broke in two. It was a ring I had chosen as a present from my great aunt. Angus had always admired it, and said he wished it had been a present from him.

The following day on the Monday we had lunch with friends at the Pier Restaurant. Afterwards we went shopping to stock up *Demon* before setting off for Annapolis in Maryland.

We left Newport on the Tuesday, heading out into Rhode Island Sound and began our voyage south. We wended our way through the islands before passing inside the northern tip of Long Island. We spent the night at Clinton in Connecticut, Sally and I having spent the day sunbathing.

Wednesday night was spent at Stamford, further down Long Island Sound. We ate in a restaurant where Angus' jacket was messed up. It was hanging over the back of his chair when a hapless waiter dropped a plate.

The following day was still sunbathing weather. We took on fuel and water before leaving Stamford. There were several boats there that we recognised from Newport. We headed on south putting in to City Island, the Bronx, New York at around lunchtime. During the afternoon we went shopping and went ashore again in the evening to eat. Angus left us in the restaurant to go and buy some wine to have with our meal. Sally felt too hot and went back to the boat before we did. Just as we got back it started to pour with rain, we were lucky not to get soaked.

On Friday morning we left City Island and headed into the East River. Planes were taking off over us as we passed La Guardia Airport. Later a light aircraft amazed us by flying under one of the bridges over the river. Motoring down past Manhattan was like being in a film. The views were fantastic as we passed all the rush-hour traffic ashore. We took so many photographs.

I was still on deck when we were crossing New York harbour. The water we had taken on at Stamford had a strange taste and looked a bit yellow. I decided to go below and boil some so that we had decent water to drink. As I stood up I saw the packing case submerged just in front of us. Too late to avoid it, it was then that we hit it and the propeller shaft was damaged. The vibration throughout the boat was alarming. Angus went into the water to inspect it and decided that from there we must sail and not use the engine any more.

Angus sailed us past Liberty Island so that we could photograph the Statue and then headed out under the

Verrazano Narrows bridge into the Atlantic. As I looked back at the bridge in the distance the sun in the east was reflecting on the car windows as they drove over it. It looked as if the bridge was lit up with fairy lights.

Leaving New York, we sailed all day, heading along the New Jersey coast. During the night we passed the bright lights of Atlantic City in the distance. We were on automatic pilot and took it in turns to be on watch.

During Saturday there wasn't much wind. We were overtaken by the odd empty Coke can as Sally and I lay on deck sunbathing. By evening we were off Cape May in New Jersey. This was our destination for repairs but the wind had dropped completely and we were becalmed.

Angus tried without any luck to signal to a passing yacht that we would like a tow. There was nothing for it but to anchor for the night. Angus gave us three bearings to check. We took it in turns to get up and check these during the night to make sure we hadn't moved. We passed around an alarm clock to wake us up, and make sure no one missed their shift.

In the morning there was enough wind to sail into Cape May harbour and manoeuvre *Demon* into Utsch's Marina under sail alone. She was lifted out of the water and put on a cradle by the roadside. The damage to the prop shaft was inspected. It was definitely bent.

A ladder was provided for us to climb back on board. Across the parking lot was the Lobster House Restaurant, where we ate that night. Sunday was the first of four days we spent living at the Marina, climbing up and down our ladder.

On Monday the bent shaft was removed and we waited for a new one to arrive. We started a big search for batteries for the echo sounder. A man came on board to ask if we had any fuses. He put me in mind of the detective Colombo. We ended up talking religion.

We had a plague of flies on board. It was a fifteen minute walk into town where the staff in the supermarket were very friendly and helpful, and we bought our fly spray. That night the Lobster House was closed and Sally cooked.

Tuesday brought fine weather. The boat was getting dirty with all the grit we were bringing up the ladder. We climbed up a bank to the road and over to another marina but we were still unable to find any batteries. A new shaft was delivered but it had the wrong taper and thread, another was required.

We were starting to become known in the supermarket. We found a local bar where we waited ages for Sally's choice on the juke box to be played. It was Frank Sinatra singing 'New York New York'. She said she had a personally signed copy of the record.

By Wednesday we were all starting to get a bit frustrated by going nowhere. Sally and Angus read a lot and I just pottered. She showed me how to tie a single length of material as a very elegant evening dress and a lot of talking was done. The second new shaft arrived after five o'clock, too late to be fitted. This meant staying another night and another visit to the Lobster House.

On Thursday morning we went shopping. The new shaft was fitted and once again *Demon* was afloat. We settled up and bade fond farewells to Ernie Utsch and set off along Cape May Canal to Delaware Bay. It was a lovely sunny day and great to be on the move again. We tried fishing but had no luck.

We kept going all day and night. We wended our way along the Chesapeake and Delaware Canal. This took us from the Delaware River into Chesapeake Bay and we then went on to Annapolis. We arrived on the Friday morning at 8.30. Angus found the berth he had been told we could use in the Yacht Haven.

The US Sailboat Show takes place annually at Annapolis in October. Angus and I had attended the Show every year for several years but this was the first time we had arrived by boat. We left *Demon* and headed into the Show, collecting our passes from our friend Tom. We later met up with another friend, Malcolm, and began a very sociable weekend.

On the Sunday Sally went back on board ahead of us to sort out her packing. Her visa was running out so she had to fly home from Washington D.C.

During that morning Angus talked to me about not taking *Demon* down to Florida. He said he was feeling tired and didn't want to take on the long sail. We went to find the agent to ask her about not going but sadly she said it was vital that the boat should be there.

On Sunday night I dreamed about four separate aeroplane crashes and woke up on Monday morning knowing that Sally and Angus weren't going to see each other again. The plane crashes had put my recurring dream of *Demon* sinking to the back of my mind. I was worried about Sally's flight to London.

Malcolm very kindly lent us his car so that Angus could drive us the thirty miles to Washington. I sat in the back of the car and didn't think either of them had seen me crying.

There were no tears as we passed the field advertising 'certified sod'. It had always amused Angus and me and certainly amused Sally. But was her plane going to be safe?

We had lunch at Trader Vic's at the Hilton Hotel, and then walked to the airport bus with her. She got on, although the bus wasn't due to leave until 3.15, and we headed back to the car. As we were about to walk round a corner and out of sight, I made Angus stop and wave to her, a final wave. Her plane was safe but they never did see each other again.

We were delayed by an accident on our way back to Annapolis. Finally, we reached the Boat Show and returned the car to Malcolm. Around five o'clock Angus moved *Demon* to a more central location, we tied up alongside *Scotch Mist*. We were invited on board for drinks and found a TV on the boat. They had some amazing gadgets in the galley including a bottle crusher. I spotted a badge that appealed to me; it said 'I'll do it tomorrow'. Later we went out for supper and saw Malcolm and Tom. It seemed strange without Sally; there were just the two of us on board now.

On Tuesday we went shopping and then met up with Malcolm for lunch. We left Annapolis at three o'clock and motored out to Chesapeake Bay. We headed for Chesapeake Beach for the night. As we gently eased our way into a mooring, wary about the depth, we were greeted by some very noisy ducks. It sounded as if they were laughing at us. We ate on board.

The next day we crossed the mouth of the Potomac River separating Maryland from Virginia. We put into Fleeton for the night, heading into a beautiful sunset. We found some very luxurious showers and just sat on deck talking. Neither of us was bothered about eating. It was a lovely setting.

By contrast we put in to Portsmouth on the Thursday evening tying up alongside a Holiday Inn where we ate.

Angus was taking photographs of the places we visited as he was looking forward to giving a talk about his trip to the members of the Royal Southern Yacht Club on his return.

We caught quite a large fish that day.

The next day we walked into Portsmouth Old Town. We were very impressed that the supermarket provided us with a courtesy car to drive us back to the boat with our shopping.

It was time to take to the intra-coastal waterways to continue our journey south. The Dismal Swamp Canal was closed. It didn't actually sound very inviting. Instead we took the Albermarle and Chesapeake Canal from Chesapeake Bay to Albermarle Sound.

The weather was warm and sunny. At one point we stopped and were standing on the tow path when we heard a man's voice shout out, "Angus Primrose!" We then saw the only yacht we had seen heading north: it was a Seal 28, one of Angus' designs.

We stopped off at the Atlantic Yacht Basin at Chesapeake for oil and air filters for the engine. That night we cooked our fish.

We went from Virginia into North Carolina. We had seen numerous naval vessels and a great gathering of coastguard ships and helicopters. When I commented on all the coastguard presence Angus replied, "Yes, but they're never around when you want them." (How true that turned out to be.) We also watched a pair of dolphins in the river.

In North Carolina we were on the Alligator River when a sudden squall caught us and caused a tear in the mainsail. We had intended to go to Morehead City but instead we put into Beaufort for repairs to the sail.

We spent the next day, Tuesday, in Beaufort. It was very hot. We sat outside for lunch and had beef sandwiches with rosé wine. Once again we went shopping, getting a taxi back. We were stocking up for the trip from Beaufort to Fort Lauderdale.

I wrote and posted several postcards and phoned our friends Maria and Peter in England. I gave Maria an update on our journey; she was going to liaise with the surgery about my date of return to work. She sounded very depressed and when I went back to the boat I said to Angus that it wouldn't surprise me if they had split up by the time we got back to England.

Angus phoned his office. I asked if there was any news of Sally. There wasn't, so obviously there had been no problem with her flight. So what of my 'knowledge' that he wasn't going to see her again? I banished the thought from my mind. Angus had a sleep and I went to look round the shops.

That night we again went ashore to eat. Angus asked for pineapple with his gammon, which they had to get from the bar. I chose chicken and had enough to feed four people. I was told I was the first person to bring their own doggy bag.

After supper we collected the sail and had an early night.

I remembered our taxi driver earlier in the day, when he had wished us, "Good winds behind you."

On Wednesday, October 22 we left Beaufort at 8.30 a.m. We motored out into the Atlantic. We were about ten miles north of Cape Lookout which is midway between Cape Hatteras, the 'Graveyard of the Atlantic', in the north, and Cape Fear to the south. I tried to dismiss the names Lookout and Fear from my mind. This was going to be the longest sail I had ever experienced and I was looking forward to it. The weather was warm but it was a grey day with no sun and precious little wind.

"Right, we're supposed to be sailing so let's put the sails up," said Angus. He hoisted the mainsail, wound out the jib and switched off the engine. There we stayed, with no wind.

If we were going to make any progress we'd have to use the engine. We motor-sailed with the mainsail up but no jib.

Sometimes if the wind picked up we could sail, but for most of the day we had the engine running. Angus started a log of our engine hours so that we could keep a check on our fuel consumption.

The sea was really calm and I had no difficulty preparing double decker cheeseburgers with all the trimmings for our supper that night.

It was after we had eaten, at 8 o'clock that a pod of dolphins began to play around the boat. We were thrilled to see them.

"Come up to the bow," Angus said. "They'll play around up there." He was so glad I could see them for myself. He had often told me how they used to accompany him when he was sailing single-handed. "You know something?" he said, "I always find the same ones come back to you."

We both tried leaning over and stretching down to reach them from the bow but we were too high up. Angus went back to the cockpit, called to them and managed to stroke them as they leapt out of the water. It was getting quite dark and I wished I had a flash for my camera. They stayed with us for about an hour.

Looking back, I think that the dolphins were trying to warn us about the storm. They kept approaching the boat from the port side, towards the sea, diving under her and coming up on the starboard side, towards the land. I think they were telling us to head inland. I felt really sad when they left us but Angus said, "Don't worry, they'll be back."

At 11 p.m. he decided to have two hours sleep. He asked me to wake him at 1 a.m. or earlier if there were any problems.

We were on automatic pilot and I decided to stay on deck. We had had a wonderful evening and it was a beautiful night. It was very warm and there was still hardly any wind. What little there was came from behind us. The jib seemed undecided; it didn't know which way to go.

After about half an hour it made up its mind, it wanted to go out to port. In the past when I had been left on watch while Angus slept, the slightest thing I did to alter the boat had woken him. Would I be able to change sides with the sail without waking him? I freed the jib sheet on the starboard side and pulled in the sheet on the port side for just two or three gentle clicks of the winch. I then had a quick look down below to see if Angus had woken. He was still fast asleep so I finished pulling in the sheet and checked below again. He hadn't stirred.

I didn't have to wake him, he came up on deck at 1 a.m., looked around and said, "I see, we've been playing, have we?"

"Yes, it's great and it's the first time you didn't wake up. I really enjoyed myself."

"Are you okay for a while?" he asked, "Can you do another couple of hours?"

"I'm fine," I replied. "I'm really enjoying it."

"Well, I'll go and have another couple of hours then."

Before going back down below Angus pulled the jib in. At the time it wasn't doing us much good. Not long afterwards the breeze, still from behind us, filled in a little bit so I let the jib out again. Angus continued to sleep.

It seemed no time at all and he was back up on deck. It was 3 a.m. on the Thursday morning. Angus thanked me for giving him such a long spell before I took his place in the quarter berth to the left of the companionway steps and slept from about 3.30 till 7 a.m.

I found it hard to believe that there could be such a change in the weather in just three and a half hours. The sea was so rough I was surprised it hadn't woken me earlier. I had never seen waves so high. The wind was probably storm force and it was pouring with rain. The direction of the wind was the same, from behind us.

The radio was on and we were picking up a local station at Charleston. After the news came the shipping forecast which bore no resemblance to the weather we were experiencing. They talked of winds up to thirty knots and wave heights of four to seven feet.

I called up to Angus who was on deck and told him there was a small craft warning on the radio. "Don't worry," he replied, "it's quite normal for them round here. They always say that when the waves are expected to go over three feet."

This was the second time within twelve hours he had said "Don't worry." I wouldn't normally be worried about being in a storm with Angus in charge. I was very much aware, however, of a knot in my stomach. My dreams about *Demon* sinking were starting to have an effect.

Breakfast time was the regular time for me to take my seasick pills. They were all I ate. Angus had nothing, not even a coffee.

It was obviously going to be a thoroughly uncomfortable day. I elected to stay where I was in the quarter berth. I had to have the leeboard up to avoid being thrown out.

Angus came back down below. After a while I wondered if eating something might ease my stomach. I asked him to pass me a banana. It made no difference. I remained just as screwed up as before.

Around mid-morning Angus went back on deck, lowered the mainsail and wound in practically all of the jib. When he came down again he said, "We've hardly any sail at all now, but I reckon we're still making five knots with the wind as it is, still right behind us and the current against us."

As the waves started crashing over us he sat reading, apparently unconcerned. Few words passed between us.

At about 2 p.m. we shared a gin and tonic, Angus having spilled his when he went up on deck.

Despite the weather it was surprisingly stuffy and muggy down below. I asked if we could take out the bottom drop board. Angus agreed that it would be worth the odd bit of rain getting in to have some air. The middle and top drop boards on *Demon* had been replaced by a pair of doors, like saloon doors.

Angus had entered another Moody 33 in the 1976 Observer Single-handed Transatlantic Race (OSTAR). On that occasion he was forced to return to Plymouth after the boat rolled through 180 degrees and was dis-masted. He realised after this experience that if the hatch cover is not closed over the drop boards they can fall out when the boat is upside down. This was why he designed the doors.

Leaving out the board had made a difference, it was less muggy. Angus made himself a coffee. I didn't want one and dozed off for a while.

When I woke up Angus wasn't there. A couple of minutes later he emerged from the loo. "What an extraordinary thing," he said.

"What?" I asked.

"I've just been seasick!"

"What? You? How many times in your life have you done that?"

"This is the third time. Once when I was fourteen, then a few years ago between Plymouth and Hamble [in England].

That time the cold and diesel fumes got the better of me."

I offered him a couple of my Stugeron seasick tablets and to my amazement he accepted them. He had hardly eaten anything. We had both had two or three stackers (potato crisps) and a liquorice toffee each.

At 3.30 p.m. Angus laughed and said that the OSTAR party in London would be in full swing. "They'll all be saying lucky old Angus, sailing down to Florida."

I was up by this time and finding it very difficult just to sit at the table, the boat was being thrown about so much by the elements.

It got to about 7 o'clock and I decided to try and eat something, Angus didn't want anything. To prepare any sort of food was going to be very difficult. I buttered a burger bun and put a banana in it. This had no effect on my screwed up stomach, I was still full of apprehension.

At 9 o'clock Angus decided to have a couple of hours sleep. "Don't bother to go on deck at all, you'll only get soaked. But check the course, bearing 1-7-0. Take it from the compass on the Radio Direction finder. The easy way is to check for 10° West of North." These were the instructions he gave me before he climbed into the quarter berth.

I sat opposite him by the table, wedged in with my feet against the steps. Every fifteen minutes I struggled to stand up and check the compass. It should have been a simple task, but I was finding it almost impossible. On one occasion, as I stood I was thrown forward. I was expecting to hit my face against the steps but I was suddenly thrown backwards and the impact came against my back and not my face. At least I had ended up back where I had started. Only another fifteen minutes and I'd have to do it all again, I thought.

After an hour and a half the wind suddenly changed direction. It went round through 90°, and instead of coming from behind us it was hitting us right on the beam on the port side. This had the effect of kicking up the sea even more.

When next I checked the compass I noted with some concern that our course had gone from 170 to 203. Angus was still asleep, I wondered what to do. He had told me not to go on deck, just make a note of any change of course and at what time so that he could correct it later on the chart.

Despite his instruction I decided that I would go up on deck. I ought to have a look. I don't know what I expected to achieve, it just seemed only fair that I should do my bit. I clambered into my oilskins and on went my sou'wester. I struggled up the steps, through the doors and up into the cockpit.

The ensign we were still flying was stretched out absolutely rigid in the wind, not fluttering at all, it looked like something solid. Normally we would have taken it down at sunset.

I carefully closed the doors and just stood there hanging on to the handles either side of them. As I looked around I was horrified. I had never seen seas like it before, not even in pictures. The wind shift had thrown the waves into great confusion. As far as I could see, through the darkness and the driving rain, *Demon* looked okay.

My problem was how to get back down below to safety. How was I going to open the doors when I didn't dare let go of my grip on the handles either side. I stood there frozen for what seemed an age but was probably only a couple of minutes. Gradually I released the grip of my right hand until I built up the confidence to let go. I opened the doors and made my way back down the steps.

As I closed the doors Angus woke up.

"The wind's changed, hasn't it?" he said.

"Yes," I replied.

"What's the visibility like? Has it improved?"

"You're joking," I said, "I can't see anything further than the next wave."

"What about the course?"

I looked at the compass. "We've gone round to 205."

Then Angus said, "It's getting worse, isn't it?"

All I did was nod 'yes' to that question. I wanted him to get up and be in charge. I didn't want to be on watch any more.

"I hope that's the most adventurous thing I have to do tonight," I said, referring to my trip on deck.

"Are you okay for another couple of hours?" asked Angus. My heart sank, I wanted to say 'no' but said, "Yes, sure." Then I added "Are you going back to sleep?"

"Yes, but not right now. I can't because I've got to have a pee."

He didn't immediately get up; he just lay there, curled up in a foetal position. It must have been around 11.15 p.m. when he finally got up and went on deck.

I decided there was no way I was going to let him get back in that bunk. When he came back down I had positioned myself between the steps and the bunk.

"You climb in there," he said, "I can sleep just as well sitting down here."

I didn't need to be told twice and did as he said. Angus seemed to have abandoned any idea of going back to sleep, and went up on deck again. This time he went to the aft cabin for the radar reflector and hoisted it. He came back and started rummaging around all the lockers.

"What are you looking for?"

"It's all right, it's all right, it's here somewhere, it's here somewhere," he muttered.

"What is it? Can I help?" I asked.

"It's all right, it's all right, I'll find it, I'll find it."

Finally he produced the safety harness, something I had *never* seen him use before.

"I thought I'd better get this out, just in case I have to go on deck to do anything in the night." He put the harness on the floor, just in front of the steps. The mere presence of the harness meant that Angus was more worried than usual.

He then sat down opposite me, by the table, and just stared at me with what I can only describe as a glazed expression. He didn't blink, he just stared. I had never seen such a look on his face. It seemed to have turned grey, matching his Lionheart sweatshirt.

He knew something. I didn't know what and he wasn't saying. I needed to say something but again, I didn't know what. Instead of speaking I just winked at him, smiling as I did so. I hoped it would snap him out of whatever it was. On a previous occasion, when I hadn't known what to say, a wink had done the trick. The wink worked. Angus pulled himself back together and smiled back at me.

"Do you fancy a whiskey?" he asked.

"That's a good idea. It's time for my seasick pills, it'll help me wash them down."

I looked round at him as he struggled against the motion of the boat. To pour the drinks he had to strap himself in by the sink. He passed the belt that was fixed at one side of the sink round his hips and clipped it into a hook on the other. As the boat was tossed around, Angus had difficulty controlling the flow of water from the tap and swamped my whiskey.

"I'm sorry, I've drowned yours," he said, giving it to me as I lay against the lee board. "If there's too much water in it, give it back, I'll have it."

"No, that'll be fine, thank you," I said as he went back to pour his own.

At the time *Demon* was heeled well over to starboard. All of a sudden I found myself thrown violently against the hull to port. There was a strange but not loud sound from up on deck. By now Angus was standing beside me.

"Was that us or it?" I asked, wondering if the extreme movement was something the boat had done to itself or if it was what the storm had done to the boat.

"We just did a funny gybe," Angus replied. I was still puzzled. We rolled over to starboard again and I was lying back against the lee board.

Angus handed me his drink. "Hold this for a minute," he said, "I'm just going on deck to look."

He slid back the hatch cover, opened the doors and struggled up the steps. I was sitting up with a glass of watery whiskey in each hand. Angus had his left foot on deck and his right foot still on one of the steps; he turned to look over his right shoulder and said, "What *have* I done?"

As he was saying this we rolled over to port again. This time we did not stop. I was aware of water flooding in past Angus' legs as he fell back in on top of me.

"We're going over," he said, his face inches from mine, as he reached for hand holds. He obviously had no chance of closing either the doors or the hatch. He had opened up the boat at just the wrong moment, the very moment we were rolled upside down.

I thought I understood what was happening because Angus had described so vividly what had happened to him in 1976 in a similar Moody 33, *Demon Demo*. He had said, "There was all this water falling, we went over and it suddenly went dark."

We ended up in a heap on the deck head, which had become the floor, half submerged in water.

"Are you alright?" he asked as we struggled to our feet.

"Yes, are you?"

I knew I had knocked my teeth but that was all.

For a short while the lights, now under water, stayed on. Then they went out. "The lights have gone," he said. Luckily it had by now stopped raining and the moonlight through the water was eerily illuminating everything.

"She's not coming up, she's not coming up."

Angus' voice was full of concern. We stood there waiting for what was probably only a minute, but seemed like an eternity. What next?

"Come here, over to this side."

We both stood to the starboard side, which had been the port side when the right way up. Here we hurled ourselves repeatedly against the hull. We were trying to shift the weight distribution so that the keel, now above us, would move away from its central position and help us back through the other 180°.

"*Demon*, come on. Come on, *Demon*," we pleaded with the boat, but nothing happened. All the time we were taking on more water.

"Oh God," said Angus, looking up at the hull and then at me. "How do we get out of this?"

I knew he wasn't expecting an answer from me, he was thinking out loud. I looked back at him and waited for the answer I knew would come.

"Right, we've got to swim out of the boat," he said.

I needed him to explain. "I'm sorry but I'm a bit disorientated," I said. "Tell me exactly where to go and what to do."

"We've got to go through there," he said pointing down under the water to the cockpit. "We have to swim out where the hatch cover and the doors are, and we'll come up outside the boat."

"OK," I said, silently thanking him for his patience. I was far from happy with the idea and still having difficulty locating everything upside down.

"Just a minute," said Angus as he moved over to the radio to send out a Mayday. It seemed the logical thing to do, but as the aerial was mounted on top of the mast, way below us, if it was transmitted at all, it was probably to the creatures of the sea.

"Mayday, Mayday. Yacht capsized fifty miles off Cape Fear. Mayday Mayday," he repeated. "Yacht capsized fifty miles off Cape Fear."

As he finished he looked round at me with a questioning look in his eyes. Was I ready to swim for it?

"I don't know if that'll work or not. Wait." He had noticed something. "She's coming up," he said. I wasn't aware of any change but he had sensed that *Demon* was starting to right herself.

"Now listen," he warned, "when she comes up she's going to go down – fast." He went on to say, "Stick right with me. We've got to get up to the bow and free the life raft."

"OK," I said, nodding my head to show him that I understood.

I thought momentarily of the large bar of chocolate stored in a drawer for such an emergency but there was no time. I grabbed hold of the back of Angus' jeans with my right hand

and followed him to the companionway steps. He muttered something about a lifejacket as we fought our way there. Goodness knows where it would be in all this turmoil. The water was well above my waist, and cushions and floorboards, anything that would float, were bobbing around.

At the steps I let go my hold on Angus. I needed to hang on either side of the steps and follow him up on deck. *Demon* was still taking a great pounding from the storm.

As I stepped into the cockpit I saw that the stern was awash. I didn't see the mast, and the guard rails were virtually flattened. *Demon* was slipping away, stern first – unlike my dreams in which she had always gone down bow first. We went up the port side. I used what was left of the guard rails to help pull myself up behind Angus. We both squatted by the life raft. Angus was facing the stern and I was to his left.

He had grabbed *Demon*'s knife as we came on deck and used it to cut the line that secured the raft. He gave me the knife and tried to pick up the bulky pack. It didn't move. Angus realised there was another line to cut.

"Can you give me the knife back?" he asked.

"Hang on," I said, "I'll open it for you."

I opened it and, as I passed it to him, our eyes met and he said, "Darling, you're incredible." He then freed the raft and picked it up, giving me back the knife.

"Well, just chuck it in the water, that's what they say." Having said it, he did so, following it almost as though he were attached to it.

The raft's CO_2 cylinder inflated it right under *Demon*'s bow. This seemed to lift the bow higher out of the water, making her go down even faster.

"Get into the water. Jump," shouted Angus.

I went to lift my left leg over the rail. By now the wind was blowing the raft to the right of the boat. It had inflated, but upside down!

"No, not that side, this side," instructed Angus. I climbed over the rail on the starboard side and just stepped into the water, there was no need to jump as the bow slipped under the sea.

I felt a tremendous pull of suction as *Demon* vanished. It dragged me away from the raft. I now had to try to swim to Angus. I chose to do this backstroke because that way I could see which way the waves were coming. Angus was shouting above the wind to guide me. "Swim, swim, swim. This way, come here, swim, *swim*."

"I *am* swimming," I shouted back.

"Swim harder."

"I can't," I sputtered, as a wave broke over me. Swimming was made even more difficult because it felt as if I had buckets attached to my feet. I had been very lazy when I turned up large hems on my jeans. I had only attached them in four places, and now they were filling up with water.

All the time the wind was blowing the raft away from me and Angus' voice didn't seem to be getting any nearer. I started to wonder if I was going to make it. I then faced the fact that I could be about to drown, this was serious. My life did not flash before me. I simply thought, 'I'm only 36, I'm not ready to die yet.' I swallowed a lot of water as I struggled to swim through the monstrous waves.

"You're not trying," goaded Angus.

"I am."

"I've seen you swim better than that. Come on. Swim, swim, swim." With his encouragement I swam for all I was worth.

"Put your hand out," he shouted, sounding much closer. He grabbed my left hand and our fingers entwined. At last I had reached him.

Looped around the base of the life raft was Terylene strapping. I grasped hold of one of these straps and held on with both hands next to Angus. I was glad he hadn't given me a life jacket to wear, that would have made swimming even more difficult.

"Now we've got to get this bloody thing the right way up!" he shouted.

"Can we just wait a minute, please? Let me get my breath back." Angus nodded and looked all around at the sea.

"Hold on tight, for God's sake," he warned me. I looked up and saw the wave that he had seen. It had to be over fifty feet high. Immediately I decided not to trust my fingers to hold on to the strap of the life raft. I pushed my left arm down through the loop so that the strap was up under my arm pit. I held my left wrist with my right hand up against my body. As the monster wave hit us Angus was holding on with his hands. It wasn't enough. He spluttered as he was swept away.

"Angus!" I shouted after him.

There was a full moon shining and it was easy to see him. He was about ten yards away. Now it was *my* turn to shout to him, to guide him back.

"Here, here, here." I could see the back of his head as he swam backstroke, as I had done. The wind was blowing the raft, and me, away from him and he didn't seem to be getting any closer.

"Here, here, here!" I kept shouting to him. Gradually he came nearer. He was only about six feet away when he shouted out.

"I've got the green light."

The raft had a line streaming from it with a green water-activated battery attached. Angus had hold of this so all he had to do was haul himself back to me. Thinking he was safe I took my eyes off him for a few seconds, to look behind me. I wanted to make sure there wasn't another monstrous wave approaching. As I looked away I heard him shout, "Don't let go of the raft."

When I looked back he was gone. There was no sign of him. "Angus, Angus!" Desperately I called his name, there was no answer. Again and again I shouted, "Angus! Angus!" In disbelief I couldn't understand how he had disappeared so quickly. As I clung to the raft I felt numb, Angus was dead. Angus and *Demon* had gone. I was on my own.

I had never felt so alone. What was I to do? My situation was dire; I was fifty miles out in the ocean with an upturned life raft and no reason to believe that our Mayday had been transmitted. My first thought was that I would go too. That way we would be together and that would be beautiful. Angus had been my reason for living and he had drowned. What reason now did I have to live?

As I thought seriously about letting go, I remembered his last words. "Don't let go of the raft." If I died too, no one would ever know what had happened. Friends would think that we had just sailed away and done a disappearing act. While I hesitated, a newspaper story I had read some weeks earlier flashed into my mind. A lady known as the Lowry heiress had been flying in a light aircraft with her husband and children when they crashed into the sea, and she had lost her whole family. She survived by clinging on to the wing of the plane until she was rescued by helicopter. At the time I thought how could she do that? Having seen her family lost, how did she have the strength to hold on? This story presented to me as a challenge. If she could do it, I could do it. All I had to do was wait for the helicopter, I decided one was coming.

I had plenty to keep me occupied, getting myself and the raft over each mountainous wave as they approached from different directions. The worst bit was going through the foaming crests of the waves. I don't know how much water I swallowed. The trick was to take a deep breath in as the wave arrived and try blowing it out as I went over the summit, through the foam.

Initially, I didn't worry about the raft being upside down. I had persuaded myself that help was on the way. The water seemed quite warm and most of me was out of the wind.

I decided I couldn't think about Angus. I just had to concentrate on survival. What surprised me was the beauty of the moonlight on the phosphorescence in the water, little lights, red and green, flashing. What was I doing noticing such a thing in those circumstances?

There was quite a pain under my left arm where the strap had stopped me from being swept away. Instead of just relying on the one strap, I kept my arm down through it and reached round to the right to hold a second loop with my left hand. With my right hand I grasped another. Unless all three broke I would stay attached to the raft. I huddled there, out of the wind.

After a while the events of the night seemed to have had an effect on my stomach. It felt as if I needed to go to the lavatory. I didn't want to make a mess in the helicopter when it arrived, so I had to do something about it. Easier said than done. I let go of the raft with my right hand, undid my jeans and eased them down, one-handed, around my knees.

The next battle was to get my bikini bottom down too, this was a race against time – could I hold on? Finally I was ready. I waited and nothing happened for a while then all of a sudden I broke wind! That and nothing more. I couldn't believe it. Had anyone ever taken so much trouble for so little? I tried to make it more worthwhile but to no avail. It was much harder to get my clothes back up than it had been to get them down, all one-handed with the storm still raging.

I estimate it was after about an hour that I saw what I thought was a bar of chocolate floating past me. I grabbed it and saw that it was a silver foil pack wrapped in polythene. It felt a bit soft but I put that down to the mild temperature of the water. I tucked it under my left armpit for safety.

I realised that the contents of the survival pack were escaping through the door of the raft which was under water. By luck I was positioned by the door, anything that would float had to come past me.

The next item I rescued was a flare. This went under my arm with the bar of chocolate. Then came a polythene bag containing two sponges. This, too, went under my arm. Next up came a pump, a black hemisphere of rubber attached to a hose.

My right hand by now felt quite painful. The strap I was holding had gouged holes in three of my fingers. I decided to use the pump to alter my grip. I threaded the end of the hose down through the strap and held a double thickness of the tubing with my hand. It was kinder to my fingers. I pushed the pump between my legs and sat on it. It was a bit like sitting on a bar stool and gave me a little bit of buoyancy.

While I was doing this the next escapees exited the raft. Two paddles presented themselves. I gathered them up and attempted to add them to the collection under my arm.

I hung on to everything for about half an hour, but I decided I was holding on to too many items to be safe. I made a decision to let go of the paddles. They seemed quite small and, as I watched them float away, I thought being fifty miles out to sea, they probably wouldn't be much help.

"In seas like these, who needs paddles?" I thought.

I didn't see anything else coming up out of the raft and just clung on to it and all I had rescued so far. I stayed like that for probably another hour, waiting to be saved.

Gradually my hope of a helicopter began to fade. Even if one was looking for me, how on earth would they find me? I needed to do something about righting the life raft.

In the middle of the base of the raft I could see a strap. I would have to pull on this to lift the raft out of the water and flip it over. There was an inflatable tube supporting the canopy under the water. I hoped this would help me.

I managed to reach the strap with my right hand and tried tugging on it. The far side of the raft lifted out of the water, but no matter how hard I tried to pull it further, it only lifted up to about thirty degrees. I just didn't have enough strength one-handed and couldn't use my left arm which was busy doing other things. I had several attempts but never got it any higher than the initial thirty degrees.

Trying to do this in the stormy conditions was quite exhausting. I decided to have a rest and a think. I dared not alter the way I was holding on with my left arm.

The next time I tried I lifted my right knee up on to the base and pushed down with it as I heaved on the strap. This was no more successful. The raft didn't lift any higher out of the water. If I had been able to put both feet on the base and tug with two hands on the strap I was sure it would have been easier but that wasn't an option.

I kept trying. and kept taking rests to recover my strength. I decided I needed to get help from a combination of the wind and the direction of a helpful wave. This I tried several times. On about the fifth attempt it worked. Suddenly the raft was the right way up.

The only casualty of flipping over the raft was the loss of the pump. I lost hold of it and had to watch it float away. I still had my bar of chocolate, the flare and the sponges. These I threw into the raft through the door.

Then it was my turn to get in. I couldn't do it. The two rings of the base of the raft were only about eighteen inches high, but I was too exhausted to heave myself up. Even at the best of times I can never lift myself out of the water in a swimming pool. I never get out at the side, I always use the steps. My arms didn't seem to have any strength left in them and my clothes seemed to weigh a ton. Also I didn't want to risk losing hold of the raft in the wind.

Despite all the water that I was still being forced to swallow, I decided just to continue as I was, clinging to the raft. I hoped I would build up my strength again and felt rather stupid not being able to get into a perfectly serviceable life raft. The moon was still shining and, once again, I watched the little red and green flashing lights in the water.

There didn't seem to be any urgency about getting into the raft until about half an hour later. Suddenly I saw three solid white shapes about four feet below the surface of the water. They passed under me from right to left and then they came back the other way. I suddenly thought they might be sharks. I *had* to get into the raft. I reached in through the door and round to the left with my right hand. I found an internal strap and pulled on it as hard as I could.

I managed to lift my right knee up on to the rim of the base. I then reached in further to another strap, pulling myself up out of the water. I managed to get my head into the raft and wedged it inside the left-hand-side of the door.

There I was stuck, I couldn't do anything more to get myself in. I decided I was at the mercy of the next wave. If it came towards me I'd be thrown out again, if it came from behind me I hoped I'd be tipped in. I must have looked a comical sight as I waited. My luck was in, the wave hit me in the back and I splattered into the raft. Safe at last, I just lay there saying, "Thank you."

There had been a little light on top of the raft on the outside and I could now see that there was also one on the inside. I saw that there were two orange bags which had held the survival gear. The bases of these bags were attached by tapes to the internal straps that went all round the base of the raft. The bags had drawstrings for closure.

While hanging upside down, the pounding of the storm had caused one string to break and the other to give under the weight of its contents. This was why all the gear had escaped. I collected up the items I had managed to save and put them in one of the bags. I tied the drawstring to one of the straps so that the bag was held at both ends.

It had been so difficult getting into the raft, I decided I didn't want to risk getting thrown out again.

I lay spread-eagled on the floor with my head up against the base rings. I held on to the straps either side of my head and tucked my feet under two others. The odd wave would break in through the door to my right and the raft was tossed around like a plaything of the storm.

There was what I called a rear window in the roof of the canopy with a skirt hanging down. Water came crashing in through that too so by now there was quite a lot of it in the raft.

After about an hour I was starting to get used to my situation when, all of a sudden, I found myself doing a cartwheel across the ocean. It was my second capsize of the night. As I was bowled along, I hung on to the straps and said "Oh *no!*" out loud. I ended up suspended, facing the canopy now under the water again, my feet still hooked into the straps.

As I wondered what to do, the water was flooding in through the door. I arched my back and decided to try to weight the raft to one side in the hope that it would flip back up. I leaned as hard as I could to my right and to my great relief we came back up again, it was easy. We didn't capsize again and I spent the rest of the night lying spread-eagled on the floor.

As Friday dawned, the little light inside the raft went out. When I leaned out of the door and checked, I found the outer light had also gone out. I wondered if they would come on again when it got dark. (They didn't.)

It was time for a prayer and a serious talk with myself. I had to face up to the fact that Angus had gone, he was dead. In the past I had worried about the possibility of him being ill and in hospital dying, with family only allowed to visit. I wouldn't be able to see him. This way, as it had happened, I felt privileged to have been there when he died. I decided that he loved his boat, he loved the sea. He was near one and in the other. I told myself that it was perfect and beautiful. I thought about crying but, if I did, it would only be self-pity, so I told myself there was no need for tears.

Now I had to face up to the reality of my situation. I was fifty miles out from land and nobody knew I was there.

What was I going to do? How could I survive? I didn't really have any answers. The storm was still raging.

It was then that I received a message, like a thought coming into my mind. The message said, "You will be rescued, but you've got to wait four days." It was so clear that I believed it. I had no idea where it had come from but it was most definite.

Four days didn't seem too long to wait. I was sure I could manage without food or water for that length of time. It was important to keep track of the days, so I knew when to expect to be rescued. Around the rear window in the roof of the canopy were some little tabs with which to tie it. I decided that each day I would tie a knot in one of them, starting on that Friday morning.

Knowing that I was going to be rescued made life a lot easier. I decided to check out what I had in the raft. There was a yellow rubber quoit attached to a long rescue line of orange plastic and a knife which incorporated a can opener. I opened the bag in which I had stored the items rescued from the sea. This produced a major disappointment. In daylight I could see that my bar of chocolate was in fact a puncture repair kit! I read the instructions written on the flare and checked the two sponges.

I then looked out through the door. In the night I had seen what I thought was a white polythene bottle of water attached by a line to the raft. As it was attached, I didn't bother to collect it with the other gear. I pulled in the line and found, not a bottle, but rolled up sail cloth. When I undid it, it turned out to be like a square parachute with a hole in the middle. It was attached to the line at all four corners. Although I didn't know it at the time, it was a sea anchor. I should have deployed it as soon as possible. It would have helped cut down some of the violent motion of the raft, held it downwind, reducing drift and prevented it from capsizing. Knowing nothing about life rafts I didn't recognise what it was, and decided it might be useful for catching rain water, if I closed the hole.

There was another line streaming from the raft. As I pulled it in I wondered what it was. The end of the rope was frayed and had a piece of wire sticking out of it. My first thought was that this had been where the green light or battery had been attached. It had come away as Angus held it and maybe contributed to his death. The horror of the previous night flooded back and I just let go of the line trying to banish those thoughts from my mind.

I found out, much later, back in England, that in actual fact this line was the painter, responsible for activating the CO_2 cylinder to inflate the raft. The battery or green light had been attached elsewhere.

My next job was to try and close the raft and stop the sea from coming in. I hadn't seen any sign of a door during the night. When I looked for it in daylight I found that it had blown up over the canopy. I pulled it down and found it had four sturdy loops at the bottom. I inspected the base of the raft and found four rubber buttons on the lower tube of the base. (The raft was rather like a child's paddling pool, with two inflated rings at its base and a canopy held up by an inflated support tube.)

I managed to fit the loops over the buttons without too much trouble. The door and the canopy were orange. I found a green inner door rolled down to the base. This fitted up inside the outer door with Velcro.

With the door finally closed, I turned my attention to the window. I had to try to tie up the skirt that was hanging in.

I used the tabs that were there but I wasn't very successful. When I tied it, it hung down as a welcome pocket for each wave that broke over us. The force of the water burst through my attempts at closure.

It was a relief to have the door closed; I could no longer see the sea. The waves were still just as high as they had been during the night. I could never believe that we would be able to climb all the way up them and go over the top.

I talk of 'we'. Very early on I decided to give the raft a name and turn it into my companion, that way I wouldn't feel so alone. I called her 'raftie', pronounced in an American accent as 'rafftie'.

My next problem was that I needed a pee. It was hardly surprising as I had been forced to swallow so much water during the night. How much easier it would be if I was a man, I could just aim out through the door. I decided that my sponges could act as my lavatory. In those conditions it was a major exercise to get my clothes down and keep my balance as I filled both sponges. I rinsed them out in the sea through the door.

The base of the raft was nearly full of water. I needed to bale out. I tried using the sponges and squeezing them out of the door. Even with just one corner of the door open the waves sent in more water than I was able to put out. I looked at the bags that had held the survival gear. I still had *Demon*'s knife hanging from my wrist. I used it to cut the tape securing the bag with the failed drawstring. I put the bag between my legs as I sat on the floor and used the sponges to fill it until I could just lift it. I threaded the neck of the bag out through the door and tipped it up to empty it. This idea worked well and kept me busy for a long time. I stopped when I had got the depth down to two or three inches. I was pretty exhausted by then but also I decided to keep some weight of water in the raft in the hope that the weight would give it a bit of stability.

The sponges were then required for more lavatorial duties. I don't know if it was all the salt water I had swallowed or if it was a nervous reaction to everything that had gone on, but I also had to cope with diarrhoea. Trying to aim that into a sponge in those conditions was no joke. There was more than one sponge full and I tried to make a sandwich with the other. As I rinsed these out in the sea I thought it was probably the most disgusting thing I had ever done.

Having swallowed so much sea water during the night I was expecting to be very thirsty by morning. The fact that I wasn't made me wonder if it would be alright to keep on drinking it. Stories of ancient mariners going mad after drinking sea water rather put me off the idea. I did try drinking my own urine when I had my first pee. Before rinsing out the sponges I sucked on one of them. I had to spit it out again, it was disgusting – it was so salty. If the sponges hadn't been so full of sea water it might have been alright.

Later it started raining and I held out the sea anchor to try catching the rain. But the cloth had taken on so much salt, the little I caught tasted more salty than the sea. Instead, when it rained I leaned out backwards through the door and opened my mouth as wide as I could to catch the water. I tried to lick up the water caught in my hair, but that was very salty too.

I decided I would ration myself to two sips of sea water each morning and each evening. I was really grateful for the fact that I never felt thirsty. Maybe sitting in two or three inches of water for the first couple of days helped.

On the Friday I wasn't hungry either, I never even thought about food. I was too busy trying to keep the water out of the raft. I lost count of the number of times the window burst in. I had to keep baling.

When I wasn't baling I adopted the same spread-eagled position that I had used during the night, holding on to two straps either side of my head and with my feet hooked through two more. I felt as if we were a football being kicked in all different directions, depending on where each wave came from. I started to listen to the sound of the approaching waves and tried to anticipate which way we were about to be kicked. I braced the raft and lifted it to try to help it over the top of the waves. It was always a different side of the raft that I lifted for each wave.

At one point in the dark on Friday night while I was being thrown every which way I remembered a conversation that Angus, Sally and I had had while we were out of the water at Cape May. One evening the conversation after supper came round to Atlantic storms. Sally and I both agreed that we would like to experience one, provided there was a switch we could turn off when we had had enough.

"OK Sally," I said out loud, "Where's that switch?"

I could really have used it, I'd had enough of this particular storm.

That is how I spent all day on Friday, that night, and all day Saturday. There were occasions when I needed a pee and couldn't be bothered with all the effort of using my sponges. I just warmed the water I was lying in. Unfortunately the diarrhoea lasted until Saturday. On one occasion I lost my balance and it went all over my clothes and the raft. I was almost in tears as I rinsed out the sponges and, horror of horrors, I lost hold of the one in my right hand. It just floated away from me. They were my most vital possessions. My lavatory and my balers. I couldn't risk losing the other one and stuck it up between my sweat shirt and my T-shirt.

It was just starting to get dark on the Saturday evening when I became aware of the door flapping. The noise of the wind on the raft seemed different and I realised it wasn't just the door, the whole canopy had started to flap. I looked at the support tube, it was sagging. I felt it and it felt quite soft. The rings of the base had also gone soft.

"I've got a puncture," I thought, "we're going to sink." After surviving for two days we were now going to be swallowed by the sea. I thought about the puncture repair kit. How would I find out where the puncture was? How would I get the rubber dry enough to stick on a patch?

My mind was racing when I had a vision of the pump drifting away when I righted the raft. It hadn't seemed much of a problem at the time but, if they gave you a pump, you must need a pump. How could I manage without one? It was time to pray again.

I'd have to try blowing it up myself to re-inflate it. There were three valves where the pump could be used, one below the support tube and one on each ring of the base. I decided to try the one on the support tube. If I undid it and it all hissed out, we'd just go down faster.

My hand was trembling as I carefully undid the valve. What a relief, nothing escaped. The challenge now was could I blow hard enough to inflate it? To my great delight it was easier to blow up than a child's balloon. Six hefty puffs and the tube was all rigid again. I did the same with the other two valves and put up a very big thank you.

Just minutes later a real rogue wave swamped us. I don't know how we would have fared had the raft not been rigid again. I settled down for the night in my usual position having had my two sips of sea. It was impossible to get any sleep, as it had been the previous night.

By Sunday the storm started to abate a little. It was still too rough to have the door open, the sea came crashing in when I tried. I decided it was time to get the raft dry and baled it out completely. I was worried about the wounds on my right hand; I thought they needed to dry out if they were going to heal. There had been quite a lot of blood on the straps in the raft.

I couldn't believe how much I was having to pee. I had to use the sponge now and there was always more than one spongeful. This meant a puddle on the floor which was impossible to mop up because it was always under my feet as they pushed the floor down.

Hunger still wasn't a problem, but I'd seen the odd clump of seaweed floating by. Perhaps I ought to try some. The next clump that came near enough I fished out of the water. It had quite small green leaves. I picked off a leaf and ate it, it wasn't bad. I'm going to be asked about this, I thought, so I rehearsed what I would say. I decided it tasted like rather tough salty pickled spinach. I ate a few more leaves and left the clump on the floor.

Later, as I was lying in my usual position, out of the corner of my eye I saw something moving. My first thought was that it was a spider. I was none too fond of them. When I looked I saw that it was a minute little crab. I put my sponge over it as I didn't fancy picking it up still wriggling. I thought I'd throw it out when it was dead. It had come in with the seaweed. "Don't be silly, Dereka. It's food. Eat it."

The thought came to me that not to eat it would run the risk of not being given anything else. I lifted the sponge, picked up the crab, shut my eyes and put it in my mouth. I chewed on it briefly and swallowed. It was slightly crunchy but went down without any problems. I couldn't believe what I had just done. On closer examination there were also some minute shrimps in the seaweed but I left those.

Sunday's problem was that, right on time, my period started. I was wearing red jeans but I decided I had to do something about the bleeding. Another use for my trusty sponge. I tore a strip off the end and used it as a reusable sanitary towel. I had always been wary of sharks when rinsing out my sponges. I was even more worried when I had to rinse out blood.

During the daytime I was never cold, but at night it did feel cold. On one occasion I found that my teeth were chattering. I repeated out loud, "You are not cold, the water is warm, you are not cold, the water is warm." I tried clapping my hands and shaking my legs to warm myself up. I spread the sea anchor over my body. I could just make out its white colour and pretended it was a sheet, I was in a warm bed.

On Sunday morning I blew air into the three valves again to keep the raft rigid. I did it every evening and every morning. Air was leaking out and if I wasn't lying down bracing the raft the waves started making it jack-knife. I'd be sitting there and suddenly be hit on the head by the base of the raft kicking up.

The water had stopped bursting in so there was more time to start thinking. I was so glad that my family had no idea what had happened and what a predicament I was in. At least nobody would be worried about me. I pictured my parents watching TV with the little kitten Twiggy that I had given them just before going on holiday. I wondered how much he had grown. I thought about work, when would I get back to the practice? I thought of my flat in Midhurst – when would the rent be due?

I would really have enjoyed a cigarette. What I missed most were my cigarettes and my Madame Rochas perfume. The perfume would have really boosted my morale.

Some instructions on how to use the life raft would have been good and some writing materials would have been useful too. In the event that I didn't survive, I would like to have written down what had happened to *Demon*, Angus and me. I thought the raft might last longer than I would. Anyone finding it would know our story.

Having nothing with which to write I thought I could have scratched my message with a knife into the rubber of one of the base rings. I dismissed that thought as being too risky. I didn't want to damage the raft. There were two knives, the one from *Demon* and the one in the raft. They were both all metal so I decided I could use one to engrave the other with my message. I never actually tried it.

I passed some of the time composing a mental list for the insurance company of everything I had lost. I really needed a pencil and paper for that as in my mind I went through everything I had packed to bring away with me. I also remembered the toy I had bought in Newport for Twiggy, a very superior scratching post. I thought of my camera and all the photos I had taken. Everything was now at the bottom of the ocean.

It was now Sunday and I hadn't had any sleep since the three and a half hours on Wednesday night. As I lay in the raft I started to nod off fitfully. I don't think I ever got much sleep but I did have the odd dream. Although I was still not hungry or thirsty, in one of my dreams somebody had scraped out a jar of jam and given me the spoon to lick. I woke up holding an imaginary spoon up to my mouth. My body must have been telling me it needed sugar. I also dreamed that Angus had made me a coffee. He was passing it to me in one of *Demon*'s yellow mugs. I woke this time with my right arm up in the air reaching for the mug to take it from him. I had several dreams about smoking, always aware that I had to be careful about stubbing out the non-existent cigarettes on the rubber floor of the raft. On one occasion I woke up to find I was reaching across my body to an imaginary ashtray on my left-hand-side, down by my hip.

When I looked out of the door that day I noticed that there were several fish swimming by. They were quite big, over a foot in length. Was I going to have to try catching fish to eat at some point? Not yet. They seemed to regard the raft as a curiosity. My problem, if I caught a fish, was going to be how to kill it. I had never killed a fish before; the nearest thing had been eating that tiny crab.

In the evening I blew again into all three valves and settled down for the night. The waves rarely broke over us and the window was now more secure. I had used the line from the sea anchor to close it. I now had more time to think about the pain I was in. The underside of my left arm was black with bruising from when it had been holding on to the raft, but no longer hurt.

The main problem was my knees; they were also badly bruised, probably from when *Demon* capsized. The skin over my knees actually felt anaesthetised, and my clothes were still wet. The pain was deep down and it really hurt. I tried putting my feet up on the top tube of the base but, if anything, that made it worse. I prayed out loud, "Please stop them hurting." I almost cried with the pain.

Monday morning arrived and with it came calm seas, blue sky and sunshine. At last, for the first time, it was safe to have my door open. I pumped up the raft and tied another knot in the tab that told me what day it was. There were now four knots, Friday morning's first one and knots for Saturday, Sunday, and now Monday. I had waited three days. Just one day to go, my four days would be up on Tuesday morning.

I sat in my doorway looking all around me. The fish were still gathering around the raft. It looked as though I could just grab one, they seemed really tame. As I was still not hungry I decided to put off any attempts to catch one. I patted the water with my hand and several fish came to investigate.

I spent the whole day scanning from horizon to horizon looking for any sign of land or shipping. There was nothing to see. We were drifting east, away from land. I wondered where exactly we were on the map. How near had we been to the Bermuda Triangle? I had assumed there was a shipping lane up the east side of the United States and hoped we would drift into it and be spotted.

Occasionally I saw an aeroplane high up in the sky. The planes looked so tiny, I knew there was no chance of them seeing us.

As it became warmer I decided to take off my clothes and hang them over the support tube to dry in the sun. I spent all day sunbathing topless, in no danger of being seen.

I thought about being rescued the next day. Would I hit land or be rescued at sea? Maybe I would arrive on an uninhabited island. With that in mind I decided to pass the time selecting the records I would choose if I were on the BBC Radio programme *Desert Island Discs*. A pencil and paper would have come in handy as I found myself going over the eight that you are allowed. The first one I chose was Anne Murray singing 'Snowbird'. This was a favourite for both Angus and me. It had been number one in the charts when Angus had been in America on a Churchill scholarship. He said it was always on the radio.

When I first collected my blue Lotus from the garage, I had selected Perry Como singing 'Snowbird' on an 8-track tape to be played as I drove away. Angus knew about this. When he collected his blue MGB GT, he left the garage and put the radio on. What should be playing but Anne Murray and 'Snowbird'! He stopped the car and phoned me saying he had nearly driven into a lamp post when he heard the song. I actually named my Lotus Snowbird.

My second choice was another joint favourite, Rita Coolidge singing '(Your love has lifted me) Higher'. The words of this song had particularly appealed to us.

Number three was Dory Previn with 'Mythical Kings and Iguanas'. Choosing one track was very difficult, we used to play the album so much.

Number four was Rod Stewart singing 'Sailing'. Angus had given me a tape of 'Atlantic Crossing' the previous Christmas.

Next I chose Judy Collins with 'Song of the Whales' from her 'Amazing Grace' album.

With my 1979 Christmas present still in mind, I thought that on my desert island I'd have to try and keep track of the date. It was always a family tradition on Christmas Eve to listen to the Festival of Nine Lessons and Carols. I decided I'd like to have, as my sixth record, the choir of Kings College, Cambridge singing 'Once in Royal David's City'. I always want to cry when I listen to the lone young chorister at the beginning of the carol. That would be my way of celebrating Christmas on my own.

My next choice was the twenty-third psalm, The Lord is my Shepherd. That too would probably make me cry. Record number eight was Perry Como singing 'For the Good Times'.

I should have stopped at eight, but I decided I had to have Barbra Streisand singing 'Woman in Love'. It was at the top of the charts at the time. Whenever it came on the radio on *Demon* I would turn up the volume. One very strange thing was that on that Monday in the raft I heard the song. It wasn't just going round in my head because I heard every word and I didn't know all the words. Somehow the raft seemed to be picking up a radio station. I also heard Carly Simon singing 'Jessie'. It was most odd.

I thought of another singer to take to the island. In 1973 Angus and I had stayed with a friend near Washington. He had a wonderful indoor swimming pool in his house. We used to play a tape of Connie Francis in the pool room and referred to her as 'swimming pool music'. My last sight of Angus on Thursday night had been with the full moon shining on him. I decided to take Connie Francis singing 'Carolina Moon' with my other records. At some point I'd have to delete two from my ten.

I was distracted from all the thoughts about music by the fish around the raft. They had started getting into the stabilisation pockets beneath it. They then seemed to panic, trying to get out. They were also rubbing against the floor and I could feel them beneath me as I sat there. They pushed so hard against me that I began to wonder if the floor had two layers and some of them had somehow become trapped. After several hours it became more than a little irritating.

I thought about using one of the knives to cut the top layer and release them. Quite rightly I decided this was much too risky, there was only a single layer of rubber!

While I spent the day looking for ships, every now and again I would spot another plane flying high in the sky. They were so far above us I realised we would be much too small to be seen. If they had been lower I wondered if it would be helpful to have a mirror to try reflecting the sun to catch someone's eye.

It was such a lovely day, so warm and sunny. I was very tempted to have a swim, the sea looked so inviting. Then I remembered how much trouble I had had getting into the raft. There was no way I wanted to end up stuck in the water again, even if it was flat calm.

Late in the afternoon a light aircraft flew over us. It was heading south east. I did think we might have been visible to the pilot as the plane wasn't that high, but it just flew on. An hour or so later what I took to be the same plane flew back again. It showed no sign of having seen us.

It was a luxury to have dry clothes to put back on, even if they were full of salt. I had my two sips of water and pumped the raft up. As it got dark I closed the door and settled down for the night. The fish underneath me were really starting to annoy me by now: at least if I wasn't rescued the next day, it shouldn't be difficult to catch one. I decided that Tuesday's job would be to make a fishing net. I would use the orange rescue line and hope I could knot the plastic. I tried slapping my hand down on the floor to frighten the fish away, but it didn't work.

After what seemed like an hour or so something lifted one side of the raft. What sort of creature was it? It had to be something quite large. It happened again and I started to get

worried. Again it lifted the raft and I shouted "Go away."
I was too frightened to look out of the door.

I don't know how long it took me to pluck up the courage
to investigate what was tipping us. When I did, I felt such a
fool. It was waves! I laughed out loud. The sea had been flat
calm all day and now the waves were starting to pick up.
What a relief. There wasn't any need to brace the raft that
night. I was able to lie on my side, curl up and try to go to
sleep. What kept me awake was the pain in my knees and
the ever present fish under the raft. They were still getting
trapped in the stabilising pockets and rubbing up against the
rubber floor.

I don't know how many hours had passed when I became
aware of the sound of a ship's engine. Sound travels a long
way through water, and I knew the ship wouldn't be close. I
sat up and opened the door to have a look. Out to the left
several miles away on the horizon I saw a ship's lights. It was
steaming from right to left as I watched.

Should I use my flare? I thought about it but decided that
there might not be anyone on watch. After all, I had been
looking all day and seen nothing. I couldn't blame them if
no one was keeping a look-out. I decided that if I used my
only flare and it wasn't seen, that would be a severe
psychological blow.

To the right of the ship I saw a flashing light. I thought
they don't put flashing lights there if nothing is going by.
We must be near the shipping lane that I thought had to
exist. This was the first ship I'd seen, I'd wait till morning.
There would be more ships and we'd be more visible in
daylight. I just sat and watched until the ship disappeared.

It had occurred to me earlier in the day that I had never
been so far away from another human being in my life.

Now they were getting nearer. I was due to be rescued the next morning.

My flare was in my hand as I settled down again in the raft. I held it as my pillow under the left-hand-side of my head. I identified the top of the flare by the thicker border of its polythene cover. I had often read the instructions on it, and on the puncture repair kit. They were the only things I had to read.

I was starting to feel excited about the thought of rescue. What would I have for my first drink? Mentally I lined up glasses of water, coke, gin and tonic and Californian red wine.

At dawn on Tuesday morning once again I heard the sound of a ship's engine. I looked out of the door round to my left and there she was. I was looking at her starboard side. She was steaming from left to right as I looked, heading east into the sunrise. I estimated that she was about two miles away. I prayed out loud, "Please God, I know we're only tiny, but they don't look too far away. Surely someone can see this tiny orange dot?"

I then sat back in the raft and decided to wait a while before looking again. I hoped that after my wait she would have altered course. I found it very hard to be patient and looked sooner than I had intended. She was still heading in the same direction. Wait again, I thought, pulling my head back in. I picked up my flare and wondered about using it. As the sun rose higher in the sky we would be more visible. I couldn't help looking out again. I saw nothing. There was no ship there. Had I imagined it? I thought, "That's it, Dodson, you've cracked. You're seeing ships now."

What I didn't immediately realise was that the breeze had spun the raft round, I wasn't looking into the sunrise. I knelt up and looked over the support tube and there she was.

Instead of being out of my door at 11 o'clock she was now behind me at 7 o'clock.

And she had altered course. She was either coming towards us or going away from us. It was impossible to tell which. Was I looking at her bow or her stern? How could I possibly wait to find out?

I'd have to be really patient, not look for ten minutes, and then see if she was getting bigger or smaller. If she was smaller I could use the flare. But would they be looking behind them? I had no self discipline. I must have looked every two minutes and had no idea if the size had changed, I just couldn't keep still.

In the end I gave up. I decided to watch the ship and see if I could make out a bow wave. If I could see one I'd know she was heading straight for us. I knelt up in the doorway and held down the support tube so I could see over it. I waited and waited. After what seemed like an eternity I thought I could make it out, a little white curl in the water either side of the bow. I strained my eyes until I was sure.

As I realised we had been seen and were about to be rescued, I burst into tears. I sat back in the raft and cried my eyes out. It was all too much. I hadn't cried after losing Angus but now it all flooded out. I thanked God and I thanked the raft. I had to get it all out of my system before facing people again.

After I composed myself I looked out again. There was no doubt about a bow wave now and they were getting bigger. Whoever they were, they were coming for us.

I thought they might not take the raft so I decided to pack up all the contents. I put everything into one of the orange bags. With all my possessions in the one bag, I felt a bit like a waif.

I then pumped up the raft so that she looked her best, all smart and perky. Briefly I thought about my own appearance but there was nothing I could do about that. I couldn't even get my fingers through my hair, it was in such a tangle. I would love to have had my Madame Rochas perfume. What I could do was clean my teeth. I had previously cut off one of the Terylene tabs, dipped in sea water it made a very adequate tooth brush. After using it I packed it with the rest of my gear. I was ready.

Next I decided to watch the cavalry arriving. I leaned out of the window, cupped my chin in my hands and rested my elbows on the base of the raft. I feasted my eyes on the sight of this great grey ghost looming out of the early morning sun. I felt quite elated. As she got larger I managed to make out her registration number, written on her bow, S34. *Demon's* number was 33. I was going up one. Eventually she stopped, just upwind of us. She was huge and took up nearly all my vision.

What was going to happen next? I heard what sounded like a very British voice. Were the Royal Navy visiting?

"Little boat on our right, raise your arms if you need help."

It struck me as really funny and I was tempted to say,

"You're joking, I come this way every Tuesday morning. Carry on young man, I'm fine, don't worry about me."

I could wave them past.

Instead I just punched up at the air, over and over again using both fists. I thought it was lucky I didn't have broken arms. If I did I would have kicked my feet up. I laughed at the thought as I continued to punch up at the sky.

I was aware of a large number of the crew leaning over the rails on deck staring down at us. I heard one of them saying,

"Well, I guess it could be a man."

Was I a woman or a long-haired man? They'd find out. I wasn't really bothered. Many orders were given and there was much ringing of bells. I heard, "Prepare to man lifeboat," and said "Yes please" quietly to myself.

The whaleboat was launched on the port side of the ship and I didn't see it until it came round under the bow. I counted six men on board and noted that one of them was a diver wearing a wet suit. "They don't intend to lose me," I thought, and it was a comforting idea. I was definitely going to be safe.

They stopped beside the raft and I held the side of their boat as I stood up. Not having stood up since Thursday, my legs didn't seem to belong to me. How was I going to get into their boat? I was sure I was going to make a pig's ear of it. I leaned over the edge of the boat laughing and said,

"You do it, you pull me, I can't do anything."

I was hauled on board with the same lack of dignity as when I landed in the life raft.

"Please take my raft, she's got to come too."

"You want the raft?" said one of the men, sounding surprised.

"Yes, yes please."

As we set off one of the men leaned out and grabbed at the canopy of the raft. He was holding the near side of the door frame and the canopy ripped. He lost hold of it and we had to circle round and go back for it. This time instead of pulling the raft along by the boat it was hauled on board. The boat then seemed quite full although I was struck by how small the raft looked.

I sat next to the diver who had his right arm protectively round me. I hadn't been able to see any national flag on the ship so I said, "Who are you?"

"United States Navy, Ma'am," said one of the men.
Another asked, "How long have you been out here?"

"Since Thursday night."

They greeted my reply with silence. We were heading
towards the stern of the ship when one of them said,

"Are you hungry? Would you like an apple?"

They had brought one with them and I accepted it. I
wasn't sure what I ought to be eating first and still wasn't
hungry. Would fruit be too acid? I took a bite out of the
apple and chewed and chewed before eventually swallowing.
I took a second bite as we all got soaked. The sea was quite
choppy and was breaking over the whaleboat.

As we went round the stern of the ship I looked up and
saw her name, *Canopus*. I later found out that, after Sirius,
Canopus is the second brightest star in the sky.

Over the port side of the ship there were two huge hooks
hanging down. These were to winch us on board. With the
sea conditions it was difficult to get alongside. We crashed
into the side of the ship twice but the third attempt was
successful.

As we were winched up out of the water, everyone was
very concerned about my safety. There were several lines
hanging down from *Canopus* and I was told to hold on to
one of these with both hands. This I did, handing my way
up. Then I noticed oil or tar on the rope. I didn't want this
getting into the wounds on my right hand so I just held on
with my left. There were shouts to hold on with both hands
but I ignored them. I thought, "I'm not about to fall out,
and even if I do, they're not going to let me drown now."

When I climbed out of the whaleboat and on to *Canopus'*
deck I looked up into a sea of faces, many of them hidden
behind cameras. One of the crew put a grey blanket round

my shoulders and directed me below. My legs still didn't seem to belong to me and I decided to go down the companionway backwards, holding on to the rails on either side.

I then went deeper into the ship, down another set of steps. Here I came to the entrance to the medical unit. Waiting for me were a doctor and two nurses, Dr David Mayer and Corpsmen Angel Paris and Kathy Dean.

During our visits to Annapolis, Angus and I had seen our first lady ratings from the Naval Academy there. They must all be qualified now and serving on board ships. The member of the crew who provided me with a blanket had also been female.

The first thing I said on entering the medical unit was, "I do hope I don't smell." They said I didn't and asked me to get undressed.

"Couldn't I please have a bath or shower?"

The answer was no. I didn't realise how dehydrated I was. Dr Mayer said that was the number one priority. I needed to go on a drip. After he had examined me, I put on a huge pair of men's pyjamas and offered my left arm for a dextrose drip. While this was running in I was put into a bunk in an adjacent small ward.

One of the orderlies gave me a drink, a beaker of red grape juice. It was my first real drink since Thursday and, although I had never felt thirsty, I now drank three beakers straight down. I became hooked on grape juice and wasn't happy unless I was holding a drink.

I then had a visitor, one of the ship's officers, Chief Warrant Officer Sam Butler. He wanted to ask me about what had happened to *Demon*. I gave him details of the incident and he then surprised me by asking if I wanted them to organise a search for Angus. Part of me wanted to say yes, but I felt that would be irresponsible. I knew it would be pointless. I said, "No, I saw him drown."

After he had gone doubts started to creep into my mind. What if Angus was clinging to a piece of wreckage? No one would now go looking for him. I had to remind myself of what had happened and what I had seen. There was no wreckage and Angus was dead.

I was also asked who would I like to be notified about what had happened. I asked for Maria to be contacted. She could inform my brother, Granville, who would tell my parents. I also asked for Angus' widow to be notified and, in Newport, Murray Davis. He was Editor of *Cruising World* magazine and would know who to contact in America. It was with Murray and his wife Barbara that we had had lunch the day before leaving Newport. That seemed a very long time ago.

Somebody from the crew brought me some clothes, trousers, T-shirts and a hooded jacket. I was also given a photograph of *Canopus* in a frame. It was from the Captain. On it he had written '28 October 1980. Ms Dodson. We were all very happy to have happened along when you needed us. May good fortune smile on you always. Sincerely Hugo E. Marxer Capt, USN'.

I was so pleased to have a picture of the ship. I would love to have had a camera as she approached me in the raft. I thought at the time that was one job my sponge couldn't do!

My left arm started swelling where the drip went in and became painful. Dr Mayer asked that it should be changed to my other arm. With all the fluid I had taken in, my fingers were starting to swell. The two rings that were on my right hand were starting to get tight. Dr Mayer decided to force these off before changing the drip. He needed to use cooking oil to help ease them down my finger. He was worried that they might obstruct my circulation.

He asked the orderly to try for a vein on the back of my right hand. My veins then started to play hide and seek! On his fourth attempt the orderly apologised for the pain he was causing me. I told him not to worry, in a way I was glad to be feeling it. It proved I was alive and not dreaming.

After a while I thought I'd really love to have a cigarette. I plucked up the courage and asked, "Would it be alright if I had a cigarette?"

Dr Mayer laughed and said, "I knew if you were a smoker it would only be a matter of time before you asked." He said that it would be OK. In no time 40 Salem menthol cigarettes were lying beside me. It would have been the perfect opportunity to give up smoking – but not yet.

Word must have got out that visitors could come and see me. I lost count of the number of people who came to say hello. I became almost punch drunk with an endless stream of crew members filing in. It was such a contrast to my time alone in the raft. One of the sailors told me he had only seventeen days left in the navy. This was his last trip out to sea and he had hoped that something exciting would happen. He told me I was it.

Among my visitors was the ship's chaplain, Chaplain (Commander) Hoyt W. Swann. He knew I had lost Angus and was very kind.

I found out a little about my rescue ship. *Canopus* was a submarine tender, normally shore-based. She only spent a total of one month at sea during any one year. She was designed to support nuclear-powered ballistic missile submarines. The re-load missiles were stored vertically amidships. She had a crew of just over 1,300, with 95 officers, and weighed some 21,000 tons. I also found out that there is no shipping lane up the east coast of the United States. With *Canopus* so rarely at sea I was exceptionally lucky to have been spotted. This was when I decided to celebrate two birthdays every year, June 10 and October 28. When looking at my stars, I'd check Gemini and then Scorpio.

The weather was getting worse and even *Canopus* was rolling during an electric storm. There was the noise of gun fire as the ship practised shooting. Somebody told me what was happening so that I wouldn't worry.

A second bag of dextrose replaced the first and I was given a vitamin pill. A curtain was drawn around my bunk and I was left to sleep. I was far too excited even to doze, and just lay there listening to what was going on around me. I overheard one conversation which sent a shiver down my spine. Somebody asked about my story and queried whether there was any question of foul play.

I later found out that the possibility of my being a Russian spy had been discussed. My condition was too good for what I had detailed and it was suggested that I had been put up by a Russian submarine in order to get on board *Canopus*!

After the second bag of fluid had emptied Dr Mayer checked and decided I was no longer dehydrated. He pinched the skin on the back of my hand as he had done repeatedly. For the first time, instead of staying raised, the skin sprang back down. Now it was time for a blood test and a check on my kidney function. A urine specimen was required. It was difficult to walk to the lavatory. My legs still felt like jelly and as the ship rolled I bounced against the walls of the corridor as if I was drunk. When I finally got there I was glad to sit down. I felt faint and had broken out in a sweat. I leaned forward with my head in my hands and felt quite ill. It wasn't easy getting back to my bunk where I flopped back and lay still until I recovered.

I was then told that I could have my long awaited shower. One of the nurses came with me and then came a big disappointment. There were problems with the water supply and I wasn't able to have a shower or wash my hair. The nurse spent the best part of an hour untangling my hair for me.

Back on my bunk I overheard a discussion about what I should be given to eat. "Let her have some soup. If she keeps that down, give her some crackers."

Just after seven o'clock the soup arrived. Of all things it was crab chowder. Very filling and delicious, it stayed down and I ate the crackers.

I was given a Tetanus injection and somebody brought me a piece of paper to look at. It was an account of what had happened and was for a possible press release.

It wasn't until around midnight that I was shown to a state room where I could spend the night. I still wasn't tired and was given a sleeping pill. All the furniture in the room had been lashed down due to the storm. Sitting in a chair outside my door for the night was a sailor on guard. I did manage to get some sleep and woke seconds before reveille which was at 4 a.m. I got dressed in the trousers I had been given and a *Canopus* T-shirt and made my way back to the sick bay. Here one of the nurses asked me if I'd like to go on deck. It was still dark but nice to be out in the open.

Later I ate breakfast with some of the officers. I had fruit juice and coffee, eggs, bacon and toast. I didn't quite manage to finish it all.

At 7.30 there was a presentation on deck. I was given a *Canopus* shield which had my name engraved on a brass plaque with the date and time of my rescue. I couldn't help noticing that my surname had been spelled with a B instead of a D in the centre. I always hate it when that happens and hoped I didn't sound ungrateful when I later mentioned it to Dr Mayer. The next time I saw the shield the spelling was correct.

I was then taken to the ship's store to collect some essentials. I ended up with much more than I expected. There were two tooth brushes with a holder, tooth paste, soap and a holder, two face cloths, two towels, shampoo, Vaseline Intensive Care Lotion, a hairbrush and comb, nail clippers, emery boards and tweezers, and some tissues.

Also socks and shower shoes, a pair of jeans, a belt, three white T-shirts and a pack of three pairs of men's Y-front pants – I couldn't find any women's pants. I was also given biros and notepaper, some Charlie perfume, a roll bag travel bag, a Snoopy watch with Snoopy playing tennis, a pair of sunglasses, four hundred menthol cigarettes and a *Canopus* Zippo lighter with flints and fuel. I was presented with a green suitcase to carry everything I had been given. This had a brass plate with my name on it.

I was worried about the thought of being found unconscious wearing men's underwear, so I feminised my Y-fronts by spraying them with the Charlie perfume.

After I had stocked up in the ship's store I went up on to the bridge with Captain Marxer. We were by then well on our way up the Cooper River and nearing the Naval Weapons Station at the Charleston Naval Base.

When we reached the base I saw that there was quite a crowd waiting. There was also an ambulance. I realised it was there for me and felt like a real fraud. Before any ambulance ride I had to face a press conference. I think all the people waiting were there for that. I felt very nervous about it and asked for a loo. I spent quite a long time there and wondered if I could just stay in there and hide.

Eventually I came out and made my way to the Captain's quarters. Here I sat next to Captain Marxer at one end of a long table. I was clutching a glass of iced tea as I watched them all filing in. I thought they'd never stop coming through the door, press, radio and television. There were so many microphones and lights so bright they made it difficult to see the faces behind them.

When it was over I breathed a sigh of relief and in no time I found I was leaving the ship. All my belongings including the raft, were waiting for me. The raft had been deflated and packed up ready to travel.

As I went ashore there were more television cameras waiting. I turned to wave to the crew of *Canopus* and a huge cheer went up. A great lump came into my throat. I was asked to wave for a second time for the benefit of the TV cameras.

Once seated in the ambulance I felt a fraud again as my blood pressure was taken. During the drive to the hospital I was noticing all the traffic, the buildings and trees. These were all things that while on the raft I had started to wonder if I would ever see again. The fact that I was alive finally registered.

I was admitted to the Naval Regional Medical Centre and taken to room 724 in ward 7a. There were four beds in the room and as I went in one of the patient's visitors said,

"Gee, you're the girl from the raft." It then dawned on me that I had inadvertently become something of a celebrity, not a feeling I enjoyed.

As soon as I was able I went in search of a hospital pay phone. I put in a reverse charge call to my parents. They were on separate phones, both in tears. I had to do most of the talking and found out later that my mother thought I had been prescribed 'uppers'. Being given a second chance of life gives one a great sense of elation and I know I sounded cheerful on the phone.

I was sent for a chest x-ray and then I was interviewed by some men from the US Coastguard. They had been searching for four fishermen whose boat had been caught in the same storm as us. One of the Coastguards showed me a chart and pointed out the area they had searched. It included the area in which *Demon* had gone down. They wanted to know if I had seen anything and I, in turn, wanted to know if they had seen anything. They had found nothing and I felt justified in not having asked for a search for Angus. I still had the irrational thought that I should have asked for one. I felt a great sense of relief knowing that a search had taken place anyway.

I had no time to settle in to the hospital. Commander Brian Gray from the Navy's public affairs office arrived to take me back to the Naval Base. He said there was work to do. He had a list of people to be telephoned as long as his arm. "Number one priority is the British Consulate in Atlanta," he said.

I started what turned into a three hour session by phoning the Consulate. Then I began to work my way down the list of relations and friends at home and in the States. I didn't complete the list but did manage interviews with the BBC and IRN in London, a lady from the 'Today' programme, a nationwide TV show in New York and a lady reporter from a Canadian radio station. I was surprised by my confidence and started to realise I felt like a new person.

It was almost 6 o'clock and all the staff had gone home. Commander Gray turned on the TV and by flipping the dial we saw me on three different channels in the News. He then took me back to the hospital. Waiting by my bed was my supper, spaghetti bolognese and cakes. I gave my cakes to the son of one of the other patients who was visiting.

I made my way to the day-room and sat chatting to a sailor who was in hospital to have plastic surgery. On TV they previewed the news and mentioned two items. They talked of the English woman plucked from the Atlantic after five days alone in a life raft and a man who had committed suicide. The total contrast of the two stories really hit me and sent a shiver down my spine. I had spent those five days fighting to stay alive while the man who had killed himself had obviously found life too much to cope with.

By the time I climbed into my bed it was way past midnight. A sleeping pill was essential, the room was so noisy. One of the patients crunched through the loudest apple I had ever heard and another had a TV on until after 3 a.m. The night nurses were far from quiet but I did eventually get to sleep.

The following morning, Thursday, a group of doctors came to see me and asked me to give them a lecture on survival. I don't know if I was much help to them, but I told them what I could.

Later Commander Gray came to collect me again. He took me to the Thrift Shop where I picked up some more clothes. He then took me to the airport where I was due to catch a plane to Atlanta and the British Consulate.

I was apprehensive about being on my own on the flight. I knew I would really miss Angus on the plane. A TV interviewer at the airport started asking me some personal questions and I began crying. It was time to put on the sunglasses I had been given on *Canopus*. So many strangers came up to me with greetings. One little lady who said she was from Yorkshire had tears in her eyes which didn't help mine. On the plane people were saying, "I'm so glad you're alive, honey."

Nobody passed my seat without putting a hand on my shoulder. The kinder everyone was, the more I cried. The flight from Charleston to Atlanta was smooth and helped by a couple of gin and tonics.

On arrival there was another TV crew and I was met by the Vice-Consul, Jack Litchfield and Norma Allen, a member of the staff from the Consulate. There was much paperwork to be sorted. Before I could leave the country I had to officially arrive. Because I had been rescued outside territorial waters, technically I needed to go through immigration. It was also necessary for me to be issued with an emergency passport.

From the Consulate I was able to speak on the telephone to my brother, Granville. He was going to Wales for the weekend with his fiancée. "You're big news in the papers here today," he said.

"What do you mean?" I replied.

"Well you're front page in the *Telegraph*, the *Mail* and the *Express*. I'm afraid that at the moment you really are big news."

I found it hard to believe. Mr Litchfield told me he had accepted an offer from British Caledonian Airways to fly me home to Gatwick as a stand-by passenger. I realised if it became known I would have to face the press again at Gatwick Airport. I had been very happy to talk to the American press. I owed my life to the US Navy and welcomed every opportunity to say thank you. In England, however, I wanted no coverage of my return. I didn't want Angus' two young children to see pictures of me arriving home.

I talked of the possibility of flying with Delta instead and hoping to dodge the press. Then I thought that I really should 'fly the flag' and go with British Caledonian who had been kind enough to offer.

After speaking with Granville I phoned Maria. I explained the situation. She said, "Leave it to Peter and me. Remember Peter knows people at Gatwick. We'll manage something."

At the Consulate they had decided I probably wouldn't want to spend the night alone in an Atlanta hotel. Norma Allen very kindly took me to her home where I met her daughters, Julie and Jennifer.

There, at last, I was able to have a long lazy bath and wash my hair. Norma also washed my clothes for me.

Before leaving the Consulate Mr Litchfield told me there had been talk of my appearing on the TV programme, *That's Incredible*. This would have meant delaying my departure and we dismissed the idea.

Once again I took a sleeping pill and woke very late on the Friday morning. I went shopping with Norma to buy some postcards and a mirror, and an anorak for England's weather.

I tried unsuccessfully to phone Malcolm who had phoned me in the hospital.

Mr Litchfield drove me to the airport where I was whisked away almost before I could say thank you. Initially I was told the flight was full and they weren't taking stand-by passengers. I just waited and was then shown to the VIP lounge. I was escorted to the plane by the Airport Manager and found myself sitting next to a young American woman.

She had lost her husband earlier that year and was apprehensive about visiting London on her own. After supper I took her with me when I was invited up to the flight deck by the crew. There we were both given champagne, and missed the movie.

As we descended into Gatwick I wondered what would happen on the ground. I was told to wait on the plane until everybody had got off. There were to be two men to meet me.

I watched as all the passengers filed off. The curtains were drawn and I just stood in the aisle of this huge plane feeling very alone. All of a sudden the curtain was swept back and there was Peter, arms outstretched, ready with a massive hug. He explained the plan to avoid the press. We were to pretend to be a couple and went to collect my luggage.

In the baggage reclaim area we joined Alan Munns, the Duty Airport Manager, a porter and two policemen. Mr Munns had told the press I would be with him. The others were to take my luggage and exit the area to the right while Peter and I were to go to the left. We went past the green gate, briefly out into the public area and immediately down a flight of stairs and out into the road. There was Maria in the Princess with the engine running and a police motorcyclist on his bike. Maria got out of the car and asked if I had any luggage. She laughed when she saw the police and the porter approaching with the trolley. Sitting in the back of the car was my mother. We all piled in and sped off heading for Brookfield, the family home.

My father, who was very emotional, and my great aunt were waiting for us, and so was Twiggy. He had really grown since I had last seen him. We only had half an hour before the press started to arrive. I was smuggled away under a blanket lying in the back of the car. We drove to Beckenham where I was to stay with Maria and Peter. It was Peter's daughter Jacqui's birthday and she had waited for us to arrive before opening her presents.

I landed back in England on Saturday November 1. I spent most of the following Monday and Tuesday on the phone. There were essential calls to banks, insurance companies and the driving licence authorities in Swansea.

By the Wednesday I was able to meet up with Angus' brother, Ian. He was very kind and worried that answering his questions would upset me. But the more I talked the more it helped. Ian surprised me by asking why Angus had left his boat. I had to explain that it was *Demon* that had left us. The very fact Ian had to ask that question made me realise I had failed to get the story over to the press.

I had seen most of the newspapers and what I had read made me frustrated and angry. There was much fabrication and I had been endlessly misquoted. According to one paper I was German and the crew of *Canopus* hadn't been able to communicate with me. Another said we had lost the mast off Miami. I also read that we had had two life rafts. Angus had put me in one and then got hit on the head by the other.

After talking to Ian I decided that maybe I ought to try telling the story myself. I hoped it might be of help to anyone who found themselves in a similar situation.

I had brought the life raft back because I wanted it to go back to Beaufort, the manufacturers. I hoped they would be able to learn from it. I found out that it was a Porpoise life raft. How odd that I had been standing on a Porpoise on the bow of *Demon* while we had been playing with the dolphins the night before the storm.

The raft went up to the factory on Merseyside where it was examined. I went up there with Granville and Doug Bence, who helped me with the manuscript *For Those in Peril*. I had a few recommendations to make and, as a result, changes were made. The bags containing the survival gear were to be attached to the base at both ends so that they would not hang down if the raft was upside down, putting pressure on the closures. A boarding stub was to be added to the standard raft. These boarding aids were added to more expensive rafts, but were not on the basic version. There were some modifications made to make it less likely that a raft would inflate upside down.

While at the factory I was enrolled as a member of the Porpoise Club. Anyone whose life has been saved by one of the rafts is entitled to become a member. I was given a certificate and a scarf by John Maltby, Beaufort's Sales Manager.

The day after I met Ian, I had an emotional reunion with Sally. She asked me why I had been crying in the car. I told her. I asked if she had seen us waving as we rounded the corner but she hadn't been watching.

Then on the Friday I went to the Foreign Office to pay my repatriation fee and collected a replacement passport from Petty France.

On my way to meet Ian in London on the Wednesday morning, I went to Victoria Station. There in the rush hour I was struck by the blank expressions on the faces of all the people milling around and suddenly I felt about ten feet tall. I remembered one of the newspaper headlines, 'Raft Woman Alive'. Indeed I was!

After Angus died I held him very close to me. I felt so in touch with him that I saw no need to consult a medium to make contact. It was some five years later when I finally did. A friend had lost her husband and wanted to have a reading, so I went along too.

I found out that I was holding on to Angus too much. He had work to do and I was stopping him. I had to let him go. He also told me, through the medium, that he didn't drown; he had a heart attack in the water. This explained why he disappeared so quickly. He also apologised for leaving me in such a situation but said he didn't think I'd have been able to manage the boat on my own. He was quite right.

Knowing that Angus had a heart attack that night also explained why he was sick earlier in the day. That is sometimes a warning sign. I once had a patient who was sick while waiting to see me. We sent her home where she proceeded to have a heart attack, luckily not fatal.

I was very tearful after the reading. I had no idea that I was impeding Angus and really tried to release him.

Through the years I have had several readings and he always comes through. In 2001 in Egypt, Isabelle asked me who the chap was that she kept seeing with me. It was Angus. Isabelle is a medium.

When I was first introduced to crop circles I interpreted some of them as being messages from Angus. I found this rather overwhelming and didn't dare mention it to anybody. It took me seven years to pluck up the courage to say anything. In 2005 I asked through Mavis if I was right. The answer given by the energies was 'yes'.

Five years passed before I had another reading with Mavis, my psychic counsellor friend. I asked what was Angus' role with the formations. The answer was, "What is important is that these formations create energy. Now you're either going to understand it intellectually, or you're going to understand it emotionally, or you're going to understand it physically. His role was to create the emotional connections. And that is why you found them fascinating, because it started to trigger your feelings. It was like you had a passion about this. And for you, you have found very little in your life to be passionate about. So this was the gift of those to start to open your heart chakra. And that was the purpose of his connection. Because you started out doing it in your head and you ended up doing it in your heart."

I then asked if other people would appreciate what Angus had put into the formations. I was told that people have to be willing to make the connections for themselves.

"The opportunity is there, but people may not take that opportunity."

CHAPTER FIVE
An Aborigine speaks to me in my dream

After 1980 I had no further premonitions until the year 2003 when I had the same very short dream three times. They all occurred during the month of October.

In the dreams I was driving with my mother sitting in the passenger seat of the car and I had fallen asleep at the wheel. I awoke, still in my dream, saw that we were about to have a head-on crash and had no time to avoid the impact. All I did was to fling out my left arm in front of my mother as some sort of protection and say, "I'm so sorry." At that point in the dream I would wake up for real, never knowing what we were about to hit.

I had spent most of the previous month, September, in Peru and been surprised by the number of eucalyptus trees growing there. We were told they had been brought from Australia many years ago. The trees grow fast, tall and straight and are used in the construction industry in Peru. We have one in the garden of which I am very fond. I pick up the leaves and the bark it sheds to burn for their smoke.

In November I bought up the entire stock of Eucalyptus incense sticks from a shop that was closing down in Devizes. I really enjoyed burning them.

One night I had a very vivid 'vision' dream. An Aborigine was blowing Eucalyptus smoke into my face. He then said to me, "If you walk the lines of truth, you will be guided."

After waking up I thought about this and decided that it might have been a reference to getting help while trying to write this book.

On the third weekend in November 2003 I went to Phoenix for their annual Signs of Destiny Conference. This was my first visit. Shortly after getting back to England I was due to drive my mother to visit friends in Devon.

Mike and Priscilla had moved from Surrey to Devon at the same time as we moved to Wiltshire. Once a month we visited them and while we were there Priscilla did our hair. During our October visit Mike noticed that the near-side front tyre on my car was illegal. My first job the next day was to have new tyres fitted to the car.

Our next visit was at the end of November. We were within two miles of their house when my car-crashing dream became reality and I found out what we were to hit.

Driving west on the A303 road there are two signs about ten miles apart which warn that tiredness kills. I fell asleep about two hundred yards short of and in sight of the second sign. There is quite a sharp right-hand bend.

I woke as the car clipped the near side verge, I flung out my left arm and said, "I'm so sorry," just as the car drove into the end of the hedge separating the road from a farm track off to the left. The hedge caught us, stopped us gently and then slowly tipped us out on to the farm track, rolling the car onto its side.

Looking down at my mother I checked that she was unhurt, then undid my seat belt and tried to stand up to open my door above me and push it up. It's quite surprising how heavy a car door is – but help was all around us in no time at all.

As fellow motorists, the police, ambulance and fire crews gathered, swiftly followed by our friend Priscilla, whom I had telephoned, all I could think was how lucky we'd been. If you have to have a head on crash, is there anything better to hit than a hedge? I'm sure people were wondering why I was so happy about the whole event.

The sun that morning had been exceptionally bright and low in the late November sky. On occasions it had been quite blinding and I had tried putting on sunglasses – something I never normally do. The senior police officer said that they had had problems with the sun that morning driving on the Exeter bypass. When giving my statement to the officer I told him that I had fallen asleep while driving. I did not blame the sun for blinding me as I approached the bend in the road. He took me to one side and very kindly said that he didn't want to take things any further, hinting that I should not mention falling asleep.

It was tempting to lie and avoid prosecution but I remembered the words of the Aborigine, "If you walk the lines of truth, you will be guided."

"But it's the truth," I said, giving the poor officer a problem.

When I finally heard from the police I was offered an alternative to going to court and facing prosecution. I could pay to go on a two-day Driver Improvement Course. This I did and would thoroughly recommend it.

The firemen managed to get my mother out of the car through the boot – with the car still on its side. She was given oxygen and taken by ambulance to hospital in Honiton. Priscilla took me there in her car. Hospital staff seemed happy for her to leave so my mother decided she'd rather go to the house and have her hair done than wait to see a doctor. I cringed and slipped lower in my seat as we listened to the traffic report on the car radio – delays on the A303 due to the recovery of a car involved in a single vehicle accident.

The car was written off by the insurance company – how grateful I was to Mike for spotting the illegal tyre. The car's registration number was Y167 UMR. I used to think of it as a question, 'Why 167 um, er?' After the crash something made me look up the three numbers 167 as a page number in a book recommended by a friend. On that page I found reference to Aboriginal guidance.

CHAPTER SIX

The Dragon Energy pulls me back to Wiltshire

When she realised how totally hooked I was by seeing and visiting my first crop circle in May 1998, Bridget made it her business to introduce me to the locally-based group of people studying the phenomenon. Their next meeting was in early June. I was unable to attend because I had already booked a week's holiday in Kenmare, Southern Ireland, visiting one of my former dental nurses who lived there with her husband and family.

In mid-July the Study Group was staging a weekend event. This was to be held at Alton Barnes in the Vale of Pewsey and included two days of lectures by various speakers and, amongst other attractions, the opportunity to take a helicopter ride and view the formations from the air. Bridget organised tickets for me for the weekend, and a flight.

Having checked into the Bear Hotel as usual on the Friday afternoon, I decided to do a recce and try to find Alton Barnes. I spotted two marquees beside Coronation Hall and stopped by the gate into the field. There were two people standing talking just inside the field.

"Huh," said my mother, "there's weirdo one and weirdo two." I said nothing.

Back at our hotel room in Devizes who should be on the TV news but weirdos one and two! I suspect it wasn't very long before I was regarded as weirdo three.

I wouldn't have thought it was possible to be provided with so much information and to have so many doors opened in just two days. I happily sat for over nine hours on the Saturday on a hard chair trying to absorb all the knowledge on offer. Half way through the Sunday morning my brain was protesting. It was as if it needed more room, it was trying to expand but my skull wouldn't let it! I think I had been expecting to learn about crop circles, but had no idea that I would be hearing about Hopi prophecies, sacred geometry, the New Jerusalem, Revelations III and more and more and more besides. I bought all the books, videos, cassettes and back copies of the Group's newsletters I could find.

My first ever flight in a helicopter would have been exciting enough without the added bonus of being able to look down on the crop circles. Although the oilseed rape had long since been harvested, the design showing the 'thirty-three tongues of flame' could still be clearly seen near the West Kennet Long Barrow. All the formations we saw were in wheat.

While feasting my eyes I was trying to juggle two still cameras and a video camera. As we returned to land back at Alton Barnes we saw the 'seven pointed snowflake' design there in East Field. It looked amazing but then it suddenly seemed to jump up out of the field, sparkling like a diamond. Initially, cloud had been blocking the rays of the sun. Only when the sunlight hit the crop could you see the intricacy of the hidden pattern in the lay of the wheat as it reflected the rays in different directions. Sheer magic.

A closing ceremony for the Conference was held within the formation, a wonderful way to watch the sun go down.

After July I started to attend the monthly Saturday meetings and the mid-month Wednesday evening lectures put on by the Group. I used to leave work early on Wednesdays and drive to Devizes to Bridget's flat. She always had a light supper waiting for me, after which I would drive her to Alton Barnes. After the lecture, Daphne would drive Bridget home as I set off back to Surrey. I began to think of Bridget as my mentor and valued any time I was able to spend with her.

It was while driving from Devizes to Alton Barnes for the September evening talk that I saw my first mini-rainbow. It was a beautiful sunny evening when we spotted this tiny oval-shaped rainbow which looked to be roughly above the hall in a cloudless sky. Neither of us had ever seen anything like it before. For me it was to be the first of many rainbow experiences.

On several occasions Bridget said to me that if ever I got a chance to hear Isabelle Kingston speak, I must go. As I recall, the words 'bees' and 'knees' came into the conversation. She is a teacher, healer and medium of international renown and does a lot of work with earth energies and linking energies 'as above, so below'.

I didn't have to wait long. Isabelle came to talk to the Group on Saturday October 3. Bridget and I had front row seats. After her talk I heard Isabelle chatting to T.C., the Group Co-ordinator. Isabelle told her that the following day she and her group were going to be working to awaken the Dragon Energy.

It came as a great surprise to me to find myself going up to Isabelle and saying, "Excuse me, but can anybody come?" Never before had I been so pushy! Yes, I could join them, meeting in the car park at Hackpen Hill at 2.30.

Back at the hotel I got out a map to try and find Hackpen Hill. I wasn't too popular as 'Plan A' for Sunday had been to check out of the Bear, have lunch, visit Beryl my Godmother and then drive back to Surrey, 'Plan B' saw me checking first the location of the car park and then making a morning visit to see Beryl. In the afternoon I dropped my mother off to spend more time with Beryl while I joined the people at Hackpen Hill.

The hills that run through the Vale of Pewsey are part of the Dragon Hills. We were at the head region of the Dragon and other groups of people were gathered at different points along the length of its body. We walked a short distance from the car park along the Ridgeway and then went into a field above the white horse carved in the chalk on the hillside. As we linked in with the other groups I was aware of a real sensation of the Dragon actually lifting its head and turning to look to its left.

All the people involved were going to meet up for a supper at Coronation Hall. I'd love to have joined them but it wasn't possible that day. I headed instead to Kingston House (coincidence!) to collect my mother and say goodbye to Beryl for another month.

It was dark as we set off for home. As I drove a strange feeling came over me – I didn't want to be leaving Wiltshire. I became aware of a physical force pulling me back to the county like a magnet. This feeling stayed with me throughout the week. I didn't mention it to anybody but I just knew that as soon as possible I had to return. I couldn't understand how I could be experiencing such a strong physical pull.

My first opportunity to drive back was the following Saturday. The weather forecast was for severe storms that day with a risk of structural damage, but I was determined to go. I couldn't say why I was going and had no idea where I would end up.

The car found its way to the car park and viewing area at Silbury Hill. I got out of the car and looked up at the hill. There were about 20 people on the top standing in a circle holding hands. I wondered who they were and if I was supposed to be up there with them.

I next drove to Devizes and went to see my friend Dawn who had a shop in the Ginnel. I needed to buy a good mackintosh as the weather was getting worse.

From there I headed for Avebury, the village amidst the Neolithic standing stones of the ancient temple, not far from Silbury Hill. I had some lunch at Stones Restaurant and then visited the Henge Shop there for the first time. I looked at the crystals on display and felt drawn to buy a small piece of snowflake obsidian.

My eyes then fell upon a selection of L-shaped copper dowsing rods. I decided to buy a pair and a little green 'Teach yourself to dowse' booklet. I went back to the car and headed once again for the car park at Hackpen Hill.

The wind up there was so strong it was rocking the car as I sat in it trying to learn the basics of dowsing. I decided to retrace the steps we had taken along the Ridgeway the previous Sunday and see if, with the aid of the rods, I could find the spot where we had stood.

As I went I tried asking questions and assessed the way the rods responded giving 'yes' or 'no' answers. Holding the shorter arm of the rods, one in each hand, I pointed the longer arm straight ahead. To indicate a 'yes' answer the rods would diverge, for a 'no' they would converge and cross over each other.

I was so engrossed that I wasn't really aware of any other walkers. I did laugh though when a couple of lads went by on mountain bikes. As they threaded their way through the puddles one of them said,

"I don't know why you're bothering, there's water everywhere up here!"

When I found the place I'd been looking for the rods started to whizz round like a couple of helicopter blades. Once again I could feel the Dragon energy I had first experienced the previous weekend.

As I drove home I saw several places where trees had been blown down during the day. I was thinking about the strength of the forces of nature when I realised I was no longer aware of the force or energy that had compelled me to go back to Wiltshire. Somehow it seemed as if the Dragon Energy had wanted me to return in order to show me that it was real.

Towards the end of 1998 Bridget became unwell and was in Devizes Hospital. Some members of the Group were going to meet up on December 21, the Winter Solstice. The plan was to meet at 7.30 a.m. and/or 3.30 p.m. and climb up to the long barrow at Adam's Grave, just above Alton Barnes, for sunrise and sunset. I didn't fancy getting up at 5 a.m. and driving all the way in the dark for sunrise. Instead I decided to leave at around 9 o'clock and visit Bridget. By the time I found the hospital it was nearly lunchtime. The staff were very kind and said I could go with Bridget and sit at the table while she ate. Then, even better, they brought her lunch to the Day Room on a tray. We talked and talked and she was delighted when I said I was going to meet up with T.C. and others for the sunset. The next day Bridget was due to leave hospital and go into a nursing home.

My mother and I went to Wales to spend Christmas with Roy and Peg (from King's College Hospital). Roy had taken early retirement, and they had bought a hotel at Ammanford which they ran for several years before moving into a property they had had built in the hotel grounds.

On our way back to Surrey we popped into Kingston House to visit Beryl. She was very upset and greeted us with the news that Bridget had died on December 22. It was a real shock to me – she had seemed so bright and alert the previous day. I'm not proud of the fact that a little part of me felt quite cross with her. How could she go when she had so much more to teach me?

She didn't go far though, as I found out some months later when I had a reading with a medium.

The strange thing was, I didn't realise the lady *was* a medium. I knew her as a shaman and a healer, and had booked an appointment for what I thought would be a shamanic health check or MoT test. How surprised and delighted I was when she described both Bridget and Angus to me, descriptions so accurate there could be no doubt, as were those of many other people or energies who are now in another dimension.

CHAPTER SEVEN
"These are for the children"

Over the years of driving to Wiltshire, I became fascinated by the white horse carved into the chalk hillside, that first came into view about ten miles before Devizes. It seemed odd that it took me several months to realise the white horse on Milk Hill at Alton Barnes was the same one. It had been calling me for years, yet when I went to Alton Barnes in July 1998, I did not recognise it.

The following year I looked forward to the first crop circle formations of the season wondering which of the fields of oilseed rape they would choose. I went with members of the Group to help measure a new one at Milk Hill. It seemed to depict an alignment of celestial bodies and was joined by another in the same field some days later. The second one put me in mind of a seahorse and had the number nine written fifteen times within it. T.C. had flown over the first one and noted that a very fine circle had been laid down. We searched for it on the ground and found that it was all of two stalks wide.

I visited another yellow field on my own – beside the A361 near Bishops Cannings. I took photos and video footage, totally unaware that, in the distance, I was also photographing the house to which we would move the following year. This crop circle seemed to represent the solar eclipse due later that summer.

In June a double formation came in barley in East Field. I saw a picture of it on the Tuesday and couldn't wait to drive down on the Friday afternoon. Climbing over the fence below the Knapp Hill car park, a long pictogram design beckoned. I explored this and on reaching the far end, looked over to the right; several tramlines away and further on was the second formation, a serpent.

It was a long hot walk to retrace my steps and then walk along the field to get into the tramline that would take me into the serpent at its head. The body was curled up in a series of nine bends. When I reached the tail I sat down for a while. To get back to the car was going to be a long hot slog. I wished I had brought some water with me.

Not far from the formation I noticed a bird flying beside me. It was about six feet to my right, level with my head and travelling at the same speed as me. As I turned to look at it I was so surprised I just said hello to it. It was a hawk and with its left eye it was looking me straight in the eye and continued to do so for about forty yards. When it finally stopped staring at me it flew off to the right at 90° to the direction in which we had been heading. It seemed to be making for the adjacent field, below Golden Ball Hill. I got the distinct impression that the hawk was trying to draw my attention to this other field. As soon as I saw T.C. I asked her if formations ever came in that field. She told me there had been some.

(I shall add here it was in that very field, along the direction of the flight of the hawk, that the UFO landed at my feet in August 2004, five years later.)

Back in 1999 I had not yet met Grandmother Twylah Nitsch or heard of her book *Creature Teachers*. I did not then know of or possess a set of Animal Medicine cards, or the book that accompanies them, written by David Carson and Grandmother Twylah's grand daughter, Jamie Sams. I just knew that it had been a significant meeting with the hawk on that June afternoon.

I joined other members of the Group on June 21 for a Summer Solstice night-watch up at Adam's Grave Long Barrow. Some people started to leave at first light and I accepted a lift back to where I had left my car. I wanted to go back, however, to watch the sun rise and take photographs of the two formations in East Field from the top of the hill. I passed the last people leaving as I started to climb up to the Barrow on my own. When the first rays of the sun hit the formations, it made a beautiful sight. I think barley is the most graceful of crops as it wafts in the breeze.

Later when I went to collect my photos from the chemist, I was very disappointed when they couldn't find them. I was told my pictures must have been sent to another branch. Eventually they turned up and I was able to look at them. There was more to see than I had been expecting. If I'd known what was on them, I would have been even more upset when they went missing!

On one there seemed to be a little blue light, quite near me in the grass. Others showed tiny round white lights. On one picture they were arranged like an arrowhead, pointing to the field below Golden Ball Hill. Several pictures of East Field showed what looked like little plumes of smoke – as if there were tiny fires burning, some around the edge of the field, others in the field. In the sky there appears to be a tiny object that does not look like a bird, and some white traces.

Somebody told me that these traces look similar to what is called Angel's hair – observed on occasions after UFO sightings.

I spent a lot of time using a magnifying glass that day, checking out the pictures. It was the first time I had had any anomalies on my photos. Since then it has happened on many occasions.

It was a few months later, in the November, that I had my first vision dream. In that dream I was driving my favourite car of all time, my 1969 blue Lotus Elan S4SE convertible. I was half a mile from home, driving up a small hill. It must have been winter because the soft-top roof of the car was up. As I got to the brow of the hill I was blinded by the brightest light I had ever seen. Unable to see, I knew I had to stop the car. Knowing the road to be straight, all I had to do was brake and stop – where there used to be a bus stop. As I braked to a halt with the light still in my eyes, what I could see looked as if it was a film negative.

Through the passenger window I could see a being standing, as if at the bus stop. I lowered the window and the 'person' leaned forward and, through the open window, placed something in my left hand. A long-sleeved, hooded garment hid both the face and hands of whoever was there. Still in my dream it crossed my mind that it might be Bridget placing whatever it was into my hand. As she did so she said, "These are for the children." After hearing those words I woke up. What had I been given 'for the children'?

It took me several years to come up with an answer. I think it was films – or photographs. In the dream I was seeing or looking at everything as if it was a negative and on so many occasions since I have had anomalies on my photographs. As I understand it, I am to show these pictures to people in the hope that it will help them accept that we only see part of what is really there.

I have never used a digital camera or Adobe Photoshop on a computer. If people want to try to explain away what is on my photographs that's their problem, not mine!

One other thing that puzzled me about the dream was the car. Why was I driving my blue Lotus? The original Elans used to come in kit form. Mine had been built and registered in Scotland in 1969. I bought it second-hand in 1971 at a local garage. I called her Snowbird and together we travelled very nearly a quarter of a million miles before I crashed her in 1989. At the time of the dream, ten years later, the car was in several boxes and hundreds of pieces. A friend had dismantled her and was hoping to put her back together again one day.

She was painted in a metallic mid-blue. The UFO that presented on my photograph in August 2004 was exactly the same colour.

In July 1999 we once again held the closing ceremony for our Conference in East Field. We walked from Coronation Hall to the Serpent formation, entering through the tail. We danced the Serpent and as the sun went down, looking up at Adam's Grave, standing there silhouetted against the sky, we saw a lone horse and rider. I don't know who the choreographer was but they certainly provided a magical ending.

That summer, at the age of 94, Beryl decided that she wished to die. She had no living family and thought she was a burden on her friends and carers. Seeing no reason to continue living, she stopped eating.

Ever considerate, she started her fast a week before she knew we were going to be spending two weeks in Wiltshire.

She hoped to die while we were near and save us the bother of having to return.

Initially it was a shock to see the deterioration after her first week and we tried to encourage her to eat, not immediately realising what she was trying to do. As she declined offers of even ice-cream, it was obvious that our tempting her to eat caused her distress. Reluctantly we had to respect her brave decision.

We returned home after our two-week stay and I would pop down to visit her during the fourth and fifth weeks. That is how long it took, five weeks.

She had been the perfect Godmother. A year earlier I had booked my 'annual' reading with the medium who had described Bridget and Angus to me so accurately. Just one week after her death, Beryl presented herself with Bridget and another friend who had died before either of them. The medium laughed as she described the three of them going off for a drive in the country, taking a picnic in the car. That is exactly what they used to do when they were all down here in their 'Earth Suits'!

There is no need to mourn them when I know that they are right behind me – pushing me forward – probably not as fast as they would like me to be going!

CHAPTER EIGHT
First contact on St Valentine's Day

It was during the year 2000 that I first started to feel as if communication was developing between me and some of the energies that were putting the information in the fields in the form of crop circles.

February 14, St Valentine's Day, was when I initially became aware of this interaction. It was a weekday and all the nurses at the Practice were swapping stories about the cards, flowers or presents that they had received. The one exception that day was my nurse, J, who had recently broken up with her boyfriend.

When she went to lunch I noticed that on the blotting paper on her desk she had drawn a solid black heart. This looked so sad and bleak, I felt I couldn't leave it like that. I picked up a red biro and drew red lines or rays all around the black heart.

As I drew the last ray a tremendous crushing feeling of love came down over me. It was so intense it made me cry. While I sat there in the grip of that extreme awareness, I was told we would have a heart-shaped crop circle that year.

The message reminded me of the one I had received in the life raft – from the dolphins. It was very clear and I believed it.

The next time I saw her I asked T.C. if there had ever been a heart-shaped formation. She said there had been one representing the mathematical Mandelbrot set that looked a little bit like a heart.

"No," I said. "I mean a *real* heart shape."

The energies involved with the crop circles are very strong. They are exciting and almost seductive – it is easy to get carried away by them.

Not long after being told about the heart I started to wonder when and where it would appear. I thought maybe I could get more information by dowsing with a pendulum.

Dowsing an Ordnance Survey map I found not only the field but also the position in that field where my pendulum told me to expect the formation. In addition, I got a date and even a time when the wheat would go down.

In 1998 I had been so smitten by crop circles that I wanted all my friends and colleagues to share my wonder and joy. I couldn't understand why none of them seemed to resonate with the formations. The idea put out so relentlessly by the media that they are all man-made hoaxes seemed to satisfy them and make them more comfortable.

If only I could gather a group of people together to watch the heart formation being laid down, if several people filmed it on video, from different angles, maybe people would start to believe. I wanted the whole world to know what was happening, and still is.

With my pendulum working overtime I asked how many people should be there, and exactly where and on which side of the two roads bordering the corner of the field we should stand. Proving what a sense of humour they have, the energies gave the date of April 1 – April Fool's Day!

I had tried to gather thirty-three people and, despite the

date, twenty-two people turned out at 5.30 a.m. that Saturday morning at All Cannings. The local milkman seemed very confused to see us all.

No wheat went down although some people did see lights and others caught a blanket blue light or energy on video. All I saw was a hare loping along the field.

A few hours later I found out that my idea had very nearly ended in tragedy. One of my friends, in the early morning mist had driven her car into a river shortly after leaving home. She could so easily have died. Never again would I allow myself to get so carried away using a pendulum to dowse for answers.

Having said that, I was really grateful to all those who made the effort and turned up at such an early hour. It was a good gathering and an indication of the intent of all those people so interested in the phenomenon, a suitable prelude to the season.

In the summer two formations appeared in the field beside where we had met. One a double ring, on the spot that we had watched and another, a six-petalled flower, down near the canal end of the field, the Kennet and Avon Canal.

The heart formation finally arrived at East Kennet and the day it appeared was the Saturday of the Group's Conference. The following day we held our closing ceremony within the heart, watching the full moon rise.

Early in June a formation had come in barley in almost the same position as the 33 tongues of flame, or Beltane Wheel formation as it was named, opposite Silbury Hill. A friend, L.J. and I visited it on the day it was discovered, a Friday. Within the circle there was a triangle laid down, a narrow path denoting its three sides. I followed L.J. as we walked along it. She was sensing with her hands where there were vortices in the energy. To test these I had removed a pendant that I was wearing on a necklace and was using it like a pendulum. At one point I heard her say,

"It's very strong here."

Sure enough, when I held my pendant over that spot it spun round so fast it was flying almost horizontally. L.J. turned round, saw what was happening and said,

"Why are you testing there?"

"Because you said it was very strong here," I replied.

"No I didn't," she retorted.

"But I heard you say it."

" I *thought* it," came her reply!

That was the first time I heard her thoughts – but the only time I said what I heard. So far it has only happened with two other people – but it hasn't been appropriate to say what I had heard.

Lying in the formation that Friday afternoon, I looked up and saw a mini rainbow in the sky. It wasn't oval like the one Bridget and I saw above Coronation Hall. It was like a typical rainbow but in miniature and with no rain involved.

I have seen them on several occasions since – always above formations. During one of my readings with Mavis Meaker, my psychic counsellor, I asked about these tiny rainbows. In replying the energies started by defining how a rainbow usually occurs – then said,

"But there is no rain. What does a rainbow mean to you?"

As I formulated my reply I was about to say beauty, love and joy. Before I could say these words they said "Joy?" Then they said that the rainbows are there as their signature. I can think of no signature more beautiful.

The next day was our Saturday meeting, and afterwards quite a few of us went to visit the formation. L.J. and I had a surprise – it had changed overnight. The large triangle now encompassed nine smaller triangles. This was the first formation I had seen that evolved over two days, although I was told it was not the first time it had happened.

Three of us decided to meet up that night and watch the formation to see if there might be any further activity. From the road we could hear people in the formation. As we watched we saw tiny lights that seemed to be in the circle.

When the people we had heard in the field came out they walked past us heading for their car. We asked them if they had been using torches or lighting cigarettes. They hadn't and were somewhat spooked when we told them about the lights we had seen.

Earlier that year a UFO had been seen above Silbury Hill. This was well documented at the time, with several people having seen its lights. In May, a hole appeared in the hill. This was first spotted by some American tourists who had climbed the hill. Although it was officially closed to the public, a few of us carried out a pre-dawn recce to investigate this hole. To me it looked as if the hill had been uncorked – to a depth of thirty-three feet (as measured later).

One of the formations that came in wheat in 2000 was at Honey Street, near Alton Barnes, very close to the canal. There had been a lot of rain and as L.J. and I went to visit it we had to wade through water in the field and squelch through mud that threatened to pull off my wellington boots. I had heard that the formation depicted a four-bladed propeller with a ring around it. Outside the ring there were three much smaller little circles, or grape shots. They were roughly in a line with the furthest, slightly offset to the right – a mirror image of Orion's Belt. The furthest circle had a standing centre. I really wanted to photograph this so I persuaded my boots to come with me to the edge of the circle. It was by then starting to get late and the clouds were very dark. There was a small bright portal in the sky which I tried to include in my picture.

When I saw the resulting photograph I noticed there was an anomaly on it. In the wheat standing around the edge of the small circle there was a white pentagon. Mentally I added the five triangular points around the pentagon to make a five pointed star or pentagram. With the bright portal in the sky above it reminded me of the first record I ever bought, 'Catch a Falling Star' by Perry Como. The song on the other side of that old 78 r.p.m. record was 'Magic Moments'. Little did I know way back in 1958 how many magic moments I would start to have forty years later!

The day before our 2000 Conference a formation was found below Golden Ball Hill in the field indicated to me by the hawk a year earlier. This was described as having six flames, one of which was curled up like a bud that had yet to open. Within that bud it looked to me as if there was an eye, a left eye – but it took me four years to make the connection with the left eye of the hawk! At the time I read that it looked like a comet that had gone into the sun. Different people see different things in the designs of crop circles, this is part of their fascination, they have so much to teach us from whatever background of knowledge or tradition we come.

One day that summer I gave T.C. a lift to Knapp Hill car park. She was due to be picked up there by helicopter in order to photograph several new formations. I was surprised when the pilot flew her off to the left over East Field and circled around above South Field at Alton Priors. As he flew in to pick her up he had noticed a brand new formation within the barley there.

After she landed we drove to Alton Priors and explored the new arrival. It put me in mind of a stained glass window in a cathedral. There were sixteen paths as I saw it, leading into a central eight-petalled flower. To enter any one of the paths you had to walk through what looked on the ground like a gothic arch. The lay of the crop was quite exquisite; it made me think of someone just leaving the hairdressers having had their hair blow-dried with not one single hair out of place.

I walked along several paths in and out of the centre. On the fifth one, walking in, I saw something on top of the flattened crop. There was a small circular ring which was three inches across. Six ears of barley had been woven together to form this amazing little detail. To be in that formation was to be in a very special space.

When I learned later that in ancient times there used to be a temple in that field, South Field, it made sense. The original location of the temple shows in some aerial photos, and several crop circles have been positioned over the site.

Beyond South Field, at Woodborough Hill, a superb formation came in a field of wheat. This looked like the seed head of a sunflower plant. Right in the centre the crop had been woven into three little nests. I took numerous photos because I could see these nests as a face – with two eyes and a mouth.

Something I really enjoy doing is visiting formations on my own, with no other people to distract me. Very early one Sunday morning I went to the sunflower. I lay in the centre resting my head on one of the nests as a pillow, the sun was coming up and there wasn't a cloud in the sky as I fell asleep.

When I awoke I looked up and was treated to the most amazing display. It was like an aerial ballet with swallows wheeling in the sky, white birds underlit by the sun as they flew and danced in pairs with perfect timing. I was overwhelmed by their performance and found tears rolling down my cheeks and going into my ears! The birds never flew away, they just went higher and higher in the sky until I couldn't see them any more. As I closed my eyes again all I could say was, "Thank you."

Some while later when I next opened my eyes there were two narrow bands of white cloud above me. The one to my right was made of a line of angels, the one to the left contained dolphins. Never have I had such a magical morning. In the distance I could see people heading for the formation, it was time for me to leave.

We had to change the venue for our Conference that year as Coronation Hall had been awarded a grant from the National Lottery and was undergoing a facelift. T.C. and I went to a Yoga Weekend staged at Devizes School. We were impressed by the site and the Group was lucky to be able to book it for mid-July.

The helicopter could land on the sports field which was perfect for anyone who wanted to take a flight to view the formations.

Two weeks after the 2001 Conference, on the Saturday evening, the Group had a post-conference party for all the helpers. The following morning a huge formation was reported at Milk Hill. It was above the white horse and covered the top of the hill, an area the size of a village. One crop-circle enthusiast had spent the night at the edge of the field, sheltering in his tent from the rain and looking in the direction of Silbury Hill. He heard and saw nothing, packed up on the Sunday morning and left without checking the field behind him!

L.J. and I heard about the formation on the Monday and went to investigate. I stayed near the edge as I watched her walk up and past the centre and out of sight as she went over the top of the hill. We had no idea of the design because nobody had yet flown over it to take photographs.

There were numerous circles of differing sizes. In one of the larger circles I found another 'face', three nests – two eyes and a mouth.

Aerial pictures showed that the formation contained 409 individual circles arranged along six swirling arms. Despite being laid down over the top of a hill on an area that included a hollow dew pond, the design was perfect when viewed from above. It looked as if it had been placed on a flat surface.

CHAPTER NINE
Counting nine colours in the rainbow

In 1999 I heard a new age audio tape that had been recorded some time earlier. From this I learned that as the result of pole shifts of several suns in other universes, there would be changes in our universe. We would receive a new sound and a new colour. The sound would be of a frequency that the human ear is unable to detect. The colour, however, we would be able to see. It would present as a new colour in the rainbow – aquamarine (a very pale shade of green).

I had mentioned this to a few people. During the spring of 2000 I was walking with L.J. near her home. We had crossed a footbridge over the River Thames, walked along the tow path and were climbing up a hill, enjoying the sunshine. Unexpectedly it started to rain, sun plus rain equals rainbow. We stopped and turned around to have a look and, sure enough, there it was – a beautiful rainbow above the river down below us.

"I wonder when we're going to see the new colour in the rainbow," I said to L.J. As we stood there looking at it, the new colour started to appear. The eighth colour, a band of aquamarine, came in below the band of violet. In awe L.J. and I agreed that if either of us had watched this alone we'd probably have thought we were imagining it!

I was really excited and couldn't wait to tell people at the Practice. You can persuade yourself that crop circles are man-made but not that someone has climbed up to add a colour to the rainbow. I particularly wanted Andrew, one of the other dentists, to see the new colour.

I don't think I convinced any of them! As I drove to work for my last day at the surgery I was only a mile away when I found that I was driving through rain with the sun shining. There *had* to be a rainbow. I'd go straight to Andrew's surgery and make him have a look. I parked in front of the house and quickly checked to see where the rainbow was.

There was no rainbow – I looked everywhere, I couldn't believe it. I literally stamped my foot on the ground as I looked up to the heavens and said out loud,

"I *really* REALLY wanted one." I went in and told no one.

At lunchtime they all gave me a farewell party. I saw my last few patients and by tea time I was busy taking down all the crop circle pictures in my surgery. All of a sudden Andrew appeared in the doorway and said,

"Right, where's this new colour in the rainbow then?"

"Why do you ask?" I said.

"Have you looked out of your window?"

I hadn't but very quickly did – and there it was, a beautiful rainbow. His nurse had come along too, and with my nurse, the four of us stood by the window. Silently I said a little prayer, "OK guys – please show them, let them see."

I then explained that they should look beneath the violet and hopefully they'd see the aquamarine colour. As the colour came in, there was much excitement and several exclaimations.

"I can see it – can you see it?"

As I was putting up some thank yous, Andrew went to

fetch his camera from his surgery. Then he said,

"What's this other colour coming in?"

I literally felt my knees buckle as I watched a band of pink fill in below the aquamarine. We were looking at a very wide rainbow with nine colours. I could hardly speak as I said,

"I don't know anything about that one."

Several years later I asked through Mavis about the pink colour that we'd seen on my last day working as a dentist.

"It was our way of celebrating with you," was their reply. "The closing of the door."

I'm always disappointed with the numerous pictures I try to take of rainbows. But on occasions, when the rainbow is really bright, all nine colours have registered on my films.

It seems amazing to me that we neither read nor hear anything about this new rainbow. If it has received any publicity I am unaware of it. I probably bore people by the way I try to promote it. I wear nine different coloured 'feathers' around my watch, have tied nine ribbons on all my luggage, knitted a bedspread and a wrap and even made a rug, again using all nine colours. Maybe if anybody reads this and looks at the next bright rainbow they see, the word will start to get around. We really are living in exciting times of change, a magical time.

My mother wanted nothing to do with the sale of Brookfield, our family home. She sheltered with our next-door neighbours while I showed a couple of estate agents round. She also said she didn't want to show any prospective buyers round either.

I remembered reading in Simon Peter Fuller's book, *Rising Out of Chaos*, that once you commit to the right way forward, the Universe steps in to help. I didn't realise how much help would be given until the day the agent put the house on the market. He phoned me that afternoon to say a buyer had offered the asking price and didn't even want to look around the house! The buyer's only condition was that we wouldn't try to put the price up if a higher offer was made. I gladly agreed to this.

The following day another would-be buyer offered an extra ten thousand pounds. I told the agent that I felt obliged to stick to the agreement with the first buyer. The next day the second 'buyer' offered to pay twenty thousand pounds above the asking price. Again I said No but I did start to wonder . . . !

When he was little, my brother had planted two acorns in the garden, half way down towards the wood where he'd found them. For about two feet, they grew joined as one, before separating and continuing to grow normally. This tree was now nearly forty years old, and very tall. I had always thought of it as a magic tree. Double rainbows sometimes appeared to end in the tree. I had watched a foal being born under it and also a deer giving birth to a fawn beneath its branches.

It was the one thing in the garden that I was really going to miss. I was preparing supper one evening and looking out of the kitchen window at the tree. Telepathically I apologised to the tree for leaving it. At the time I was washing a Sainsbury's organic Heart of Romaine lettuce. Having 'spoken' to our tree, I removed the next leaf from the lettuce and found – I couldn't believe my eyes – two oak leaves! In a Sainsbury's lettuce! Magic.

I brought my mother down to my cottage in Devizes and planned to return to Surrey to empty the house on the Monday, after a weekend workshop put on by the group of

dowsers to which I belong. Leading the weekend was
Dr Patrick MacManaway. It was an extremely interesting
two days, interactive and practical.

One of the things we were taught was how to
communicate with trees, with the spirit of the tree. I decided
then that I would spend my last night at Brookfield sleeping
under the oak tree and trying to bond with it in the hope
that I'd be able to link in with it from Wiltshire.

I planned to leave Devizes really early on the Monday
morning and arrive at Brookfield before the removal men.
I hadn't reckoned on the storm that came during the night.
I drove through deep flood waters, had to turn back at
Upavon due to a fallen tree – back through the floods which
were by then even deeper!

Twice I ended up back at Devizes. My third attempt via
Marlborough was successful. It took ages but I finally arrived
at Brookfield around 3.30 in the afternoon. The removal
men had started without me and already made at least one
trip to the Council tip. Long gone was the black bin bag in
which I had carefully packed some of my most special
possessions – the ones with huge sentimental value. I had
left it in the kitchen so that I could put it safely into my car
as soon as I arrived!

I did spend my last night at Brookfield under the oak tree.
It was a beautiful starry night. The following afternoon I
decided to go down to the orchard and pick up some
windfall apples. On the way I passed the oak, it was about
ten yards to my left. As I came level with the tree I nearly fell
to my left, so powerful was the force that it exerted as it
pulled me in.

By the time I had loaded up my car and was finally ready
to leave the empty house it was dark. I wanted to have one

last look at the back garden and say goodbye and thank you. There was a switch in the sitting room to turn on an outside light. I put it on and walked out of the back door from the kitchen. The garden and the woods beyond looked magnificent – as if they were floodlit. When I eventually turned round to go back into the house, the light went out. I thought I should turn off the switch even if the bulb had gone. When I reached the sitting room I found that the outside light was still shining. As I switched it off the realisation hit me – it had never been anywhere near as bright as the light I had just enjoyed . . . and it wasn't the moon.

CHAPTER TEN
To Egypt with a broken leg

In the autumn of 2000, I was invited to join a small group of people for a visit to Egypt early in 2001. The organiser of the trip was the medium I had consulted on two occasions in the past. I knew very little about Egypt but was keen to be one of the group of eight.

Not long after booking my place I went to a workshop with Simon Peter Fuller in Glastonbury. On my way from Devizes, I had just driven through the village of Seend. Going down a long hill, I saw a white football travelling beside me on the other side of the road. My first thought was that there must be children around. I looked and checked in my mirrors but couldn't see anybody. It was early on Sunday morning and there wasn't even any traffic. After a while I overtook the white sphere and it took me a while to realise that I had probably seen a ball of light – not a football!

One of the books on display in Glastonbury had been written by a German author who gave details of channellings from Princess Diana. One thing stuck in my mind, Diana had said, "I am only a breath away."

A few nights later, just before falling asleep I remembered that line and wondered how frustrating it might be in the next dimension, wanting to communicate but to have nobody 'tuning in'. I put the thought out, "If anybody will do, I'm here."

That night I had one of my vision dreams. In my dream I was in Egypt standing in a temple at the foot of a narrow flight of stairs. At the top of the stairs I could see a small rectangular portal which I took to be aligned with Sirius. Coming slowly down the stairs was a being in a long white hooded robe that hid their face. The being was carrying a rolled up scroll. As it reached the lower steps it started to unroll the scroll, and I knew it contained a message for me. I felt quite apprehensive about what I was going to read. At the bottom of the steps, having fully unrolled the scroll, the being slowly turned it around so that I could see what was written. At the top there were two words, the rest was blank. The two words read, 'Chapter One'.

When I woke up I thought long and hard about my dream. (It was two years before I saw the cloud that indicated the notebook and pen when photographed.)

Just over three weeks before going to Egypt I met up with five friends at Avebury. We walked about two miles out of the village to a dolman connected with Sirius. Once again it was a Sunday morning, the sun was shining and it was crisp and frosty. The night before I had had a dream about Silbury Hill. In my dream the hill had been like a firework with hundreds of silver stars shooting up into the sky, like a Roman Candle.

Standing by the stones forming the dolman we invoked the four Archangels – Michael, Gabriel, Raphael and Uriel. Then I linked in to Sirius. I heard a voice saying, "Welcome child – but you must go back." I felt so welcome that I wanted to stay. I didn't want to come back down to earth.

Again, I heard, "You must go back *now.*" Reluctantly I tried to ground myself.

The six of us decided to walk on further to a collection of sarsen stones representing the constellation Delphinus, on the other side of the Ridgeway, at Temple Farm.

Still 'with my head in the clouds', I began to recount my Silbury dream. I was very soon brought back to earth. The mid-day sun was thawing the frost and my foot slipped into a deep rut left by car wheels on the path. As I fell I knew I had done something nasty to my leg, but was determined to limp on to the sarsen stones.

I was grateful to V for the Arnica, also to Simon Peter and Diana for the helping hands on the walk back. My boots seemed to be picking up pounds of sticky mud but I wasn't able to shake or kick it off. V went on ahead and drove her car back up the track to save me having to walk all the way. I was never more grateful for a lift.

Four days later, on the Thursday, I had promised to drive a friend to Sussex and back. He was giving a lecture there and I didn't want to let him down, so I did the drive.

Ten days after my fall I was due to take my mother to see her doctor. Seeing me limping and my swollen leg the doctor decided I should have an x-ray. I drove my mother home then took myself to Devizes Hospital for x-rays.

A fractured fibula showed on the film. What also showed on the film was that, after ten days, the fracture was starting to heal. Although not perfectly in line, new bone was forming around the broken ends.

I took my x-rays back to the doctor and was told that now it was known I had broken my leg, I could no longer drive! My insurance would not be valid; also, I had to use crutches.

Next stop the fracture clinic at the Royal United Hospital

in Bath. The Consultant told me either they could operate and realign the bone, and 'pin and plate' it, or I could carry on as I was. It was an easy decision to make. I then asked about going to Egypt in ten days time. He said he'd have another look in a week but thought it should be okay – as long as I was going on a cruise, because I wouldn't be doing much walking. I laughed and didn't say we *weren't* going on a cruise. A letter from the Consultant ensured that I was given a seat on the plane with enough space to put my leg up to avoid swelling.

Thinking I might not be able to go, made me realise just how much I wanted to make the journey to Egypt.

We stayed first at Cairo and then at Luxor, going on day trips either using a couple of taxis or a minibus. I was very struck by some of the poverty we saw. In places it looked as if nothing had changed since biblical times. Some dwellings did exhibit one 'improvement' – the addition of a satellite dish.

In the Cairo Museum I joined the queue to walk past King Tutankhamun's sarcophagus. I found my attention strangely drawn to the Canopic jars. Was there a link with my rescue ship *Canopus*? Until then all I had known was that Sirius is the brightest star in the heavens and Canopus is the second brightest. When preparing the Pharaohs' bodies after death, some of their organs were placed in these Canopic jars. I later found out that there is a town in Egypt called Canopus, and wonderd if this was where the jars had been made – hence the name.

At Giza five of the group travelled out to the pyramids by camel or pony, while three of us went in horse-drawn carriages. There were some risks I wasn't prepared to take with my leg and some that the group leader wasn't happy for me to take. Although I had managed to get into a couple of pyramids earlier in the week, as we all prepared to enter Menkaure at Giza, Isabelle suggested that she and I walk around behind it and try to link in with the six inside. As we headed for some rocks on which we could sit, Isabelle said to me, "Who's the chap I keep seeing with you?"

I laughed and asked, "Has he got a beard?" I told her it was Angus she was seeing.

Sitting there on a rock I noticed a green disc in the sand. I picked it up and studied it. The diameter was about two and a half inches and it was a quarter of an inch thick at the centre. The contents of my pockets were already a joke with the group. At every security checkpoint I had to tip out about half a pound of assorted stones and crystals from each pocket. We decided my green disk was probably just a piece of old glass and I decided to leave it where I had found it. At the time it did cross my mind it might be a piece of Moldavite, but I'll write more about that later.

When we all flew to Luxor I experienced a very strange feeling. It felt as if I had come home and I knew I had lived there before. I remember thinking that if I ever returned to Egypt – this was the one place I'd want to visit. Back home in England after the trip I found myself feeling homesick for Luxor.

During our first visit to the Temple there I was following a couple of people in the group. In the corner of one room we entered, I saw what looked like the same rectangular portal I had seen in my dream.

"The energy is very strong here," said one of the two standing beneath the portal, holding out her hand to sense the energy. The second put out her hand and agreed. I doubted that I'd be able to feel anything but thought I'd have a go anyway. I held out my left hand as I walked towards the corner – wondering if maybe I might feel a tingling sensation.

An invisible force from below grabbed my arm and pulled me into the corner. I was never more surprised. I stood under the portal and closed my eyes as my body was moved round and round in a spiral with my feet fixed to the ground. It didn't feel as if I was straying far from the vertical but I was being moved in a clockwise direction.

When I first learnt to dowse with a pendulum, I read that usually a 'No' answer is indicated by the pendulum swinging in a straight line, and a 'Yes' answer by it swinging round clockwise in a circular motion. I could never understand why my pendulum always went round in an anti-clockwise direction to indicate 'Yes'.

After the incident in the Temple at Luxor it was almost as if my polarity had been changed. Since then, if I dowse with a pendulum, it now goes round clockwise for 'Yes'.

One day all eight of us took part in a meditation in the Temple. Just after this I felt a hand on my right shoulder. I don't know if I have spent more than one lifetime there, but the feeling of the hand on my shoulder brought back memories. It signalled that I was 'under arrest' and the end (of that lifetime) was nigh. Strangely there was no fear attached to that memory.

Crop circles don't only occur in crops. Some have been reported in sand. I've heard of two in Egypt and seen photos of one of them, and drawings of the other. We were chatting one day and Isabelle said,

"Shall we make a crop circle while we're here, Dereka?"

We were due to fly back to London from Luxor the next day. I replied saying, "We'll have to make it just at the end of the runway or we won't see it!"

Imagine my surprise a few months later, in May, when the first oilseed rape formation arrived in England. It was right at the end of an airport runway, not Luxor but Hurn Airport near Bournemouth.

The number of the runway was 35, which reminded me of *Demon*'s number 33 and *Canopus*' 34. I have only landed once at Hurn, on a flight from Jersey to Gatwick, which was diverted due to fog. The design of the formation put me in mind of a ship's wheel or a seven-pointed star. It was right beside a tourist attraction devoted to Alice in Wonderland. Sometimes I feel very like Alice, in a land full of wonder.

CHAPTER ELEVEN
A reply for SETI

Two months after the ship's wheel formation at the airport, a nine-pointed star appeared in wheat below the white horse at Milk Hill. It arrived on July 12, a few days before our annual Conference. On day one of the formation a group of us went to visit it in the early evening. As we walked up the field we noted how dry and cracked the earth was. We wondered how the wheat could be growing in such conditions.

It was decided to hold the closing ceremony for the Conference in the formation. As I walked up one of the tramlines I began to think my eyes were playing tricks on me. As I looked down into the deep wide cracks in the soil I saw a red light shining up at me. It ran the length of all the fissures and they looked like red serpents. I rubbed my eyes and thought maybe I was overtired and imagining it. I said to Jean who was following me that there was something funny going on with my eyes. "You can see it too!" she exclaimed. It wasn't just me. The red glow continued for quite a distance.

After the ceremony Jean and I were talking about the red light we had seen. T.C. overheard us and said she had seen it too, but she had been walking up a different tramline. While we had all been feeling sorry for the earth, for the state of the soil, we had been shown her red energy. I have been told that Milk Hill represents the heart of the dragon in the Dragon Hills. Was the dragon opening its heart to us?

It was a month later, on August 12, that the huge 409-circle formation appeared above the white horse and covered the top of the hill. I had tried to make a face out of three nests in the centre of one of the circles. A real face was to arrive two days later on August 14. This came in a wheat field next to the Observatory at Chilbolton in Hampshire. It put me in mind of a postage stamp with the picture of the face made up of standing circles of the crop arranged like pixels in a newspaper picture. Five days later the face was joined by a long narrow script. This came in the same field above the face and slightly over to the right, nearer to the Observatory, yards from the radio telescope.

The script was written in binary code and seemed to be a reply to a similar message sent out in 1974 from the Arecibo Observatory in Puerto Rico, to the stars in star cluster M13. It was sent on November 16 by the Search for Extra-terrestrial Intelligence (SETI). It gave to any off-planet intelligence capable of receiving it, details of the numerical nature of the message. This was at the top of the script.

Below this were the atomic numbers of the primary elements of Hydrogen, Carbon, Nitrogen, Oxygen and Phosphorus. Then came the chemical composition of the nucleotides that make up human DNA. Below that was a representation of the double helix of the DNA. And under that was a stick figure representing a human being. To the left of this figure was the binary number showing the population of humans on earth and to the right the number showing the average height of a human being. Next came a representation of our solar system with the nine planets to the left of the sun, placed on the right. The third planet from the sun is shown elevated, indicating our planet. At the bottom is a representation of the radio telescope by which the message was sent, the means of communication, and its diameter.

The radio message beamed out from Arecibo will take over twenty-two thousand light years to reach M13. Any reply sent in a similar way would not reach the earth until the year 47574. Yet here in 2001 is what appears to be a reply, arriving just beside a radio telescope as a crop formation in a field of wheat.

In this reply there are several differences. Included with the primary elements is Silicon. The senders' DNA includes a million more nucleotide sequences than human DNA. The representation of the double helix has an extra strand. Their population is larger than ours. The stick drawing of the extraterrestrial being has a larger head than the human and the height is indicated as 3' 4". If their solar system is the same as ours, the script in the field indicates that there may be life on Mars and the moons of Jupiter. Where the means of communication is indicated, the reply appears to depict a representation of a crop circle that appeared in the same field a year earlier, in 2000.

This was all very exciting and yet little space was given to it in the press and SETI prefer to ignore it.

T.C., L.J. and I flew above the two formations to photograph them and then set about trying to find them on the ground. We weren't sure if visitors were welcome at the Observatory and tried to think 'invisible'. Several military helicopters flew over us but we carried on. From the air we had seen a herd of cattle near the field. When we found them we knew we were close. L.J. put her hand up in the air to sense the energy of the formations, and thus we found them.

As we walked into the field we reached the face first. It was impossible to tell the design at ground level, it just seemed a real mess, a number of circles of wheat standing in no apparent order and of different sizes. With some difficulty, after a while we managed to find the region of the third eye and lay there for some considerable time, absorbing the energy and enjoying the sunshine. After the face we explored the script and were left undisturbed for over three hours.

Unusually the 2001 crop circle season extended well into October. A formation came in wheat at Wabi Farm near Etchilhampton that was still uncut at the beginning of the month. A friend of mine, Maggie, came from Surrey to stay. She said she'd like to go into a crop circle. I told her when we visited it that she was very lucky to find one so late in the year and on the land of such an obliging and friendly farmer.

On October 18 the *Gazette and Herald*, our local newspaper, reported on a crop circle in the grass of the cricket pitch at Coate. My bedroom window overlooks the cricket pitch but I missed seeing any of the action because I was involved in an eleven day 'tree protest' in the Market Place in Devizes. I always look out of the window at night towards Silbury Hill in the hope of seeing any strange lights. The protest had finished on Wednesday October 17.

A couple of days later I met with some members of Isabelle's group in the evening. One of them, P.B., asked me about the formation on the cricket pitch and, not having seen the newspaper, I didn't know anything about it.

During the crop circle season T.C. used to fly regularly to take photographs. The helicopter took off from Thruxton and landed at Knapp Hill, near Alton Barnes, to pick her up.

In 2001 we had the problem of Foot and Mouth disease, and the helicopter was not allowed to land on farmland. I thought the answer would be for it to land on the cricket pitch. I contacted the Chairman of Bishops Cannings Cricket Club and got his permission for the landings on their pitch at Coate.

I somehow thought P.B. was referring to this when he asked me the question. But he insisted there was a crop circle on the pitch and told me to look in the paper. This I did as soon as I got home. It was dark by then so I had to wait until morning to investigate.

It was still dark when I awoke but something made me take a couple of photographs out of my window, looking towards the pitch. At first light I went to have a look. I was really disappointed, the grass had been cut and there was nothing to see.

When I saw my photographs, however, one had two converging beams of light on it and another had several anomalies or orbs.

The weather at the time was good for grass-growing and I hoped that the energy in the circles on the pitch might affect the grass and make it grow stronger, thus showing up the circles in the new growth.

And that is what appeared to happen. The circles grew stronger and taller than the rest of the grass. There were over a dozen rings with a diameter of about a yard. The rings were two inches wide, all situated on the roped off area of the wicket. Some friends who are dowsers came to check them out and I filmed them as their rods spun round. Sadly there was no aerial photograph.

They quoted the Chairman of the Club in the newspaper. He is a farmer who has had crop circles appear on his land.

He said the grass on the pitch had been laid down just like the crops in the formations he had seen.

The tree protest started in Devizes on Sunday October 7. There used to be five ancient London Plane trees in the Market Place. One had been cut down and there was talk of cutting down the other four. A couple of years earlier over four thousand people had signed a petition to save the trees. The Town Council had the idea of turning the picturesque Market Place into an Italian Piazza with pavement cafés.

The public were ignored and it was announced that the trees would be cut down at 9 a.m. on the Sunday. A silent vigil was organised for people to gather at that time.

I heard a rumour that to avoid any possible confrontation the trees were to be cut down earlier. I decided to arrive before 6 a.m. and reached the Bear Hotel at 5.45 a.m. As I got out of my car the chainsaws started up. I could hear a man shouting for people to wake up and come and help, he was in one of the three trees by the fountain. I went to the tree and asked him if he was okay. The sound of all the saws was deafening. The police were in attendance and I appealed to the Senior Officer. I said surely they couldn't be allowed to make all that noise at such an early hour on a Sunday. He told me I'd have to contact the Council about it.

Gradually more people trickled into the Market Place and we all gathered around the tree with the man in it. We defended this tree while the other three were cut down. Eventually the tree surgeons left. The people of Devizes were very angry and we decided to continue the defence of the one remaining tree. By this time a second man had climbed up into it.

It proved a very popular protest. People of all ages were involved and they came from all walks of life. We had shopkeepers, a hospital consultant, the manager of one of the Market Place banks and a music examiner amongst our number. One of the group had a contact with the BBC and we were due to be featured on the Monday morning *Today* programme on Radio Four. This was cancelled because Mr Bush decided to start bombing Afghanistan on that Sunday.

There was a storm during the afternoon and it ended with a beautiful rainbow above us. I took this as a good sign.

I felt sorry for the people living around the Market Place because drivers started hooting their horns in support as they drove past.

I decided to stay night and day for as long as it took. I thought some gray hairs might help curb any over-enthusiastic young protesters. At night I parked my car under the tree and slept in it.

After eleven days the tree got a stay of execution and we all disbanded. As I left there was a huge clap of thunder over the Corn Exchange, down Station Road. The rain was torrential. I was due to attend the Crop Circle Study Group Wednesday lecture that evening. People who had driven from London said they stopped their car to watch the lightning as they passed Silbury Hill.

Although the initial protest was over we didn't just disappear. We got together and formed ourselves into a political party. The Devizes Guardians were born. We adopted the tree as our logo. Initially it was a picture of the Devizes tree. Now in 2011, it is a more modern design and we have five councillors on the Town Council, and three of the six Devizes Councillors on Wiltshire Council are Guardians.

After the eleven day protest, we were described in a letter to the local paper in October 2001 as 'rentamob who have gone away'. Far from it!

Four new trees were planted around the fountain although the 'Devizes One' was still standing. Its fate was to be decided at a meeting of Kennet District Council the following spring. It had to go.

After my experience trying to connect to the spirit of the oak tree in Surrey, I decided to link in to the Market Place tree. I asked a friend who is a shaman to do the same. She told me the tree was going to have to go, but that the spirit of the tree had agreed to transfer to one of the new trees.

When the day came for the old tree to be cut down, the same young man who had climbed up into it previously, did so again, and it wasn't felled. It wasn't going to happen while there were people around. This meant it would be vulnerable at night.

I was the only one who didn't have to get up and go to work every day so I volunteered to do the night watches. I drove into town every night at around midnight, parked beside the tree and waited till people started to appear in the morning. I had some phone numbers to call if I was worried.

At around 5 a.m. each morning, a car would arrive and park. Sometimes the driver would get out and walk around. On one occasion he walked behind my car, then got back into his and used his phone. I found this intimidating and was quite worried. I didn't want to wake anyone up at that hour but I pretended to be using my phone. He wouldn't know that I wasn't calling for help.

About ten minutes later a second car arrived and drove towards me. I was really quite scared as it pulled up beside me. In the glare of its headlights I couldn't tell who it was. It stopped with both drivers' windows side by side. What a relief – it was Mark. He had woken up and sensed I was in trouble, and decided to drive into town to see if I was alright. The other car drove off.

After the sixth night, as the town was coming to life, I set off for home. As I drove out of the Market Place I got a message from the tree. It said it was going to go but that it would come back as a crop circle.

When I arrived home, I felt full of energy. Instead of going to bed I decided to defrost the fridge, a major task. It was the day of the Queen Mother's funeral, April 9, and I had the television on in the kitchen. I didn't go and lie down until late afternoon. I fell asleep and didn't wake until midnight. I still felt really tired and when my mother said she hoped I'd spend the night in my own bed, I said I thought I would.

Not long after 5 a.m. the phone rang. It was Carroll, my neighbour in Devizes. She had been woken by the chain saw. The tree had gone. I felt too upset to go but phoned Keith who went to investigate. The first night I hadn't been there, the tree surgeons moved in.

A week earlier, the day the tree was supposed to be cut, I had taken several photographs. On two of them there were light anomalies. Above the tree just to its right there is what looks like a white five-pointed star with a diaphanous tail. It is heading to the left. It reminded me of what the shaman had said about the spirit of the tree transferring to one of the new trees. On the second picture the star is above one of the new trees.

During the summer one of the Councillors on Kennet District Council died and there was to be a by-election on Thursday July 18. The Devizes Guardians put up a candidate. I decided if the tree was going to come back as a crop circle, that would be a good time to come. I sent up a telepathic message to the energies involved to that effect.

Early on the morning of Monday, July 15, Lisa phoned me and told me to watch GMTV on the television. She said there was going to be an item about a crop circle. Sure enough there was the reporter in East Field at Alton Barnes. He was interviewing the farmer who said he had no idea what the design was. There was no aerial photograph and, as usual, on the ground it was impossible to tell what the formation represented. All I could see on the television were several fairly small flattened circles, some with standing centres.

The next day I was flying with T.C. above East Field. We came to the formation and there it was, *our tree*! I think I shouted as I said, "It's the tree!"

It looked like a fruit tree; I later counted 105 circular fruits. If you looked at the tree upside down, the root area represented a mushroom. The tree in the Market Place was said to have been diseased and this mushroom made me think of Honey Fungus. I took numerous photographs but felt pretty stunned. When we came in to land Peter, the pilot, asked me if I was alright.

"I'm in awe," I replied.

I felt really excited as I collected my photographs later in the day. I crossed the Market Place and took one into the office of the local paper. They had been very supportive of our protest. I was greeted by a very snooty young lady who didn't even look at the picture and dismissed me by saying that they got all their pictures from the internet.

Needless to say, on the Thursday, the Devizes Guardians' first councillor was elected.

Chapter Twelve
"Home, phone ET"

The drama with the Market Place tree was all over
before the 2002 crop circle season began. On Sunday
April 28 I was driving along the A361 road towards
Beckhampton from Bishops Cannings. It was just after 7.30
p.m. and I was on my way to Isabelle's for a meditation
meeting. Unusually there was no other traffic on the road.

Looking in the direction of Silbury Hill, I decided to
check where you get the first glimpse of the top of the hill.
Almost immediately my car started to lose power. As I
wondered what on earth could be wrong, it gradually came
to a standstill. A warning beep sounded, and a red light
indicated that I was out of oil. The car was only one year old
and had just had its first service. Had the garage forgotten to
replace the oil when changing it? Before finishing the
question in my mind I dismissed the idea – the car wouldn't
have come quietly to rest if that had been the problem. At
that point the beeping noise started again and the red
battery warning light came on. As I rejected that idea I
remembered stories of how the cars of people who have seen
UFOs came to a mysterious halt.

Feeling very excited at the idea, I looked up through
the sun-roof. I didn't see anything other than sky. The car

re-started when I turned the ignition key and gave no further trouble. When I told the people I was meeting what had happened, Isabelle laughed and said that would teach me to have spiritual thoughts while driving!

A week later Monday May 6 was a Bank Holiday. I had arranged to meet a friend in Glastonbury that day. I awoke early with a strange feeling of a strong connection to the energies responsible for the crop circles and wondered when the first formation would arrive in Wiltshire. Unusually it was a 'bad hair day'. One section of hair above my left ear insisted on lying flat and pointing forward.

As I reached home that evening I noticed a microlight plane circling in the sky the other side of Bishops Cannings and wondered if there was a new formation there. I found out a couple of days later there was indeed, in oilseed rape, at North Down.

Only as I drove past it for the third time did I suddenly realize that the formation was in the very field beside which my car had ground to a halt a week earlier.

I was talking to L.J. about all this a few days later and she jokingly said down the phone, "They have obviously got their eye on you!"

I thought no more about it until a week later when I looked at a photograph I had taken in the formation.

On Wednesday April 16 a speaker came to talk to the Study Group. One of his thoughts was that the complicated work of mapping out the design of crop circles was probably done prior to the moment when 'a button' is pressed and the crop then goes down in a few seconds. After the talk I told him about what had happened to my car a week before the North Down formation. We joked about it being yellow, the same colour as the oilseed rape.

The next day T.C. asked me if I would take an overseas visitor to see the formation. She was returning to Canada from Italy and had given herself a day in England to try to go into a crop circle.

The design of the formation was the outline of an oval nestling in a crescent of downed crop. Beneath this there were three smaller circles of flattened crop. We walked up past it, walking at the edge of the adjacent field of young wheat. From the top of the hill looking down over the formation the tramlines were hardly visible, just a slight indentation in the six foot tall yellow jungle.

To find a tramline to walk in we had to look at the base of the stalks, to find a gap. We then had to 'swim' through the plants sticking our arms forward and parting the entangled flowers. We were covered in yellow pollen from head to foot. When I got home later I got a very disapproving look from my mother. "You were wearing black when you went out, where did you get *that*?!"

It was well worth the struggle. After ten days the flowers of the downed crop had turned up towards the sun, forming a beautiful carpet about ten inches deep. We explored the oval and the crescent and then tried to find the three small circles below the crescent.

I particularly wanted the Canadian lady to see the standing bouquet that I had heard was a magnificent centrepiece in one of these circles. I photographed it but was told by a couple of friends who visited the formation on day three that what we saw was but a shadow of what it had been, beautiful as it was.

When the friends had tried to photograph it, their brand new camera refused to work. The next day the camera was fine. Cameras and electric equipment often malfunction in crop circles. Also on day three they said the temperature was much higher in the circle with the bouquet than in the rest of the formation.

I included my companion in a couple of pictures in that small circle as a reminder for her of her visit. One of them showed some anomalous lights. A white 'necklace' crosses her head and face, and from her waist down there is a multi-coloured area of pink and green [photo 56]. This could have been due to the sun but in the centre of the pink and green area was something very strange. Level with the lady's right hand is an eye, a left eye.

At first I thought it might have been a dolphin's eye; whatever it was, it wasn't a human eye. L.J.'s 'eye on you' comment came back to me and really made me think. I thought about all the time that she, T.C. and I had spent in the third eye area of the enigmatic face at Chilbolton the previous August.

My 'bad hair day' lasted for more than a day. By day thirteen I had got used to the flat patch. My mother and I went down to Devon to see Priscilla and Mike. After washing my hair Priscilla was having trouble blowing it dry. "Dereka, I can't do anything with it, the back is insisting on going in a circle and this side bit is growing forwards."

"Is it going clockwise?" I asked.

The following year when I was asking questions through Mavis I was told that when my car was stopped, the energies were working on my crown chakra.

After oilseed rape, the next crop to receive formations is barley. In early June T.C. and I visited two of these. One opposite Silbury Hill had a central eye-shaped area and the other at Avebury Trusloe was described as a Celtic knot design. In the one opposite Silbury I was walking around filming while T.C. was lying in the eye. As I approached she described seeing some curious amorphous blobs in front of her eyes. I lay down and as soon as my head hit the barley I could see the same thing. The black spots were joined by fine filaments.

It is very hard to describe but it was as if we were under water looking up at a film about eight inches above our eyes. It was like being in an eye looking through a viscous solution. All the dots and filaments were joined as one body. By moving our eyes we could both make the whole mass move around, following the eye movement.

The following evening we experienced the same phenomenon in the Celtic knot formation. It was in no way the same as seeing those little 'floaters' one can often see. Our sight was affected by the energy in both formations.

When I looked at the video film I had taken in the Silbury formation, I saw that for the first few seconds there was a small white light floating just above the standing crop. It came in from the left and it was almost as if it saw it was being filmed because it suddenly dropped down out of sight. Maybe they can keep an eye on us more easily than we can keep an eye on them.

On July 17 T.C. and I were flying above the white horse at Pewsey. Below us we saw a new formation. Peter the pilot said it hadn't been there the day before. It was a beautiful shell design including numerous very fine lines. That evening we visited it with L.J. On one of the photographs I took you can see a round white luminous globe or orb below the white horse.

Our Conference at Devizes School was held on Saturday 27 and Sunday 28 July. For the first time Mavis was there giving readings. I made an appointment with her on the

Sunday morning, and towards the end of our session came the link with the energies involved in some of the formations.

The last speaker of the morning was a semi-retired Church of Scotland minister. I went into the hall to hear him. He started his talk wearing a cravat which he soon removed to reveal his dog-collar. He asked us if we would like to sing 'Jerusalem'. We said yes and all joined in. He then invited us to go outside onto the grass quad with him.

He got us to stand in two circles, one inside the other. There were too many people which made the circles too large, so we ended up standing in three concentric circles. He asked us to focus our attention and direct our thoughts to the centre.

Each circle was then given a different note to sing, and a lady helped the speaker organise us as we harmonised and put up a beautiful sound.

I don't think any of us looked up, but some of the stallholders watching us saw a whole flock of seagulls circling above us. They stayed above us the whole time we were there. A couple who had been to visit a formation saw the birds as they were driving back to Devizes.

Throughout the weekend a helicopter had been taking people from the School sports field on tours of the nearby crop circles. The pilot always followed the same route, taking in as many formations as possible. There was a great deal of excitement when the helicopter got back at lunch time. A new formation had just arrived, in a field the pilot had flown over frequently during the morning. It seemed to be a representation of the workshop we had just taken part in, with three concentric circles and numerous lines running into the centre.

It was not our usual helicopter company, Fast from Thruxton, and the pilot was so impressed by this new discovery, he joined the Study Group.

Through Mavis I asked about this the following year, during another reading (see The Transcripts, February 2003). I was told that we had put up the energy and that they had been able to use that energy for the formation.

It came in a field at the Gallops at Cherhill. It is unusual for a crop circle to arrive during daylight, they are normally found in the morning having come overnight.

On the Sunday afternoon of the Conference I also saw a healer. He told me that, like him, I was part E.T. This was certainly food for thought.

About ten days later I was lying in bed one night and remembered what the healer had said. Keen to make contact I thought of the film *E.T.* and how, at one point, the extra terrestrial had said, "ET, phone home."

I decided to reverse this and put up the request for "Home to phone E.T.", me being E.T.

A week later I was talking to T.C. on the phone. She told me about a new formation in wheat at Sparsholt, near Winchester in Hampshire. She was looking at a picture of it on the internet as we talked. She said it was very strange and looked like the back view of a cat with a disc above it and to the left. It came on August 15.

The next day I saw it on her computer. The photograph had been taken upside down. Turning it the right way up, I took one look and exclaimed "It's E.T!" The disc was below the head, to the right. It looked as if he was holding the disc forward in his left hand.

There was a message spiralling out of the disc, which was later found to be in binary code. Decoded the message read,

Beware the bearers of FALSE gifts and their
BROKEN PROMISES. Much PAIN but still
time. Believe. There is GOOD out there. We
OPpose DECEPTION. Conduit CLOSING
(BELL SOUND)

Needless to say I was absolutely delighted by the arrival of
the formation and couldn't wait to visit it. Before going in
on the ground we flew over it. We booked a larger helicopter
and five of us went. Having asked for home to phone E.T,
I couldn't believe my ears when we were told that the
formation was beside some telephone masts. Many
photographs were taken and much filming was done. We
didn't leave until sunset.

Whereas the face at Chilbolton was made up of standing
circles of wheat, this one was achieved by numerous lines of
flattened crop going horizontally across the design of the
being. Some were only two inches wide.

On the ground we first entered the centre of the disc. I
left to go and film around the being. T.C. and L.J. decided
to walk out of the disc by following the spiral path. They
timed how long it took them and estimated that the path
was two miles long.

We noted that the left eye of E.T. was open but the right
eye was closed, almost as if he was winking. As we were
flying back to Thruxton we saw three other formations in
Hampshire. One of these, at Beacon Hill, was a pyramid
surrounded by thirty-three points. At the top of the pyramid
is an eye, a left eye, once again. It made me think of the
anomalous left eye on my photograph back in May and how,
anatomically, the left eye is connected to the right side of the
brain. When I later saw my photograph of the pyramid

taken as we flew over it, I found there was a light anomaly on it.

The day before the E.T. crop circle was found, a new formation appeared in East Field at Alton Barnes. The tree formation was joined by two dolphins swimming in a circle. They were level with the tree but further along the field to the right. Within the dolphins were three concentric circles of standing wheat with a flattened central circular area. L.J. went to great lengths to convince me they were sharks, but the formation made a big splash on the internet as dolphins.

By the time I was able to visit it, the combine harvester was in the field. In the central area there were two standing tufts of wheat. Incorporated into one of them were two peacock tail feathers. One tendril from these feathers was wound so tightly around a wheat stalk that it looked like a corkscrew on a climbing plant. As the field was being cut I thought it would be in order for me to take the feathers. It was with the greatest of difficulty that I pulled them out of the earth. A year later when I asked about this through Mavis, I was told the feathers had not been put there by humans.

I had recently telepathically asked our next door neighbours' peacock, as it passed under the kitchen window, to leave me one of its feathers. Later I went out and got into my car before I noticed that a feather had been left for me just by my door.

It had been such a wonderful crop circle season that I didn't want it to end. I have only mentioned a few of the formations. By mid-September everyone was saying the season was over but I didn't want to believe them. The previous year I had been able to visit Wabi Farm and the cricket pitch in October.

I drove around but the combine harvesters had been busy and I couldn't find any wheat fields that hadn't been cut. All that was left to receive a formation was maize. I had seen a photograph of a crop circle in maize in America, so that is what it would have to be.

One Sunday L.J. phoned and said that she had been shown a picture of a maize formation near the Milk Hill white horse at Walkers Hill below Adam's Grave, the long barrow above Alton Barnes. She described it as a simple circle. I drove to investigate and thought I could see two circles in the field. It was getting dark so I would have to wait until the next day before exploring further.

I set off on the Monday to visit them. My problem was how to find where they were. The crop was eight feet tall and there were no tramlines. It seemed my only hope of locating the circles was to dowse. I took off the pendant I was wearing and used it as a pendulum. I walked along the top edge of the field and tried to find the nearer circle. I thought I was walking too far before turning into the crop, but the pendulum was adamant. As soon as it indicated a left turn I was more than happy to take cover as there were three military helicopters above.

For several yards the maize at the edge of the field had been planted in rows at right angles to the way I wanted to go. I had to separate the leaves carefully and step through each row. It became somewhat easier when the rows changed and were going in the same direction as me. It was still very difficult to make any progress, it was more of a jungle than the oilseed rape had been back in May. I was continually being slapped in the face by the large leaves, still wet from the previous day's rain.

I became convinced I would never find it and would walk

straight through the field. Then, all of a sudden, there it was, on my right.

There was a large standing circle in the centre and these eight-foot high plants with their thick red stalks were laid down just like barley, sweeping around in a clockwise flow and reflecting the sunshine. I walked all the way around the edge of the formation and looked back up towards the white horse to the left of the standing centre which seemed so tall with its big green leaves, red stalks and corn husks flecked with purple. Under a blue sky it all looked quite magical and felt very welcoming.

The flattened ring was approximately eighty feet across and the centre was thirty feet wide. The stalks were one inch thick. The plants had been bent at ground level, some were detached from their roots, others still partially or fully attached. I took many photographs of the formation and then set about threading my way through the plants to find the edge of the field again. I assembled a little pile of stones to mark the entry point for finding my way in another time. I didn't try to find the other circle that day.

The following morning I booked a microlight flight so that I could take aerial pictures of the formations. Above the field I could see there was a third circle of downed crop, a tiny one about twelve feet in diameter.

I took my film in to be developed and that afternoon, with the aid of an aerial photograph, T.C. and I managed to visit all three of the circles. I had to dowse once again to find two of them.

I was glad I hadn't been led to the largest circle the day before. I wasn't comfortable in it, it didn't feel nearly so welcoming as the ring had done. The lay of the crop was radial, with the flattened plants all pointing from the centre to the circumference. It felt as if there had been an explosion of energy and there were a few lines that extended beyond the edge of the circle. These reminded us of a formation known as the 'Medicine Basket' in the same field in 2000.

There was something of a standing centre, all of four plants. Either side of the four there were other plants bent over at lower and lower levels, in effect two rows with the tallest at the centre.

Definitely my favourite place to be was in the tiny circle. How on earth do you persuade eight-foot plants to lie down and bend round neatly in a clockwise direction in a circle with a six-foot radius? Sitting in it with these huge plants towering above me was like being a child in my own very special secret hiding place.

I revisited all three circles a couple of days later with L.J. and was very pleasantly surprised at how much nicer the energy felt in the largest circle than when I had first entered it. There was a big change in the energy in a short period of time. From the air the red stalks of the crop made the formations appear to be pink. The ring looked just like an iced doughnut!

During that summer I had been adopted by a robin in the garden. It would come to me every time I went out of the door, landing on my hand. Daphne gave me a tip and said that I should keep a bag of biscuit crumbs in my pocket, so I did. Sometimes it would come into the kitchen, either through the window or the door. I tried to practice communicating telepathically with the bird.

One day the kitchen window was open and the robin was standing on the frame. I decided to take a photograph of it. When I looked at the picture later there were several anomalous white orbs to be seen. They started with one around the beak, and went just to the right. They reminded me of the thought bubbles you see coming from people's heads in pictures in comics. Coming as 'thoughts' from the robin's beak they struck me as a perfect representation of telepathy.

Sadly, another robin regarded the garden as its territory and used to attack 'my' robin viciously. The bully won and the little bird stopped coming, ending a beautiful friendship.

I had been collecting seeds from some of the crop circles that summer. I had nine cardboard drums labelled and containing grains of wheat and one with maize. The next year with the help of Lyndon, our gardener from Surrey, I planted the seeds in ten large containers, and put them on the flat roof above the garage.

The maize didn't grow very well but some of the wheat was amazing. Lyndon was very impressed with stalks that bore ten ears of wheat. The seeds that did least well were from a drum I had labelled 'Sharks' from East Field. I later found that there were still two grains of wheat left in the drum. I took these out and apologised to them for having used the word Sharks. I labelled a new drum 'Dolphins' and popped the seeds in. I planted these two seeds at the same time as sowing crop circle wheat for wheatgrass to be juiced. I put them in the corner of the tray so that I could watch them compared to the rest of the seeds.

It was very noticeable how much better these two grew. They were much stronger and taller than the rest of the tray. It really made me think about the consciousness of the seeds and about the effect of talking to them. It was these two that Domino the cat chose to eat!

I grew several trays of wheatgrass. These I took to our Conference and gave them to Peter Vaughan, the Devizes-based chef who used to cater for us. He juiced the grass and it proved very popular with people attending the Conference.

In crop circles the grains of wheat from the downed crop are often spilled onto the ground. When it rains these can germinate and young green plants appear. After a few weeks the floor of a formation can be quite green. Following the harvest, if the field is not ploughed, these young plants become quite sturdy. You get a replica of the original design in green.

Four of us visited one of those formations at Windmill Hill near Avebury in November 2002. It was a sunny afternoon and we had a magical time. There was a hare in the field as we went through the gate. The energy in the formation was dowsable and, at one point, we had a beautiful rainbow above us. I had finished the film in my camera before the rainbow appeared. We had a short meditation after which I looked up. There in the sky, backlit by the setting sun was a small white cloud. It looked just like a golden bearded sun god. By this time nobody had any film left. Maybe some things just aren't meant to be photographed.

I visited another green formation in January 2003, at Coate, below Etchilhampton Hill. It consisted of five circles and had been called 'The moons of Jupiter'. I was in there late in the afternoon and a mist was coming down. One of the circles had had more energy than the other four. I stood in this circle and with no-one around, decided to sing three OMs by way of making contact. The first one sounded really loud and surprised me. I hesitated before the second, wondering how it was that the first one had been so loud. The second sound was even louder and I found that my lips were vibrating. It felt very strange. I felt quite apprehensive about putting up the third OM. This proved to be an amazing experience; the sound was so loud and was coming back to me. Not only my lips but my whole body was vibrating, and over and above it I could hear what I can only describe as a celestial sound.

I felt as if I was in shock and have since found out that there is a vortex there. In February, through Mavis, the energies said, "You shout at us, we shout at you!"

CHAPTER THIRTEEN
The fires that lit themselves

The 2003 crop circle season in Wiltshire began with a formation in oilseed rape at Woodway Bridge at All Cannings. I went to visit it but, just as I was about to enter the field, it began to rain and all I did was take a picture from the bridge over the Canal. There was a boat passing as I took my photograph, with someone holding up an umbrella.

Shortly after this I joined some of the members of Isabelle's group above Cherhill. At one point while we were all standing in a circle, I felt energy coming into my left hand. The palm became warm and then hot, almost uncomfortably so. As we left to walk down the hill there was a beautiful sunset. I stopped half-way down to take some photographs.

I finished the film in my camera at a celebration party. All five Devizes Guardians candidates had been elected, either to the District or Town Councils. I took my film in to be developed, and when I collected them, they were very strange. The first picture, from the bridge over the canal, came out fine. The next few of the sunset were extremely blurred and upside down. The rest of the photos were less blurred and the right way up.

The man in the photo processing shop told me the machine that printed them would have sensed they were upside down, and righted them automatically. I checked the negatives and all but the first one of the boater with his umbrella were upside down.

What on earth had happened to my camera? The next film was fine. One of the photographs of the sunset (Photo 93) had some anomalies. There are some grey triangles and a red and a green light. A cloud in the sky looked yellow and made me think of a snail. A large snail had mysteriously appeared on the inside of the windscreen of my car when I was returning one day from Glastonbury!

On May 21 I had a phone call from one of the people at the Crop Circle Connector website. They had received on their computer the co-ordinates giving the location of a new formation. It had been sent to them anonymously so they were a bit suspicious about it. I was told roughly where to look and set off to investigate.

I drove past Silbury Hill and from a high point looked in the direction of West Overton. I was hoping to see a shadow in one of the fields, indicating where the formation was. At first I couldn't see anything but then, in the distance, there was a field of barley wafting in the breeze. At times I thought I could just detect the slightest of shadows and tried to work out how to reach the field.

I parked at the edge of a very narrow lane and went up the bank and through a hedge into the field. I walked along the edge of it, dowsing to locate the formation, and turned into the crop along the tramline where the pendulum indicated. When I found the formation I saw that the barley had been very lightly indented. The stalks had been bent half way up, not near the ground as they usually are.

I started to take some photographs and then looked behind me. There was a huge black cloud, it was about to pour with rain.

I decided to hurry back to the car and wait for the rain to pass. Just as I reached the car, of all things, a bus drove up behind me. I wouldn't have thought the lane was wide enough for buses. I'd have been very unpopular had I not returned when I did, as he could not get past until I moved the car.

After the rain I went back to investigate the formation further. As always, on the ground, it was impossible to work out the design. I managed to locate the centre and there I found a charming little detail. Six heads of barley had been gathered together in a circle and bent outwards just above ground level; a little arrangement that was only about four inches wide.

I finished my roll of film and drove back to Devizes to get the pictures developed. I was just in time to catch the post and send a set of prints to the Connector website office. They arrived the next morning, not as fast as digital photography, but not bad!

When T.C. flew over the formation later, she could see the design was of a six-petalled lotus. It looked as if it had been mapped out by tyre tracks. L.J. joined us a couple of days later to go into it. The tyre effect was achieved by the crop being bent in bands. In one band the crop was bent at right angles to the left, and the next band bent to the right, but only from halfway up the stems.

Much later, through Mavis I asked the energies about putting the information on the computer. They said they didn't do it often because normally the formations are found. This one they said could not have been found.

They have also altered information on my computer in the past. I had the Study Group membership list on it and, wanting to telephone one of the members, looked up her number on the computer. I had phoned her previously using, as I thought, that same number, but that night I found myself talking to her next door neighbour. Another time the name of her house on the list had been altered.

When I asked about this through Mavis, I was told it was to draw my attention to this particular person. She and I share a past-life memory of fire.

A few days before the local elections in May 2003 I was once again visiting a friend in Glastonbury. As I was leaving, I got into my car and started the engine. Looking up I saw a rainbow at the end of her road. I could see all nine colours in this rainbow so I went back to the house to get Francesca so she could see it too.

"Why don't you take a photograph of it?" she suggested. I told her it was too faint. "You really need a very bright one to show all the colours." Soon I got back into the car and set off for home.

I was just leaving the town when out of the corner of my left eye, through the hedge I caught sight of something bright. As soon as I could I stopped the car and got out to look. There by the base of the Tor was a really bright wedge of rainbow. This one I did photograph, and used it on the jacket for this book, and again as Photo 91 in the colour plate section. If you look hard, you can just see the nine colours.

The rainbow came with me all the way back. I stopped off to visit Daphne at Seend and saw that the wedge of rainbow was over Devizes. This I took to be a good omen for the Guardians in the forthcoming elections.

After the lotus design crop circle I had been asked to find at West Overton, another lotus formation appeared in mid-June. This one came in wheat and was much easier to see. It arrived in the field below the white horse at Milk Hill. Incorporated in the design was a six-pointed star. T.C. and I flew to photograph it and on some of our pictures that included the white horse, we both found a distinct pink colour in the white clouds.

The previous autumn we had been so impressed by a firewalk in Scotland that T.C. asked Stephen who organised it to bring a firewalk to our Conference in 2003. It was arranged to take place on the Saturday evening, August 2, at Alton Barnes. The main Conference was held at Devizes School, but we met in the evening at Coronation Hall. The firewalk was to be in the field next to the Hall.

Remembering what had happened in 2002, when a formation appeared at the Gallops on the Sunday of our conference, I thought the energies might mark the firewalk in some way. I didn't tell anyone about this but put up a request for a formation in East Field.

2003 was my year of getting fit to go to Peru and do the Inca Trail so, as well as attending the gym, I did a lot of walking. I would drive to Knapp Hill, walk up that first, and look down into East Field and focus on the formation I hoped would appear there. Then I would climb up to Adam's Grave and from there again look down into East Field, and ask for the formation.

On the Saturday morning of the firewalk, word went round the Conference that there was a new formation in East Field! I felt really excited and wondered what it looked like.

Later in the day I saw an aerial photograph. The formation was rectangular and looked to me to be surrounded by a path of flames. This path had right-angled bends and followed six directions before a 45° bend led to the centre of the rectangle.

As I understand it, the six directions represent north, south, east and west, followed by above and below. The seventh direction is within. I was told that one of the purposes of a firewalk is to open the heart.

When I visited the formation on the Monday morning, I walked the six directions round the edge, and then along the seventh, into the centre. There in the downed crop I found two centre pieces. Both exhibited a heart shape. One was like a bouquet of wheat; the other was a standing centre. When I looked down through the middle of it, the visible area of soil was also a heart shape.

I counted fifty-five flames of standing crop around the edge. These were all separated by circles of downed crop and each circle had its own standing centre.

Needless to say I put up some mega thank yous and, after the harvest, I buried a crystal under one of the two centrepieces in the middle, in the heart region as I saw it.

On the Monday after our August Conference another beautiful formation arrived at Walkers Hill, below Adam's Grave. It was in wheat and in the field above where the maize formations came the previous October. It became known as 'The Swallows' because it depicted three birds that looked as though they had swooped down a hill leaving trails of circles in their wake. This really was a wonderful formation to visit. I lost count of the number of times I went into it.

The Study Group met up as usual for the winter solstice. In 2003 it fell on a Sunday. For several years we had held a celebratory Christmas lunch on the day of the solstice at

Peter Vaughan's Healthy Life cafe in Devizes. We were unable to do so that year, but the plan was to gather and perform Agni Hotra fire ceremonies at sunrise and sunset up at Adam's Grave Long Barrow, above Alton Barnes.

Knapp Hill Car Park was cold and windy when we met at 7.30 a.m. It was also raining and I wondered what chance we would have of lighting the two little fires in their copper pyramids up on top of the hill. We crossed the road and climbed up to the Barrow.

I failed to light my fire. It was so cold that my ghee (clarified butter) was rock hard. As I tried to scoop it out of the tin and spread it on the pieces of dried cow dung, I kept bending the little copper spoon. It didn't matter though because T.C. and L.C. were successful in lighting the other fire. The rain had stopped and the flames and sacred smoke greeted the first rays of the sun as we sang the mantra and threw the rice into the fire.

Afterwards we moved just below the two copper pyramids and formed a circle. We sang and danced and sent up some fantastic OMs with our prayers.

The result was quite dramatic. When I had tried to light my fire I had failed completely, it didn't catch at all. At one point I turned round from the circle to look at the two pyramids and saw flames roaring from my fire, shooting out horizontally in the strong wind. I couldn't believe my eyes; the flames had come from nothing.

Down below us East Field was still displaying the rectangular fire formation in green. Now, not only had the fire on the hill self-ignited, but a portal had opened in the clouds above the field. A small circle of blue sky could be seen.

Lisa noticed that at the left of this blue circle, a tiny faint rainbow had formed, very similar in shape to a cloud formation photographed exactly five years earlier in 1998, again above East Field. It was thought at the time to represent the Ken rune.

During the next forty minutes or so the light of the little rainbow intensified and its shape changed. At one point the cloud arranged itself so that it looked like a breaking wave in the ocean. The rainbow positioned itself along the leading edge of the wave, like a very bright 'white horse' in the sea.

Later the increasingly bright light turned itself into a ball shape. As we all watched in awe this ball of light separated itself into two and each half took on the shape of a flying saucer.

By the time we were back at the car park it was one amazingly bright light, the two halves having united.

I tried to photograph these different shapes and hoped they would show up on film. As usual the rainbow didn't really register but I need not have worried about the light, people looking at the last few pictures initially thought I had been trying to photograph the sun.

The last two pictures, for whatever reason, make the light look as though it was enclosed in a huge bubble containing bands of pink and green energy. There is also the hint of a lightship in the cloud to the right of the light. Through Mavis I was later told that the bubble effect may have been caused by my camera.

What a privilege it was to witness light coming through that portal into our dimension, to be bathed in its rays and hopefully to have absorbed them. It is my belief that the light brings truth and information. I was reluctant to drive away from the car park.

In the afternoon, prior to leaving home for the ceremony at sunset, I put the ghee on the dung while still in the warm. This time we had three pyramids and two of the three fires lit. T.C.'s refused to light, just as mine had at dawn. After the ceremony we stood in a circle around the three pyramids. As we sent up the OMs I was actually watching T.C.'s fire as it suddenly burst into flames. What absolute magic!

We were then treated to gale force winds and pelted with hail before retiring to Mipo At Home at Lydeway for hot soup and drinks . . . a perfect ending to a truly amazing day.

A few days later I noticed that photo number 23 on one of my films had not been printed. This should have shown, in green, the formation from August 2 in East Field. I persuaded the man in the photo shop to print it regardless. Whatever energy was still there produced a mega blur, you can just make out a bit of hedge.

This drew my attention to photos number 24 and 25. In the top left corner of both there is a very narrow beam of light directed down into the field. The beam comes from a much higher elevation than that of the sun at the time of taking the pictures. It was from the light that came in as the mini rainbow, but none of us saw it. I wondered if we were being directed to Alton Barnes for our next Conference. Devizes School was unable to accommodate us in 2004.

Just before the end of the season, T.C. was showing a group of Australians around. I joined them after lunch and we went into a couple of formations at Woodborough Hill. Both had arrived in July. The first was described as a scarab and the second, heading towards it, represented a serpent or sperm.

We also visited the church at Alton Priors. In the churchyard is a magnificent yew tree, said to be seventeen hundred years old. It flourishes despite being separated into two halves. You can walk between the two and stand within each one. I took several photographs before leaving the churchyard and heading for the sacred spring nearby, below

East Field. Here too I took photos trying to capture on film the ripples in the water.

I didn't finish the film, so ended up taking those photographs still in the camera to Peru. I used up the remainder taking pictures in the Swissotel in Lima. When I had it developed I had a few surprises. A photo of the yew tree, in the top left hand corner, has a white light anomaly on it. And two of the pictures of the spring show a column of energy coming up out of the water.

I feel that the energy present at the time of taking those pictures continued to affect my camera, and enabled other energies to be seen on subsequent pictures taken in Peru.

The one that gave me the greatest food for thought was of a display of arum lilies in the lobby of the hotel in Lima. I took two pictures. The second one shows what I was expecting – arum lillies! – but the first is quite different.

There is no atrium above, no tables with lamps or flowers. On the left hand side of the picture is a column with what looks to me like a female light-being in it. In the centre of the picture you can see another being wearing a white robe with a black belt. He has his arms raised as if his hands are behind his head. It is difficult to make out the head.

To the left of the being is what looks like a large roman numeral; the number one in black. To the right of him is a number two. Both numbers reach up to the ceiling. Beside the horizontal at the top of each number is an orb. The being is only shown down to just below hip level where there are over twenty orbs in front of him between the two large numerals. One of these orbs at the forefront of the picture appears to be blue.

A year earlier I had been drawn to buy a book by Maurice Cotterell entitled *The Lost Tomb of Viracocha*, published by

Headline. What caught my eye was the cover of the book which had on it a golden crab man. It made me think of Angus whose star sign was Cancer, the crab. Viracocha translates to 'foam of the sea' which is where crabs live, between the sea and the shore. The book talks of various incarnations of Viracocha, who is described as wearing a white robe which is belted – just like the being in my photograph. The raised arms are also mentioned in the book.

The dates given by Maurice Cotterell suggest that Viracocha would have been walking the earth at the time when the yew tree at Alton Priors was starting its life. The energies of both seem to have been linked on my film.

There is a table of Supergods and Sun-Kings in the book which shows Sipan I and Sipan II, both as incarnations of Viracocha. This I took to explain the I and II in the photo.

Also in the book is a section on reincarnation with a diagram showing small spheres as souls. I thought of this diagram when I saw all the orbs in my picture.

The pillar shown on the left-hand-side of the photograph reminds me of my Mayan Sun Glyph, Ben. There are twenty Mayan Sun Glyphs, the equivalent of our star signs, and my 'sign' is Ben. One of the meanings of Ben is given as 'pillars of light'.

Referring back again to the book, there is a chapter on the mysterious Nasca lines in Peru, in the desert. I have always been drawn to the monkey and have it as a silver pendant on a necklace. Maybe my liking for it is because I was born in the Chinese year of the monkey. Before reading the book I had never noticed that the monkey only has four digits on its right hand. Were it not for the plastic surgeon, I would have had only four digits on my right hand, and was so fortunate that he had been able to save most of my ring finger.

A statue of Viracocha is described as only having four digits on each of his hands and the link is made by Maurice Cotterell, the author, between him and the monkey.

Another of my photographs put me in mind of 'foam of the sea'. I was in one of the hotel lifts which was on the outside of the building. It had glass walls and I was looking down at the hotel pool when I took the picture. There is a reflection in the glass of my right foot and it shows my trainer half over the water and half over the land, an urban version of the seashore. The shape of the swimming pool reminded me of the Mandelbrot Set crop circle back in 1991.

The blue orb on the photograph with the being on it made me think of the blue colour of the throat chakra and wonder if I was supposed to talk about it all. I asked the energies about this through Mavis and the answer was 'yes'.

When reading of the 'bearded white man' in books on Egypt I can't help but think of Angus who had a beard. Viracocha is also described as a bearded white man. He is said to have ended one of his lifetimes by walking into the sea. He died in the Pacific Ocean, Angus is in the Atlantic. Were it not for my rescue I would also be in the Atlantic. That is where I have asked for my ashes to be scattered.

Something else happened that year that was remarkable, and that I could not explain until I later asked the energies about it through Mavis.

When T.C. and her husband had moved to a house with no garden, Domino, the family cat, went to Wales to live with one of T.C.'s sons and his family. I visited her at her house in May and found the cat back home, curled up on the settee.

"What's Domino doing here?" I asked.

"Oh, I've got to find an old lady for Domino," said T.C.
"It's done!" I replied.

Apparently the family in Wales couldn't cope with her any longer. I had always been sorry we hadn't taken her when she first needed a new home.

Taking in an eighteen-year-old cat was not like arriving home with a kitten like Twiggy, and I hoped my mother would be pleased. With a cat that age, every day would be a bonus. T.C. took the cat to the vet for a check up and then L.C., her husband, brought her round to us at Coate. For a few days Domino and I had to keep a low profile but she soon won my mother round.

I can remember saying to T.C. in Cusco in the September that I felt totally happy about having left Domino in charge of my mother.

In October, only recently back from Peru, I was trying to work out how to break the news to my mother – and the cat – that I was going away again in November, to America.

One afternoon I got home and went up to my mother's room. The bathroom door was wide open and I smiled as I saw Domino fast asleep beside the washbasin. She had both front paws curled round together, supporting her chin.

The first thing my mother said was, "I'm very worried about Domino – she's spending too much time in the bathroom."

I hadn't been living at Brookfield when the family cat died of kidney failure. Before dying she spent nearly all her time in the bathroom, and the vet had said this was quite common when cats know their kidneys are packing up.

When my mother told me how worried she was, I said the cat looked alright to me. It took maybe twenty seconds for me to go into the bedroom and then into the bathroom to re-check the sleeping cat. And she was dead. Her head was hanging down and her neck had no muscle tone at all, just like a dead chicken in a butcher's shop.

I scooped up her head, cradling it in my hands, and restored it to its natural position. She wasn't breathing; I just saw one single hair in her fur do a slight twitch.

Then I did a very selfish thing. I opened up a telepathic link and told her she couldn't die yet, I needed her to look after my mother in November. I really prayed that she would come back and put in a few more months on earth.

And that is what happened. She came back, as I thought, and woke up. I was so grateful to her. I will continue to call her Domino here to avoid confusion, but I found out later that her soul had gone home, and another soul had come into her body as a 'walk in'.

When I was discussing this over a year later with Clarisse, a clairvoyant at the Signs of Destiny Conference in Phoenix, she had a great way of putting it. She quoted the incoming soul as saying, "OK, I'll drive for a while!"

It was during one of my readings with Mavis that I asked about what had happened. On two separate occasions, when wondering about the possibilities of two souls in one body, I had selected twin matches out of a box. Each time I had been about to light a candle, took a match and discovered I had two sticks with one shared head.

Through Mavis I asked about two lights in one being, and the energies said, "What do two lights make?"

"One flame," I said. Another soul had come in to replace Domino's. I asked if it was a soul I had known before. The answer was yes.

"Was it our previous cat?"

"Yes."

It was Twiggy who had volunteered 'to drive for a while'. This was not the first time Twiggy had been back. We were still living at Brookfield when I was awoken one night by the sound of foxes in the woods. There was such a spectacular full moon that I decided to get up and go outside to look at it. I stood just beside the front door, and became aware of what I thought was a black cat sitting a couple of yards to my right.

"Hello," I said to this visitor, "who are you?"

After a few seconds the cat disappeared. It didn't walk away, it just wasn't there any more. As I went back to bed I was puzzled about this cat. I closed my eyes and just before falling asleep I was head-butted by Twiggy. Then I knew who had been sitting in the drive.

When Domino did finally die we were lying together on my bed and the rays of the setting sun were shining in on her. When Twiggy died I had taken him to the vet to be put down. I was in pieces in the waiting room holding him. He comforted me by putting a paw up on to my shoulder. This time it was a natural death, in his own time. All I can say is,

"Thank you, Twiggy and Domino."

CHAPTER FOURTEEN
A crystal for Lake Titicaca

In the autumn of 2002, T.C. and I went up to Scotland to Lendrick Lodge, a centre at Callendar run by Stephen and Victoria Mulhearn. We went to attend a five day Shamanic course which was to culminate in a firewalk. As soon as I heard about the course I wanted to go – the main attraction being the firewalk, which was to take place on the night of the full moon. We walked barefoot across hot coals and it is rightly considered as a rite of passage.

Also attending was Adriel, a delightful Andean Priest and Shaman from Cusco in Peru, and one of the guides for the tours Stephen organises to Machu Picchu. Towards the end of the course we all had individual coca leaf readings with Adriel. I found him very accurate. At one point he looked up from the leaves in surprise and told me I was talking to people not of this planet. This confirmed to me my links with the energies responsible for some of the crop circles.

T.C. and I were persuaded to go on the September 2003 trip to Peru. I knew the Inca Trail would be tough and that I needed to lose weight and get fit – the gym had to be joined!

During one of my readings with Mavis, I asked about going on the trip. I was told to go with an open mind. I decided to do just that and deliberately did not read up anything about the trail beforehand. I was so uninformed I thought you had to climb up to Machu Picchu rather than spend the last day climbing down to reach it!

Had I read about the trail and the climbs before the descents, I wouldn't have gone because I would have thought I couldn't possibly do it. When I looked up at Dead Woman's Pass I just accepted that I was going to be that dead woman!

The flight from Lima had given me my first glimpse of the Andes. As the clouds parted and I looked down at the mountains, I found myself involuntarily saying, "Oh mother!" The words came out quietly but were full of wonder.

When we first landed at Cusco and left the plane, the altitude felt very strange. Walking to the arrivals hall was like trying to get my land legs back again having spent several days at sea.

Waiting to greet us was a group of local musicians who entertained us while we waited for our luggage to come through. Then out into the open air, a reunion with Adriel, and we were on our way to our base hotel. I was delighted to see that the flags flying everywhere were rainbows, although as yet they only display seven colours.

We had several days to get used to the altitude and the lack of oxygen, before setting off for the trail. We explored Cusco, its shops, markets and restaurants. Together with Adriel we visited Saqsayhuaman, a sun temple on a huge site with amazing stonework. We also went to the Temple of Water and the Temple of the Puma, guarded by a puma-shaped rock.

We set out early one morning for a visit to the sacred site of Tipon. We drove for about an hour out of Cusco and up into the mountains. I marvelled at the way the farmers are able to cultivate the land on such steep slopes without terracing. We saw llamas, cattle, pigs and ponies. After a while we left our coach by a waterfall and set off on foot to climb up towards the sacred spring.

The Incas had diverted the water from the spring into two channels. Adriel explained to us that this represented duality. After a short distance the two were divided into four, representing the four races and the four directions.

Adriel and High Priest Adolfo performed ceremonies for harmony as we lay on the ground in a circle looking up at a cloudy sky with some sun and very fine rain. They then gave us healing one at a time, during which we were each given an egg. We could put whatever we liked 'into the egg' before placing it in the water and watching it disappear down the mountain.

At one point I looked up to see an eagle circling above us, and down to see a plane coming in to land at Cusco Airport. The whole area was very busy with people doing restoration work near the site of the sacred spring.

On the night of the full moon we were privileged to be taken to the underground Temple Di Luna, where Adriel and Adolfo conducted the Despacho ritual for us.

The rock walls of the cave had been worn quite smooth. For how many thousands of years had people been gathering there for ceremonies, I wondered? Not all the locals were happy about us being there and we had a discreet police escort for the evening.

For the ritual, Adriel and Adolfo spent a long time praying and assembling and wrapping the package to be offered to the Apu, the Mountain Angels. We followed the two priests out of the cave to the place where they lit the fire upon which they placed the offering. As we watched we were joined by four horses and, according to Adriel and Adolfo, the Apu accepted our offering with great alacrity. They were surprised that the fire burned in double quick time.

The Despacho ritual reminded me of Lendrick Lodge the previous autumn when Adriel had performed the same ceremony in Scotland, in preparation for the firewalk.

Another reminder of the Course in Scotland came the night before we set off for the trek to Machu Picchu, when Stephen had produced a bag full of arrows. I had watched in disbelief when, as part of our preparation for the forthcoming firewalk in Scotland, Stephen had placed the sharp end of an arrow into the softest part of his neck just below his Adam's apple. With the other end of the arrow against a firm surface he then lunged forward – breaking the arrow. Still doubting what I had seen him do, I turned round and saw a pile of arrows on the floor – one for each of us!

So what had helped with preparation for the firewalk in Scotland, had to be done again now in Peru, in preparation for the trek to Machu Picchu. All thirteen arrows were duly broken.

Our Inca Trail guide was another Adriel. One of his first questions was to ask if anybody had a fear of heights. Mine was the only hand I saw go up.

"A big fear?" he asked.

"Quite big," I replied. What had I let myself in for?

The porters who accompanied us were amazing. They went ahead and prepared our lunch. Having eaten we would start off again and after clearing up and washing up they would overtake us and pitch our tents for us and prepare the evening meal. After breakfast they would clear up, pack up the tents and chase after us again. They did this for four days.

Some of the views were magnificent, with snow on the distant mountains, while our path and camp sites at the same altitude had no snow at all. The plants and flowers were beautiful.

In the past, when watching any TV programme about mountaineering, I had often said I might be able to climb up, but didn't think I'd be able to climb back down again.

Before leaving England I had bought a strong wooden staff from Dawn's shop in the Ginnel in Devizes. This survived three flights – not the easiest thing to take on a plane these days. Two sticks were recommended and necessary, so I bought a second stick from a young girl eager to supply us all as we joined the trail. Long sections of the trail consist of steep steps many of which are similar in height to a chair. I did indeed find it easier to climb up than down.

The second day was the climb up to Dead Woman's Pass. I wasn't looking forward to it but couldn't understand why I was so lacking in energy as we set off. I was sure there was no way I could complete the climb. It only took a few minutes for Stephen to notice that I was in difficulty. He asked someone to carry my sticks and held his out behind him. I grabbed the ends of the sticks and he pulled me up in his wake. Not a good start to the day!

After a while we all stopped for a mid-morning drink. Refreshed by a coffee I then set off again unaided. It started to rain and people disappeared under waterproof ponchos. I caught up with one member of the group who had stopped to look at the view. As I approached she pushed back her hood because she sensed I had not recognised her. Not only did I not recognise her, but when I answered her I was aware that I was talking utter gibberish. Had I had a stroke?

Thinking sense and hearing rubbish coming out of my mouth was very disconcerting.

Adriel was quickly on the scene trying to snap me out of it – holding his hand in front of my face and asking me to count how many fingers he was showing me. Thankfully I got the numbers right. He then produced a bottle of pink liquid and put several drops on his hand. Rubbing both hands vigorously together he then wafted the strong smelling vapour into my face. The Andean equivalent of smelling salts did the trick. I reached Dead Woman's Pass alive, having found out what it feels like when sufficient oxygen does not reach the brain.

While I was wondering if I had had a stroke, I was surprised to briefly remember the words of a friend many years earlier. She had told me her step-father was recovering from a stroke and how difficult it was to understand what he said. On one occasion he asked for a lorry with three planks. It took a long time to work out that he wanted an omelette made with three eggs.

As we all joined up at Dead Woman's Pass Adriel borrowed everyone's cameras and took group photos for each of us – proof of our successful ascent.

Several members of the group suffered from food poisoning on the trail and had to be carried part of the way. I managed to avoid this and only had a minor problem with my left knee on the last day.

That whole day was spent climbing down to Machu Picchu. Going down the steep steps I had to lead with my left leg as it was painful to bend that knee. This meant I had to face towards the right, always looking over the edge of the narrow path and the drop below. I'd have been a lot happier looking at the rock wall of the mountain to my left.

After an hour or so I slipped and fell on the steps. Adriel was worried because I very nearly hit my head on one of them, although the only thing I dented was my aluminium water bottle. In a strange way it was a relief to have fallen and not damaged myself. I just sat there on a step and burst into tears. Once I started crying I couldn't stop. Adriel looked worried and told me I couldn't be hurt because there weren't any more 'men with poles' – all the stretchers were in use.

I promised him I didn't need the men with poles. The problem wasn't with my body, it was in my head. I continued to cry until I caught up with all the others at lunch time and T.C. gave me a homeopathic Arnica tablet.

(I found out, some six months later, that that fall had triggered a past life memory of a fall in Wales, on slate, in Puritan times. I then understood all the tears in Peru.)

Arriving at Machu Picchu was quite magical and a real feeling of achievement for us all.

That night we stayed in a hotel just below at Aguas Calientes. Real beds were very welcome but not as welcome as real loos – modern plumbing and running hot water, not only the water in the hotel but also the sacred hot springs. Just as we were about to leave the hotel after a quick freshen up, and planning to bathe in the hot springs, a power cut hit the town.

It was very dark as we climbed the road up to the springs and changed into our swimwear. The baths are open air so it was a real bonus having no electric lighting to detract from the beauty of the night sky. I have never seen such a beautiful starlit sky. It included a perfect heart just above us, mapped out, as I recall, by ten twinkling stars. There were also two amazing shooting stars. I only saw the first one, but

I'll never forget it. As it flashed horizontally past us it seemed very close and had a tail like a comet of smaller starlets, a mega firework.

When he was trying to persuade us to go to Peru, Stephen had asked us to visualise relaxing in the warm waters of the hot spring, having completed the Trail. The actuality was far and away more wonderful than my visualisation.

As we walked back down the hill the electricity was restored just as we entered the town – perfect timing! After a celebration meal we all appreciated being able to sleep in beds that night.

The following day we were free to revisit Machu Picchu before catching the train back to Cusco and our base hotel.

I returned from Peru with eleven rolls of film to be developed. I tried to photograph everything in the Temple that was pointed out to us by Adriel. What had an unexpected effect on me was a very sturdy forget-me-not plant. As I took pictures of the blue flowers I wondered if the plant's message 'remember me' was from a person or the place. Was it a command or a question? Had I been there before?

After returning to Cusco the last few days of the trip were to be spent preparing the members of the group to take Ayahuasca, the hallucinogenic drug from a rainforest plant. At the time the idea didn't appeal to me. I decided I'd like to go instead to Lake Titicaca and visit Sillustani to see the towers there, the Chullpas. I found a travel agent in Cusco and booked a bus ride on the Inca Express to Puno on the shores of the lake. I asked the agent to book me into a hotel beside the lake for two nights.

On Sunday, September 21 I got up early and waited outside the hotel for the bus to pick me up at 7.40. It was to be a long journey of ten hours. There were five breaks along the way. I didn't go into any of the museums but did buy some souvenirs: a few miniature bells and a couple of Inca calendars. One of the stops was at a restaurant. A very good buffet lunch was included in the price of the bus ticket. It was a sunny day and I sat outside to enjoy my meal.

Back on the bus I sat next to a man from the Wye Valley who had also just completed the Inca Trail. We swapped stories of the mosquitoes at Machu Picchu and I managed to steer the conversation around to crop circles. He seemed quite interested. As we approached Puno the bus driver announced that the Hotel Libertador was the most expensive hotel in town. This was the hotel into which I had been booked.

"Oh, we'll all be staying there then," joked my companion. I hoped he would get off before the bus dropped me. He didn't. I felt quite embarrassed as we swept up to the hotel and I stood up.

"Pamper yourself!" he said, and I promised to do so.

It was dark by the time I arrived and from reception I was impressed by the lights of Puno. There were no such lights to be seen from the window of my room. The whole of one wall was a huge window and all I could see in the distance was two little lights, one red and one green. No night time view, I thought.

I took advantage of having a telephone beside my bed and phoned home to speak to my mother. She told me that Daphne and my friend Lisa had come up trumps looking in on her.

Deciding I would pamper myself I then went to the hotel bar and treated myself to a gin and tonic before going to the restaurant for supper. I ate a delicious vegetarian meal before retiring to bed for an early night.

I was awakened at 3 a.m. by the loudest clap of thunder I have ever heard. It was directly above, an electrical storm with torrential rain. 'Wow, that's quite a welcome!' I thought. The storm didn't move away, it stayed above us, very noisy.

Monday dawned, September 22, the Equinox. I got up and saw that the view through my window was superb, out across the lake. I watched the birds and numerous little boats before having a bath and going down for breakfast.

The hotel arranged with an agency in town for a private trip to Sillustani for me, leaving at 2.20. The agency later phoned me to change the time to 2.30 and told me that my guide would be Eduardo. I didn't feel too well and thought I was going down with a cold. I spent the morning writing postcards sitting by my window. For purely medicinal reasons, of course, I took a Red Label Johnny Walker Whisky from my mini bar for my throat.

The hotel is actually on an island, Esteves Island, on the shore of the lake. There were several llamas down below my window and I watched a woman wearing a traditional bowler hat, collecting firewood. She was breaking the sticks by throwing a rock down on them.

At 2.30 I met Eduardo in reception. As we went out I thought someone was polishing his car. It turned out to be my driver and I set off in style with a driver and a guide. It was a drive of thirty-five miles and a very hairy one. We were dodging potholes at 120 km per hour. The speed limit was 60. I was told the potholes had only appeared ten years earlier, until then the road had been fine.

On the way I mentioned the previous night's storm. Eduardo said it had been very unusual. Such a storm would normally occur in March or April. He had wondered about it and put it down to global warming and the ozone layer.

As we neared Sillustani, with my permission, we stopped to pick up the daughter of the leader of the village, the No. 1 girl in town. She unlocked the Museum so that Eduardo and I could go inside. It was very interesting but through the windows I could see the Chullpas up on the hill and was worried this was the nearest I was going to get.

There were pre-Inca relics, preserved mummies, some in the foetal position and babies wrapped in reed bags. One corpse was minus its skull, a good luck trophy for someone, I was told.

Outside the Museum there were several rocks from the hill on which the towers had been built, with animal carvings on them. I photographed a lizard, a frog and a serpent. Before setting off for the hill I bought some mini pottery towers as a souvenir.

I was known as Mrs Jane to Eduardo. There had obviously been a mix up when the Cusco travel agent made the hotel booking, Jane is my middle name.

We left the Museum and drove to the foot of the hill. We then climbed up to the assorted Chullpas, walking through a graveyard to another graveyard. There were exposed bits of bone and pre-Inca pottery relics. Eduardo picked up some pieces of pottery for me.

As we walked the conversation came round to crop circles. He was very interested and had seen them on TV. He wanted to show me the stone circles there. As he did so three eagles flew above us, he had never seen three before.

I then visited all the towers, first grade to fourth grade, two built as squares around a circle. Not all were finished and some had been partially destroyed. Eduardo told me he was giving me the esoteric tour, pointing out all the animal carvings and the symbol for water. The openings into the towers were just big enough to crawl through, and all faced east towards the rebirth of the sun every morning from mother earth.

Human bones were clearly visible through one of the entrances. One large rock was the shape of a lion, and on it was carved the Milky Way and a comet. I was also shown a fountain. The site was on the shore of a lake, Lake Umayo. It was a spectacular place.

The afternoon was cloudy but also sunny. Eduardo kept pointing to the sun's rays and talking about the clouds. As we got back to the car I told him about some of the cloud formations I have seen including an ouroboros, the notebook, a turtle and an eagle. Just as we left he pointed up through the windscreen and turned to me with a look of amazement on his face. There in front of us was a large cloud that was a representation of one of the towers that was falling into disrepair. Luckily I still had enough film to photograph it. We then saw a cloud that looked like the Milky Way. They really were a superb finale to our visit.

Two suicidal dogs tried to pick a fight with the car as we drove away. Eduardo then talked of a TV channel he liked to watch which deals with UFOs. We talked about the squaring of the circle in some crop circles and the square towers built to surround the circular towers.

As we neared Esteves Island and the hotel, I asked how I could get down to the water. I had a crystal I wanted to put into Lake Titicaca. Eduardo told me that the hotel had a dock, I could do it there. He showed me where it was. Afterwards we returned to the lobby and I settled up for the trip. I was able to use some Amex travellers' cheques, and Eduardo was very happy to be given $60 instead of the $50 he asked for. As he left he said he would take me in his heart.

I had a coca tea and then went up to my room. When I came down later to find the dock it was dark and there was nobody about. The crystal I wanted to give to the lake was a Rainbow Obsidian. I had carried it with me for three years. After my little ceremony, quite a wind blew up as I went back to the hotel and into the restaurant. I had the same supper as I had had on the Sunday night and went up to my room for an early night.

At 1.51 a.m. I was again woken by a storm, thunder and lightning directly above. This time it didn't remain over the hotel, but gradually receded across the lake. There were flashes of wall-to-wall sheet lightning, and then vertical flashes of lightning coming straight down, amazing to watch. They came down not only as single streaks but in twos, threes and even four at a time, close together and parallel. I just lay on my left side staring out of my window. Every now and again I would say "Wow!" out loud. I had never seen anything like it.

All the action seemed to take place in a narrow band as it slowly moved further away, just to the left of the red and green lights on the lake. On one occasion the lightning traced a number 9 as it came down. On another, two vertical lines came with a horizontal line above them. It made me think of the Sun Gate at the other end of the lake. It seemed to be quite interactive.

At one point I wondered how long it was since my ceremony with the crystal. Just as I worked out that it had been seven hours, so the lightning traced out a number 7. I really felt very involved and invigorated by the storm. It receded into the distance and was over by 3 a.m., but not before one flash of lightning went up instead of down! All in all, an equinox to remember.

I didn't get much sleep after the show and got up early on the Tuesday morning. I decided to check out before having breakfast. The Inca Express was due to pick me up at 7.50. My bill was horrendous, over 4,000 soles, around £900 for the telephone. I had been charged for a nine hour phone call to England! I tried pointing out that just after the call they had charged me for my meal in the restaurant on the Sunday night. This was going to take a lot of sorting so I ducked away for a very quick breakfast, bringing my fruit juice back with me to reception. We finally got the phone call down to ten minutes and 74 soles.

Meanwhile at the other end of the desk a receptionist was searching for a Mrs Dodson for the bus driver. They didn't have one registered at the hotel. I settled my bill as quickly as I could and then presented myself to the other receptionist as Mrs Jane, aka Mrs Dodson! I hoped the people on the bus hadn't had too long a wait as I climbed on board and found a seat. Ten hours later, after the same five stops, I was back in Cusco. As I rejoined some of the group in the hotel I was told I had obviously had a wonderful time because it showed in my face.

The following day we were all due to leave Cusco and fly to Lima. There T.C. and I were to say goodbye to the rest of the group. The other eleven had come to Peru from Scotland flying via Holland. I had obtained free flights for the two of us with Continental Airlines, having cashed in some of my rewards on their frequent flyer scheme. We had flown out from Gatwick to Houston and from there to Lima, where American Express had booked us in for a couple of nights at the Swissotel some eight miles from the Airport.

Once we'd settled in, T.C. and I were tempted by the Alpaca Shop and the sauna. T.C. arranged to meet a

Peruvian couple who practised Agni Hotra, the ancient Vedic fire ceremony, and who were interested to learn about crop circles. Above the lobby there was a large oval atrium. While we were talking to the couple, sitting beneath this atrium, I found it quite disconcerting to hear my own voice booming down at me as if from the gods. I could hear myself as others hear me.

It was here that I took the photograph that was meant to show a display of lilies but which showed the being in the white robe.

When I had booked our flights to Peru I asked to return via New York, and reserved a room at the Newark Airport Marriott Hotel to break our journey back to England. I had stayed there several times.

Those members of the group bound for Holland and on to Scotland left us in the departure lounge. I was worried because Newark wasn't on the departure board. I went to enquire and was told that, since booking, Continental had cancelled their daily flights from Lima to Newark. We had been re-booked to stop over in Houston. I pointed out that we were booked into a hotel that night and they put us on a flight from Houston to Newark.

The following morning T.C. and I were in separate lines, queuing to go through U.S. Immigration at Houston Airport. T.C. went straight through with Mr Nice, while I found myself face to face with Mr Nasty. I must have been through immigration in America over forty times and knew only too well that you have to fill in the forms perfectly. You have to give the name and number of the street where you are going to stay. I had written the name of the hotel and said it was at Newark Airport. (It wasn't on a street and didn't have a number.)

This wasn't good enough for Mr Nasty, I was told to fill in the form again. When I argued and tried to explain, I was sent off across the hall to a lady at a desk who would look up the address for me. After making a phone call she couldn't come up with the street or a number either.

Back in line, Mr Nasty, who was not amused, withheld my passport and told me to go over and stand by the wall. There I stood, feeling like a naughty child, for nearly ten minutes before a passing official asked me what I was doing there. I told him and he carried on, taking no further interest. I was worried about T.C. and missing the connecting flight.

I plucked up courage and walked back to Mr Nasty to point out I had a plane to catch. He told me that if I missed my flight, Continental would put me on another one and sent me back to the wall. Eventually a more senior looking official asked me what I was doing. I told him and was taken off into a small room where half a dozen other passengers were waiting. I was convinced I would miss my flight. Luckily he dealt with me first, went and collected my passport, stamped it and let me go. T.C. was duly waiting for me and by running we just caught our flight. The whole incident had had an effect on my stomach and I barely made it in time to the loo on board.

That was my worst experience entering the U.S. and I hope not to repeat it. I see that the Marriott at Newark now boasts the proud address of No 1, Hotel Road. I probably wasn't the only person to have had a problem. I refused to let it spoil what had been a wonderful trip, but the incident certainly brought me back down to earth after the high of Peru. We arrived back in England on September 27, exactly three weeks after we had set out.

In mid-November I was due to fly to America again for my first Signs of Destiny Conference at Phoenix. Before that though, I had a reading with Mavis. I talked about putting the crystal in the lake and the storm that night. I was told it meant my intention, when placing the crystal, had been honoured. The energies then went on to say I should take a crystal with me on my next trip to America, and place it in the earth there in a similar manner. They said quartz would be a good crystal to use.

I went to see Simon who runs the crystal stall in the market in Devizes on Thursdays. Most of my crystals have come from him and we selected one together.

Before the Conference I was going to visit the Grand Canyon and Sedona with two friends. Whenever I could I charged up the crystal in the sunlight. We had a meeting in Sedona with a lady who had a Medicine Wheel in her garden, just below Thunder Mountain. I felt moved to ask her if I could add my crystal to this wheel, and did so. Later that night I remembered I had been asked by the energies to put the crystal *in* the earth. I had placed it *on* the earth. It became important to me to rectify the situation, I needed another quartz crystal.

At the Conference a few days later, there was a lady selling crystals. I picked one out and told her why I wanted it. At this point she said, "I've just been given to give you this crystal," and she gave it to me.

My problem then was where could I bury it in the earth? I was literally on my way back to England. I had flown from Phoenix to Houston where I was to catch the overnight flight to Gatwick. On the way over I had entered the country at Newark where I had no problem with Immigration. Now, somehow, I had to find a patch of earth in which to place the quartz, and do so without arousing suspicion.

I went out of a door and saw an area of grass beside the building, also planted with several trees. There was a vehicle ramp that would take me down to it. I looked around, there was just one man behind me, sitting out having a cigarette. I selected a tree by which to plant the crystal, asked for protection and set off down the ramp. I tried to make myself invisible; I didn't want to come up against the authorities again. As I went I suddenly became aware of a butterfly flying beside me, just by my right shoulder. I said 'hello' to it and wondered what it was doing there in the middle of a busy airport. I was glad of its company.

At the bottom of the ramp I turned to my right, on to the grass and back towards the tree I had chosen. As I buried the crystal I prayed that no one was looking out of any of the windows surrounding me. I made my way back up the ramp, pushing my luck by photographing the tree, and was very relieved to find myself safely back inside the terminal building.

The Continental Airlines aircraft that was waiting to fly me to England was painted with some of the colours of the rainbow. As I walked in through the pink colour around the door, it just seemed very appropriate. I was told it had been painted to mark the Millennium.

CHAPTER FIFTEEN

The 2004 Conference channelling

January 22 2004 was the Chinese New Year. We were entering the year of the Monkey, my sign. When I went to bed that night I found three of my dolphin divination cards had been placed on my pillow. The remainder of the pack was still on the stool beside my bed where I had left them. I was intrigued as to how the cards came to be there and, because they were lying face down, wondered which three had been selected, and who had put them there. I carefully turned them over and saw that they were Synergy, Entering New Dimensions and Abundance.

Much later, when I asked through Mavis if the energies had been responsible, their reply was, "Well *you* didn't put them there!"

I noted well what was said about each card in the book that accompanies them.

In February I picked up a book that had belonged to Angus. It was his Reed's Nautical Almanac 1977. On the top of the book there was a dead bee. It had been caught in a spider's web. I knew that somehow this was important. Little did I know that later in the year we would have a crop circle of a bee and one of a spider. I checked where Angus had left a book mark, it was at page 981. I didn't see it, but in 2002 there was a crop circle in Hampshire near the ET formation. It was a simple tree design and looked like a seal. My Collins English Dictionary has on its front cover a golden tree within a circle. Having opened the Almanac I decided to look at page 981 in the dictionary and see if there was anything relevant. I discovered 'natural selection', which would explain what had happened to the bee.

Later that summer, I was feeling upset. I decided to take myself to the yew tree at Alton Priors, to sit in it for healing. There I was joined by a bee. It walked into the tree and then proceeded to burrow down into the earth. I wondered what it was teaching me and decided that the lesson was to keep my head down.

It was a very busy summer, having to change our Conference venue to Coronation Hall at Alton Barnes. I visited hardly any formations before August. One that I did go into was at East Field. It came on June 20, the day before the summer solstice. It was thought to look like a musical instrument and put me in mind of a bugle and a wake up call.

The bee crop circle came a week later, once again in the field below the white horse at Milk Hill. The bee was 'flying' directly towards the horse.

The spider arrived on August 3 and was 'climbing' up Etchilhampton Hill, headed in the direction of Devizes. By the time I got into the formation it had been harvested. The formation reminded me of the huge resident spider that came with my cottage when I bought it. After one of our monthly Wednesday evening lectures, I returned home to find the spider on my sitting room wall. I was really quite scared of it and tried to communicate with it telepathically, asking it to find another house to live in. I drove to Brookfield, arriving at about 7.30 the next morning.

As I took my towel out of my bag, out plopped the spider. "Oh no," I said out loud. "I didn't mean this house!"

It staggered across the kitchen floor and disappeared down beside the washing machine. It looked a bit jet-lagged having travelled eighty miles at high speed. It had obviously got my message and I realised it was my fault for not having been more specific!

February's Wednesday lecture was about the importance of the Agni Hotra Fire. Halfway through the talk I was distracted by someone sitting in the front row. He had his right leg crossed over his left and appeared very agitated. He was kicking his right foot up in an exaggerated way, so much so that I looked at his face. It was the first time I had ever seen anyone shape shift. He looked just like a lizard. I was so shocked that I nudged Lisa, who was sitting next to me, and tried to get her to look. She didn't understand what I meant and his face soon returned to normal.

One way and another it was a very strange night. Much later at home I decided to let the cat out. Domino was deaf and we didn't usually let her out after dark as there were foxes around. I quickly thought better of having opened the door for her and went out to fetch her back in. As I carried her towards the door, I can only say that I was pushed backwards by an unseen force. I dropped the cat as I fell. My fall and two ribs were broken by hitting the corner of a rectangular stone trough planted with herbs. I knew I had injured myself and was in a lot of pain as I struggled to get up. I will never know what that strange force was that pushed me over.

I didn't tell my mother about my fall. The next day I was due to see a healer in Glastonbury. I decided that what had happened was an attempt to stop me going and I became determined to go. It was a painful drive and when Francesca opened her door I was in tears. When the healer arrived she decided to concentrate on my injury. It was extraordinary as she worked on me to feel the broken pieces of bone being put back in place. I could almost hear the noise of them grating. That night I decided not to even try to get undressed when I went to bed.

Early the next morning I was woken by Domino standing on my chest. She indicated to me that I should look out of the window to my right. There I saw a small cloud, pink in the early morning light. It made me think of the Angel of Peace. I decided to take a photograph of it and found that not only had I not undressed, I hadn't even removed my camera from around my neck! I didn't have to struggle to sit up, I just took the picture.

Another cloud came by and I could see it as a monkey and thought of the 'hundredth monkey' as I took a second picture. A third pink cloud appeared. Initially I saw this as a dish of fire, but then saw it as a healing hand. It doesn't look the same as the other two on the photograph because the automatic flash went off on my camera. I was very grateful to Domino for having woken me in time to see these little clouds. I took a picture of her standing on my chest. She was too close and I didn't think it would be in focus – but it was. You can clearly see the number 7 in the fur over her heart.

During a reading with Mavis I was told off by the energies for driving to Glastonbury and back. They said this had made things worse. I should have asked them for healing. This made me think of the healing hand cloud in the sky.

I took several pictures of clouds later in the year looking in the same direction, above the cricket pitch at Coate. I was in Sainsbury's car park in Devizes when I noticed a portal in the sky. A narrow band of sunlight was shining down and highlighted a pink leather glove that someone had put up on one of the car park railings. The glove's index finger was pointing as if to say 'Look up'.

When I got home I did just that and saw a cloud that looked to me like an eagle in flight. On the photograph I took, there is something in front of the bird that I can't identify. I also saw a cloud that made me think of E.T. with his left eye accentuated. I thought I could also read the words 'I AM' in the clouds in another photograph.

Whenever I see things in clouds it reminds me of an occasion in 1999 when I was waiting at the traffic lights in Effingham. I looked up and saw a cloud that was a perfect pair of spectacles. I thought the message was to keep my eyes open. Within seconds of leaving the lights a car pulled out of an entrance I had never noticed before.

A precise ouroboros was in the sky one day when I didn't have my camera. A cloud that I did photograph in 2001 looked to me like a turtle. While photographing the clouds I noticed that the nets on the cricket pitch had been raised. This made me think of the lifting of the veil.

June 8 was a day of great celebrations. It was the day of the Venus Transit. We gathered up at Adam's Grave at 5 a.m. and greeted the sunrise with Agni Hotra fires, one of which was tended for over seven hours. If you imagine the sun as the face of a clock, Venus crossed in front of it from roughly eight o'clock to four o'clock. By wearing special protective glasses we were able to watch, and it was also projected on paper. A large number of people gathered and the weather was perfect. We were joined by a very curious herd of cows, rather appropriate seeing as we were burning dried cow dung in the copper pyramid containing the fire and using ghee.

Two days after the transit, June 10, 2004 was my sixtieth birthday. When I awoke at dawn my vision was very blurred and it was a very misty day, but I decided to go up to Adam's Grave and repeat the promises I had made when I incarnated (into this life), even though I didn't remember them.

Up by the long barrow two beings suddenly appeared out of the mist. I had heard voices and then there they were, standing about fifteen feet from me. Nothing was said. After a short while they turned to their right and disappeared. I didn't see any hands or faces, they seemed to be wearing hooded cloaks.

After seeing them my eyes became so sore I could hardly see out of them. It was with great difficulty that I returned home. They stayed sore all day. Lisa came to collect me to take me to a formation. I had to keep her just in front of me so that I didn't have to open my eyes too wide.

Three days before the Conference at Alton Barnes, I had a reading with Mavis. I received strict instructions to put my feet up after the Conference and to do nothing for two weeks in order to recover. The energies talked of my having invited their input for the event and said that they would provide it.

On the Sunday afternoon of the Conference an awesome wind suddenly blew up. Lisa and I tried to support one of the marquee poles as the sacred Agni Hotra fire on the site was extinguished. It had been burning throughout the Conference. The following channelling was received by the lady who had been tending the flame.

We wish to reiterate our amazement at the absolute joy we have perceived at soul level in many who have come together for this gathering. We are heartened at the level of understanding which is coming into flower amongst the manifest energy which are particles of the humanity. Our wish is to nurture this and we pass through you the message of appreciation to all those who have laboured and passed the tests of initiation which were flung at them. To keep one's centre under these trials and demonstrate the higher aspects of being is a great achievement, wings unfurled and hearts to the fore.

The healing here on all levels has been phenomenal. We wish you to know that. Many souls have come from across the Universe to assist in this and some have left their mark in your fields, calling cards from across the galaxy. As the people hear the call and make their way to your gathering, so the call went out in the ethers. Know this. It is important. The healing is not only for yourselves and your planet but for many, many aspects of creation, manifest and unmanifest in the fields of love which you can perceive in and around your star systems. The teamwork involved is a great harmony which could only unfold through the intent of manifest humanity.

Go in Peace and Love Each other.

Through Margaret, 8th August 2004, Alton Barnes.

When Margaret came to find me and show me what she had taken down it made me cry. I had woken that morning with my eyes as sore as they had become on my birthday. It had forced me to ask for more help during the day and I had to have the channelling read to me. Although Mavis was at the Conference giving readings, it had not come through her.

One of the speakers at the Conference flew over from America and stayed for two weeks at my cottage in Devizes. She is Flordemayo, a Mayan Elder, recognised as a priestess and a healer. She was the Saturday night speaker. On the

Sunday evening she closed the Conference by conducting a Mayan ceremony.

As if in recognition, the following morning, opposite Silbury Hill, an amazing formation was found. The design depicted Mayan knowledge and referred to the Mayan calendar. Flordemayo was taken to see it, but felt unable to enter it.

I was very good about not visiting any formations for two weeks, I only went to one. I took Flordemayo to a star design at Coate. It came where the 'Jupiter moons' had been two years earlier. It had a central star with seven points. Around this was an eleven-pointed star with an outer thirteen-pointed star. In the centre was a circle of seven ornate arrangements of wheat with one central detail. Sitting in this circle felt as if I was with others around a camp fire. After seeing the crop circle we went to Alton Priors to see the yew tree.

Flordemayo was very affected by the energy in the formation at Coate. This was where I had had the experience with sound in one of the Jupiter moons, in green, in January 2003.

On her last day at the cottage she asked me how far away Glastonbury was. Did we have time to visit it? I told her we just had time. We hurried to the coffee shop for a couple of takeaway espressos and sped to Glastonbury. We parked in the Abbey car park, visited the gift shop and then sat out to enjoy a couple of crepes as a late lunch. It was a beautiful sunny afternoon.

Back in Devizes she gave me a healing before I left her. Just as I was going she went and fetched her staff. It was a beautiful stick that had been made for her by the grandmothers. It has turtles and ears of wheat painted on it.

She held it out and said, "Would you like it?"

"Would I!" I replied. She gave it to me and said it had wanted to stay. I felt so honoured and really treasured it. It felt like a replacement for my staff that I had left by mistake in Cusco.

I had the staff for several years before Flordemayo wrote to me and said that it needed to go back, could I find a way of getting it to her? I felt as if I had been punched in the solar plexus. I wasn't ready to part with it. I didn't reply and hoped that she would think her letter had been lost in the post. About a year later Lisa told me that she had had a phone call from T.C. She was going to be meeting with Flordemayo in France and had been asked if she could bring the staff. By then, my mother had died and I no longer felt the need to keep the staff. I phoned Flordemayo and explained and apologised and told her I would be sending it with T.C.

By Saturday August 21 my two weeks of rest were up and I set out to visit three formations. I started with one in South Field at Alton Priors. It had arrived two days after I had been to the yew tree for healing. I cried while I was in the tree and when the crop circle came two days later I saw from a picture that it represented a left eye crying. There were two beautiful tears falling from it down the slope of the field. As I stood within the formation, I saw that you could look down from the hill and see the yew tree below.

As I got back to my car a tractor went along the road. The farmer glowered at me and I hoped he was going for his lunch as I headed for the whale and dolphin formation at Golden Ball Hill. I have already described my visit to this one, probably my favourite formation.

Taking with me the stone that had been given to me there, I drove to the field below Milk Hill's white horse.

It was a long walk to the bee formation which was over two months old by then. I came across a real live bee in the formation which looked old and tired, a bit like the formation! That's how I felt too as I made my way back to the car. I had to take off my left shoe as all the walking had given me a painful blister. Before I got into the car I noticed that without my feeling it, I had been stung on my left thumb by the bee.

Next stop – the Market Place in Devizes to have my films developed and printed. I was happy to see the faint band of colours on one of the pictures but thrilled with the UFO on another.

Had I not had the blister and been so tired, I would have gone into a formation at Tan Hill, just to the left of Milk Hill if you are looking at the horse. This had evolved over four nights. The original 'head' section was modified and had three trailing lines of circles added to it. The whole thing was headed in the direction of the white horse. I discovered later that if I had gone into it on the Saturday, I might well have found Mavis there!

There was a formation below the white horse at Pewsey that I wanted to photograph from the air. It depicted the seven chakras. I also wanted to take pictures of the star formation at Coate, so I booked a helicopter flight. It was a very stormy afternoon and the pilot wasn't sure if we'd make it to Coate. I urged him to try and we did just make it, even though the weather was no good for taking pictures. As we flew above the stars formation I noticed a man dressed in black striding through the wheat heading for the formation. He wasn't using one of the tramlines to gain access but following a track made by thoughtless people damaging the crop. I didn't like the way he was approaching the formation and got a bad feeling about it. So much so that a few days later I went into it myself to conduct a ceremony to try to undo what he had done.

The sun broke through as we flew over the Tan Hill formation where the combine harvester had started to cut. One of the pictures I took has on it a pink anomaly and there is a large white anomaly on one of my pictures of the chakra formation at Pewsey.

On an earlier flight I had photographed a formation very near the entrance to the West Kennet Long Barrow. It had come in mid-July and was described as a sun and moon formation. Looking at it I got the impression that it was almost like looking beneath the cap of a mushroom. When the sun was shining, the design of the laid crop appeared to show a small circle (Photo 153). This small circle was at about four o'clock in the central sun. It reminded me of the projected picture of the Venus Transit that I had photographed in June. I thought of the transit as being hidden under my 'mushroom'. When I asked through Mavis if it represented Venus, I was told that it didn't. It represented another transit that we on earth had not noted.

By the time I visited the formation it had been harvested. I wanted to see the small circle and see how it had been laid to reflect the sun's rays. The general lay of the sun was round in a clockwise direction. The small circle was also laid in a clockwise direction but with a much tighter circular lay.

In the autumn of 2004 I got another chance to photograph a wedge of rainbow with nine colours in it. I was driving past Jump Farm in Devizes when I spotted it. I stopped the car and got out to take several pictures. As always the colours appear very faint on film but you can just see the green and the pink bands below the violet.

When I went to Phoenix in the November I took with me the stone that was given to me in the Golden Ball Hill formation in one of the dolphins. I wanted to show it to Flordemayo. She took it from me, held it and told me that when you are given a gift like that you look after it. She took out of her bag a beautiful woven yellow cloth for me to wrap the stone in.

CHAPTER SIXTEEN
The red velvet heart

The 2005 crop circle season began with a bang, literally. On the night of Saturday April 30 there was an amazing storm. I watched it as I lay in bed in my cottage in Devizes. At one point I saw two streaks of lightning shoot horizontally in the direction of the Vale of Pewsey. I wondered if there would be a crop circle in the morning. At one point the whole sky lit up with one brilliant flash. Sure enough the next day, May Day, a formation was spotted in oilseed rape at Golden Ball Hill. It was said to be in the same area as the whales and dolphins formation, but much smaller.

I didn't hear about it until the Tuesday night. The following day I went to have a quick look from the hill above and finally got to visit it on the Friday. From that vantage point it looked like a six-petalled flower. Strangely, looking down on it I could see in the yellow flowers of oilseed rape a 'shadow' of the whales and dolphins formation from the previous summer when the field had been sown with wheat. How on earth could that be? The oilseed rape flowers were now over five feet high, how could they reveal the shape of last year's formation in wheat? What I could see looking down, was that the new formation was over the exact area where the UFO had landed at my feet.

Inside the formation I felt the same wonderful energy that I had experienced on August 21. It was a beautiful sunny day and a really warm afternoon. I had the formation to myself and I lay in the centre, not wanting to leave, just remembering what it had felt like as the pink energy swirled down nine months earlier.

I had parked my car at Knapp Hill car park. As I walked along the path on my way back up, I felt drawn to step to my left and into East Field. It had been planted with wheat and the young crop was growing. I tried to ground the energy and wondered what we might have by way of formations in that magical field in the summer.

A couple of weeks later I received a phone call from a reporter on the *Western Daily Press* newspaper. He wanted to question me about the formation at Golden Ball Hill, so I explained to him that I was now merely a member of the Study Group. This didn't seem to bother him and he asked his questions anyway.

The next day I picked up the last copy of the paper in the newsagents and was pleasantly surprised to see that I had been quoted accurately. There was an aerial picture of the formation and a funny thought struck me. I decided to try to reconstruct the design by using Polo mints. This I did by halving three mints and arranging the pieces around a fourth.

The day after going into the formation I visited a book fair, where I bought a book on Australian Aboriginal art. Looking through it, searching for any links to crop circle designs, I came across a picture that reminded me of a 'dragon' formation at West Overton. It was a drawing of a snake and eggs on a shield.

My attention was also drawn to pictures of Wandjina, the mythical beings with large eyes and a nose, but no mouth. In my photograph of the UFO in the formation I can detect eyes looking out, (Photo 151).

Somehow my experiences in the two crop circles at Golden Ball Hill, with the whales and the dolphins and the little six-petalled flower, seemed to have quenched my great thirst. I no longer felt the need to go into formations. I couldn't hope to better the energy I had felt there, and the stone I was given in the dolphin still holds that energy.

Having gone up to Adam's Grave the previous year on my birthday, I decided in 2005 to go to Avebury on that day. I arrived at the village at 6 a.m. and parked my car. I set off along Green Street and up onto the Ridgeway. It was a beautiful sunny morning and I wanted to revisit the stones linked with Sirius, and go on to the Delphinus stones at Temple Farm.

Between the two I passed the spot where I had fallen and broken my leg four years earlier. I had my camera with me and took lots of photographs. One of the dolphin stones I took a picture of had strange markings on it, like grooves next to a shallow hollowed-out depression.

I noticed a beautiful thistle as I approached the pod of dolphin stones. I talk elsewhere of how I had the thought that I would like to find a small stone, holding the energy. I didn't find one by the Sirius stones and turned around in the dolphins to find one right behind me.

I picked it up and instead of the grass being white beneath it, the grass sprang back up and was the same colour as all the rest. It seemed the stone had only just arrived. It is smaller than the one from the crop circle and is roughly the shape of a pentagon.

On my way back along Green Street I stopped to photograph a particularly striking poppy, and paused to look across the adjacent field. I wondered what sort of crop circle it might host later in the season. When it came, the formation was not of pentagons, but diamonds and hexagons. They were said to form a necklace surrounding a central six-pointed star made of triangles.

In the car park I found a fellow crop-circle researcher. She invited me for coffee at her home nearby in Avebury Trusloe. I showed her the stone I had been given and when she realised it was my birthday, she went out into her garden and brought me a piece of sarsen stone as a present. (The stones at Avebury are sarsen stones.)

She told me about a crop circle that had come in barley at the end of May at Stanton St Bernard. Having given my computer away, I was really out of touch. The design reminded me of a clock belonging to my grandmother, raised above a rectangular base. The barley was all laid down within the formation apart from a large letter Y that went from the centre of the rectangle base line, and divided into two in the domed area above.

I decided to visit it that afternoon. I took with me the stone from Temple Farm and Flordemayo's staff, which I had carried all day.

I was pleased to find an honesty box in the formation. The farmer had put it there with a notice asking for donations. It read 'Welcome to the corn circle. We would welcome a donation', and was signed. I wish more farmers would do this. I am always very happy to make a payment and am relieved that the farmer does not object to my being there. They always suffer a loss of some of their crop when the plants are laid down.

The day after, on June 11, another formation was found next to the Y design. It had two overlapping circles. The area of the overlap was laid flat with a central circle left standing. Had it arrived a day earlier I would have walked through it to reach the other one!

On Saturday, July 9 I decided to go to Glastonbury. Before setting off I attached to the staff the wooden dolphin that Flordemayo had given me the previous November. She had said that that was what I should do with it. I went out to my car which was parked facing down a steep slope in its usual parking area. As I walked around the back of the car, I found a little red velvet heart. It had been propped up against my offside rear wheel. I was delighted with it and on picking it up, discovered it had a distinct perfume or scent.

In 1976 Angus had gone to St Petersburg in Florida. He went for six months as a consultant to a boat building firm there. He decided that while he was there he would smoke a pipe instead of cigarettes. He asked if I would mind. I said of course I didn't mind, and when I joined him for the last month of his Contract, I found he was smoking a very sweet smelling Dutch pipe tobacco. This was the smell of the little red heart by my car!

I put the heart on the passenger seat and started to reverse up the slope. The car did an extraordinary emergency stop. It didn't stall, the brakes were applied, but not by me. I still had my right foot on the accelerator. I couldn't understand what had happened and wondered if it was a sign that I shouldn't be going. I thought of the heart by the rear wheel, and the brakes.

I decided to proceed with caution. Leaving Devizes, driving down the steep dual carriageway, there were two grey cars in front of me. I wanted to overtake them and checked in my wing mirror. There was a black Mercedes speeding up in the outside lane, so I had to let it pass.

When I looked back in front of me, in that short space of time, to my horror the two grey cars had stopped. I braked as hard as I could, but it looked as though I was going to hit the rear car. Then suddenly an extra braking force was applied. A stalk of wheat on top of the dashboard in front of me lifted over an inch in the air. With help, the car stopped in time. (The same thing had happened to me a few years earlier in a different car on the M3 motorway. Again a piece of wheat in front of me had lifted into the air.) I was ultra cautious as I continued my journey to Glastonbury. When I parked behind the High Street I found I was next to a car with the word 'Chill' written on it! I did.

On August 21, exactly a year after the UFO appeared on my photograph, a third formation arrived in East Field. It was a lovely scarab design. A couple of days later Lisa and Luke, her six-year-old son, took me for a picnic. On a perfect day we sat on the hill looking down over the field and the formation.

It was in East Field in 1998 that Lisa and I first met. We were standing next to each other during the closing ceremony of the Study Group's Conference, in the seven-pointed snowflake crop circle.

As we enjoyed our picnic I looked to my right, up to Adam's Grave. A year earlier the three of us had been sitting up there looking down at the 'bugle' formation. We had taken musical instruments up to the barrow. Luke had really enjoyed himself playing music up there.

After we finished eating we made our way down to the field and went into the scarab. The sun was really warm. Feeling thirsty we then drove to Woodborough Garden

Centre to have a cooling drink. From there we went to visit a couple of formations at Marden, but only had time to go into one of them, my last of the summer.

I was back at East Field on September 22, the Autumn Equinox, two years after putting the crystal in Lake Titicaca. I went to the field to collect sloes to make organic sloe gin, with added energy!

I propose to write about just two more experiences, and they were both with light.

The day after Halloween, November 1 was All Saints Day. My friend Anne from Honiton, and I had arranged to meet in Glastonbury. It was surprisingly warm for November and we sat outside to eat our lunch at the 100 Monkeys Café. Suddenly we saw a light in the sky above the town. Although it wasn't as big or as bright, it reminded me of the one we had seen at the Winter Solstice gathering at Adam's Grave in 2003. Neither Anne nor I had a camera with us so we just looked at the light. It stayed for over an hour and was still there when I got into my car to drive home.

Two days later I experienced an extraordinary 'light event' in my cottage in Devizes. It was thirteen days after I had been 'told' to clean the little window above my front door. I didn't know why I was doing it and used vinegar and newspaper, as instructed. I also had to clean the two crystals hanging in the window.

Then on November 3 this amazing light came in. It appeared to be almost solid. I couldn't see through the centre of it. It was rectangular in shape, and lit up the settee as it hovered above it from 10.30 until nearly midday. I was transfixed and took numerous photographs. To the left of the light, on the wall, is a picture of the heart crop circle. It was when I first heard about that particular formation on

St Valentine's Day in 2000, I felt I made my first contact with the energies.

The light gradually broke up and I photographed a rainbow that settled on my picture of an angel from the Andes. It made the angel look like a Rainbow Angel.

Six years on, the red heart I was given in 2005 still has the faintest perfume of pipe tobacco. Although we never made it to Florida in 1980, the heart reminds me of happy times there in 1976.

1. Demon of Hamble *at the start of the Round Britain race in 1978.*

(Photographer unknown)

2. The picture of the lady with twenty-five golden hearts, on the wall in my hotel room at Atlanta.

3. The lady with thirty-four golden hearts, wearing 'crop circles'.

4. *In the whaleboat with my life raft after having been rescued in 1980.*

5. On the bridge of Canopus *with Captain Hugo E. Marxer the morning after my rescue.*

(Note: Photos 4 and 5 are official US Navy photographs by
Second Class Photographer's Mate (PH2) Michael Harrison.)

6. *My first sight of my first crop circle, the 'Beltane Wheel' opposite Silbury Hill, May 1998.*

7. *Inside the formation, looking back towards Silbury Hill.*

8. The seven-pointed snowflake in East Field, Alton Barnes, July 1998.

9. The first two to arrive up at Adam's Grave for the solar eclipse in 1999.

10. *The two oak leaves that I found in the lettuce after communicating telepathically with the oak tree, planted by my brother at Brookfield.*

11. *The formation at Golden Ball Hill in 2000 in which I saw what I took to be the left eye of the hawk.*

12. *The little white pentagon light anomaly (circled) inside the formation at Honey Street in 2000.*

13. Beautiful barley lay in a formation at Windmill Hill.

14. A spectacular central swirl in a formation in young wheat.

15. The tiny circle of ears of barley entwined in the formation at South Field in 2000.

16. The closing ceremony for the Study Group's Conference in the heart formation at East Kennet in 2000.

17. *One of the arrangements between each of the nine points of the nine-pointed star at All Cannings in 2000.*

18. *A blue light anomaly in a picture taken in the six-petalled flower formation near the Kennet and Avon canal at All Cannings in 2000.*

19. A pink light anomaly in the same six-petalled flower formation, just across the road from the nine-pointed star.

20. A golden light in a formation at Horton in 2000. The formation had a spectacular standing arrangement near its edge.

21. The standing arrangement in the formation at Horton.

22. "We'll have to make it at the end of the runway." The formation at Hurn
  Airport in May 2001. (Photograph by Steve Alexander, www.temporarytemples.co.uk)

23. A helicopter on the cricket pitch at Coate in 2001.

24. A white light anomaly on a picture of a summer solstice formation at Avebury, taken on June 21.

25. The three nests making a 'face' in the sunflower formation at Woodborough Hill.

26. The huge formation on top of Milk Hill in 2001 with 409 circles within it.

27. The Milk Hill formation with the white horse just showing on the right.

28. Another 'face' in one of the 409 circles.

29. A real face, with three rings below it, at Chilbolton in Hampshire in 2001.

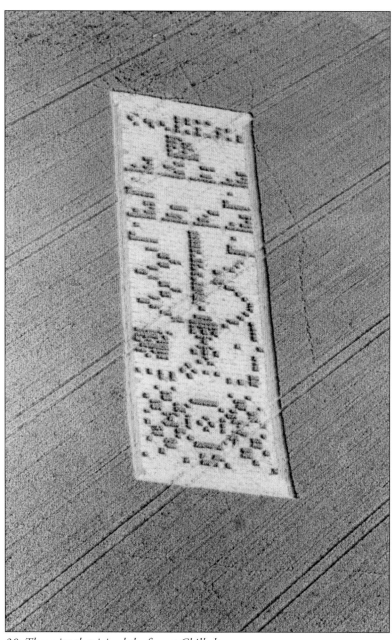

30. The script that joined the face at Chilbolton.

31. The face and the script together in the field just in front of the Chilbolton Observatory.

32. In the third eye region of the face.

*33. The standing circles,
like pixels, which made up
the face.*

34. *Inside the script, even nearer the Observatory.*

35. *My friend Maggie in the formation at Wabi Farm in October 2001. Above the oak tree are two tiny white light anomalies (circled). When magnified, the one on the left is a mushroom, just like the inkcap we had seen on the drive at Coate that morning; the anomaly on the right is a heart angel resembling the brooch I had just given her.*

36. *Ground shot in the Wabi Farm formation showing an area where there was a wavy lay of the wheat.*

37. *The wheat was woven like a basket in another area of the Wabi Farm formation.*

38. A cloud that put me in mind of a turtle.

39. A sunset in the garden at Coate; it made me think of reincarnation and I see a being on the left wading out of a red sea.

40. *Nature spirits gathering around one of the trees in the Market Place in Devizes. The tree was just about to be cut down in October, 2001. (Photograph by Dawn Bulson)*

41. *A rainbow above the Market Place on the day the other three trees were felled. One is left standing.*

42. Protecting the tree.

43. A large white light anomaly that appeared on a photograph taken during the tree protest. It was Market Day, 5 a.m. on the Thursday.

44. With the two men who climbed into the tree.

45. The 'Devizes One' after the stay of execution.

46. Some of the protestors.

47. The tree decorated for Christmas.

48. Once again the tree was saved in 2002. In the top right-hand corner of the photograph is a white light anomaly. It is a five-pointed star with a tail.

49. The star and tail now on the left of the picture, above one of the four new trees planted around the fountain.

50. The re-growth of the crop circles on the cricket pitch at Coate in October 2001.

51. *The columns of light on my photograph taken before dawn, looking across to the crop circle on the cricket pitch. Left picture shows how it was; right picture has been lightened slightly to show more detail.*

52. Our next door neighbours' friendly peacock that left one of its feathers by my car.

53. Winter Solstice sun rise at Adam's Grave, December 21, 2001.

54. *Sunset at Alton Barnes, December 21, 2001.*

55. *The central bouquet in one of the three small circles in the formation at North Down in May 2002.*

56. *In this North Down formation there is a white light anomaly 'necklace' crossing the lady's head and face, and from her waist down there is a multi-coloured area of pink and green. Also note the eye to the right of her right hand*

57. *The formation in barley opposite Silbury Hill where we had problems with our vision in June 2002.*

58. *Another barley formation at Avebury Trusloe where again our vision was affected, June 2002.*

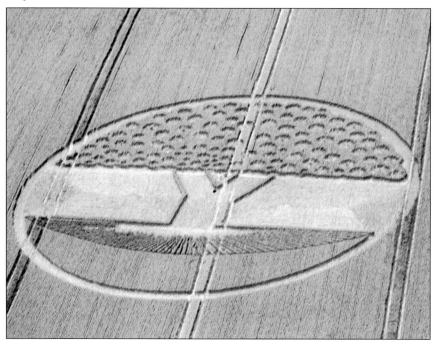

59. *The tree formation in East Field which arrived on July 15, 2002 (three days before the local election).*

60. The tree formation with the Milk Hill white horse in the distance.

61. Ground shot showing one of the 'fruits' of the tree.

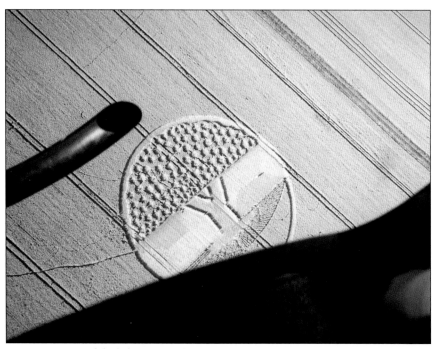

62. Leaning out of the helicopter to photograph the tree while flying overhead, later in the summer with the wheat ripening.

63. The beautiful Nautilus shell at Pewsey in wheat in mid-July 2002.

64. The Nautilus with the Pewsey white horse in the distance.

65. Ground shot in the centre of the shell.

66. In the shell with a luminous white orb below the horse.

67. The ET formation in wheat at Sparsholt, near Winchester, which arrived in
    mid-August 2002.

68. ET with a mauve light anomaly in the bottom left-hand corner of the photograph.

256

69. Ground shot in the centre of the disc held out by ET.

70. Ground shot looking out from the centre of the disc.

71. My request "Home phone ET". In the face of ET just below the telephone mast.

72. The pyramid formation at Beacon Hill in Hampshire with a light anomaly, July 2002.

73. The dolphin formation in East Field with a light anomaly. It was in wheat and joined the tree on August 14, 2002.

74. A blue light anomaly on the left.

75. The dolphins with the tree in the distance. The combine harvester is in the field.

*76. Ground shot in the centre of the dolphins with the peacock feathers
    incorporated in the standing centre.*

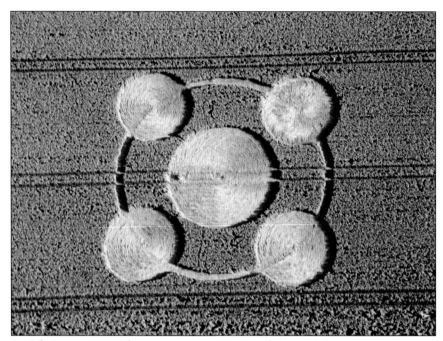

77. The 'Jupiter moons' formation in wheat at Coate, below Etchilhampton Hill in July 2002.

78. The three formations in maize at Walkers Hill, below Adam's Grave in October 2002.

79. *The maize sweeping round in the ring formation, with the Milk Hill white horse in the distance.*

80. *Finding the tiny circle.*

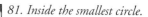
81. Inside the smallest circle.

82. A ten-pence piece on the stalks of maize.

83. In a formation at Windmill Hill in November 2002 with the design still showing in green.

84. One of the 'Jupiter moons' in green in January 2003.

85. *The robin that befriended me in the summer of 2002.*

86. *The speech bubbles coming from the robin's beak which seemed to me to indicate telepathy.*

87. *The formation at the Gallops at Cherhill which came on Sunday July 28, 2002 just before lunchtime, during our Conference.*

88. *The Gallops formation after harvest showing in green in October 2002.*

89. *The oak tree that my brother Granville planted is on the left of the picture.*

90. *The rainbow outside my surgery window on my last day at work, when the pink colour came in for the first time. Sadly, it can't be seen in this picture.*

(Photograph by Andrew Graham)

91. The rainbow below Glastonbury Tor. It just shows the aquamarine and pink bands of colour below the violet.

92. The rainbow at Jump Farm, Devizes. It shows the aquamarine and the pink colours very faintly.

93. *Sunset at Cherhill. This was from the film that had many of the pictures out of focus and all but one upside down. In the centre below the trees is a tiny green light with some anomalous shapes to the left of it.*

In the cloud above the tree in the centre, I can see a little yellow snail.

94. *The cloud in 2003 that showed the notebook and pen.*

95. *A cake at our celebration party in May 2003, after the Devizes Guardians were successful in the local elections.*

96. *Another special cake.*

97. The lotus crop circle, lightly pressed in barley at West Overton which I was asked to find in May 2003.

98. In the centre of the lotus was a tiny little posy of six ears of barley.

272

99. The barley was bent half way down the stalk.

100. The crop was hardly pressed down at all.

101. The other lotus design in wheat beneath the white horse at Milk Hill in June 2003.

102. The clouds appeared to be slightly pink above the horse, with the lotus formation below.

103. The formation that arrived in East Field on the day of the firewalk, August 2, 2003.

104. One of the 55 arrangements that appeared in between all 55 'flames'.

105. Walking along the path of flames in the firewalk formation, as I called it.

106. *One of the two centre pieces in the firewalk formation, showing a heart-shaped area of earth within the wheat.*

107. *The other centrepiece in the firewalk formation.*

108. After harvest, you can still just see the formation in East Field.

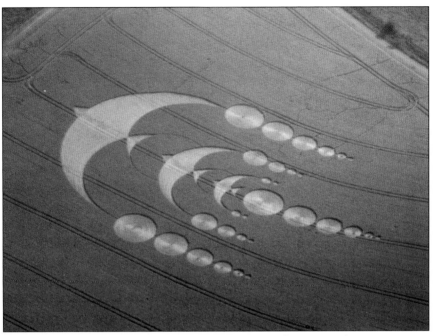

109. The swallows at Walkers Hill in wheat, which arrived on August 4, 2003.

110. The swallows from the hill with the Milk Hill white horse in the distance.

111. In the centre of one of the circles trailing behind the swallows.

112. A blue light anomaly on the photograph of a formation at Avebury in 2003.
It made me think of the book 'The Standing Stones Speak'.

113. The ancient yew tree at Alton Priors with a white light anomaly in the top left hand corner.

114. A column of energy coming out of the water at the sacred spring at Alton Priors.

115. One of the two pictures I took of the lilies in the lobby of the hotel in Lima.

116. The second picture which should have shown the lilies but which shows a being, a pillar of light and numerous orbs.

117. *The swimming pool at the Swissotel in Lima, taken from the glass elevator. I liked the reflection of my shoe being half over land and half over water.*

118. *The amazing stonework at Saqsayhuaman in Peru.*

119. The thirteen members of the group at the start of the Inca Trail.

120. Adriel on the left of the back row with all our porters.

121. In the Andes on the trail. To the left of the water you can see the top half of an Apu, a mountain angel.

122. The angel has moved forward from behind the trees.

123. Looking down on Machu Picchu.

124. The forget-me-not plant in the temple that prompted me to remember.

125. Bones visible in one of the burial chambers at Sillustani.

126. The dock at the Hotel Libertador where I put my crystal into Lake Titicaca. The
lights of Puno are in the background.

127. The Lion rock at Sillustani with the Milky Way and a comet carved on it.

128. The Sillustani skyline. Note the shape of the tower on the left.

129. The cloud that looked like the tower on the skyline.

130. The medicine wheel at Sedona, near Thunder Mountain in Arizona, where I placed a quartz crystal.

131. The tree at Houston Airport, Texas, under which I buried my other crystal.

132. The light in the sky at the Winter Solstice at dawn on December 21, 2003, looking like two flying saucers.

133. The light with a ghostly lightship just to its right, December 21, 2003.

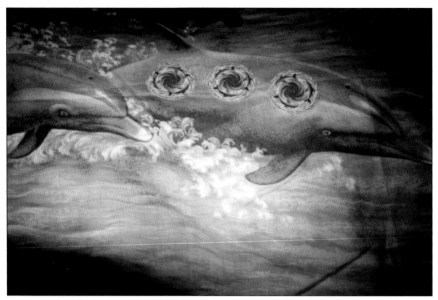

134. *The three dolphin cards that were placed on my pillow in 2004, at Chinese New Year.*

135. *The number 7 on Domino's chest.*

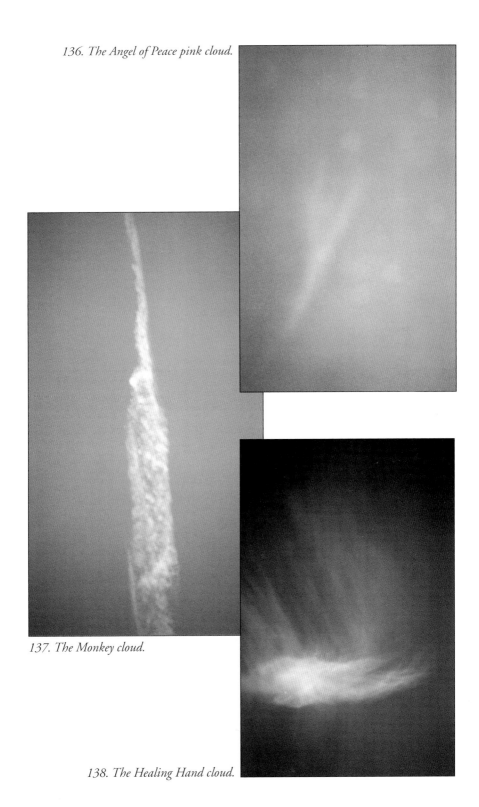

136. The Angel of Peace pink cloud.

137. The Monkey cloud.

138. The Healing Hand cloud.

293

139. A pink cross in the sky looking towards Adam's Grave.

140. Agni Hotra at Adam's Grave at sunrise on the morning of the Venus Transit in June 2004.

141. Sunrise on June 8, the day of the Venus Transit, in 2004.

142. This is the sun projected onto a sheet of blue paper, with Venus a mere dot at about 4 o'clock, having almost completed her Transit across the sun.

143. The bee trapped in the spider's web on top of Angus' almanac.

144. The bee crop circle at Milk Hill in June 2004.

145. *The bee heading for the white horse.*

146. *The Milk Hill white horse.*

147. The formation at Tan Hill also pointing towards the Milk Hill white horse.

148. A pink light anomaly on a picture of the Tan Hill formation after the start of the harvest.

149. The whales and dolphins formation at Golden Ball Hill, which arrived on July 26, 2004.

150. Standing on the tip of a dolphin's fin, with Adam's Grave up on the left. A pale band of colour rests on the standing wheat on the right.

151. The UFO that landed at my feet while standing in one of the whales.

152. The 'bugle' formation in East Field in June 2004, the day before the Solstice.

153. *The formation at West Kennet Long Barrow which appeared to depict another sun transit, in July 2004.*

154. *The left eye crying in South Field.*

155. *The Mayan formation opposite Silbury Hill in August 2004.*

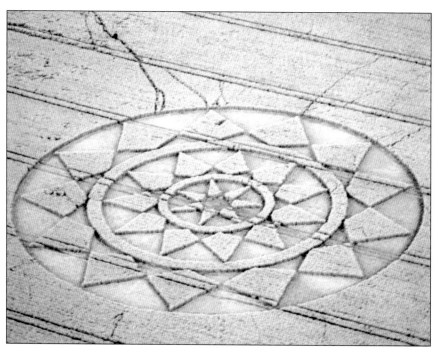

156. *The triple star formation at Coate, below Etchilhampton Hill, taken on a stormy day. It arrived on July 25, 2004.*

157. *The triple star taken from Etchilhampton Hill, showing Devizes in the background.*

158. *The chakra formation with a large light anomaly on the photograph. Note the Pewsey white horse on the hill above.*

159. The chakra formation below the white horse at Pewsey.

160. *A cloud above the cricket pitch at Coate which made me think of ET.*

161. *I saw the words 'I AM' written in the clouds, on the right at the bottom of the sky.*

162. An 'eagle' flying over the cricket pitch with I know not what in front of it.

*163. The cricket nets made
me think of the 'lifting of
the veil'.*

164. A rainbow on the channelling that came during our 2004 Conference.

We wish to reiterate our amazement at the absolute joy we have perceived at soul level in many who have come together for this gathering. We are heartened at the level of understanding which is coming into flower amongst the manifest energy which are particles of the humanity. Our wish is to nurture this and we pass through you the message of appreciation to all those who have laboured and passed the tests of initiation which were flung at them. To keep one's center under these trials and demonstrate the higher aspects of being is a great achievement, wings unfurled and hearts to the fore.

The healing here on all levels has been phenomenal. We wish you to know that. Many souls have come from across the Universe to assist in this and some have left their mark in your fields, calling cards from across the galaxy. As the people hear the call and make their way to your gathering, so the call went out in the ethers. Know this. It is important. The healing is not only for yourselves and your planet but for many, many aspects of creation, manifest and unmanifest in the fields of Love which you can perceive in and around your star systems. The teamwork involved is a great harmony which could only unfold through the intent of manifest humanity.

Go in Peace and Love Each other.

Through Margaret.
8th August, 2004
Alton Barnes.

165. In one half of the ancient yew tree at Alton Priors in 2004.

(Photograph by Flordemayo)

307

166. The little yellow flower at Golden Ball Hill which arrived on May 1, 2005.

6 – WESTERN DAILY PRESS, FRIDAY, MAY 20, 2005

Flowering harvest

...but the farmer's kicking up dust over the circle

Crop Circle: Six-petalled flower pattern in a field of oil seed rape on Golden Ball Hill which has angered farmer Jack Torrens but delighted 'croppies'

EVERY year, with summer on the horizon, they materialise in the West as if by magic to inspire awe and admiration – but in some cases anger.

Yesterday, experts were probing the first "agriglyph" of 2005 after it emerged in a field of oil seed rape in Wiltshire, the crop circle capital of the world.

But as "croppies" were expressing approval of the six petalled agriglyph – a technical term for corn circle – farm manager Jack Torrens was less than happy.

He threatened police action on anyone found making a crop circle, and stressed he would not allow visitors access onto farm land under his control.

The shape surfaced on half-an-acre of countryside at Golden Ball Hill, Alton Barnes near Marlborough, an area well

known for crop formations. Argument still rages over the causes of the often sophisticated and intricate formations, a subject of endless books, films and conventions.

But Mr Torrens firmly believes they are all man-made and considers their appearance on hard worked farmland as criminal damage. He says he and other farmers are sick to death of them.

He said: "We are all fed up with this happening every year. What they have done is totally irresponsible.

Mr Torrens, who runs the West Stowell Estate, owned by the wealthy Rothschild family, said damage is caused both by those who make the patterns and visitors who trample over crops to reach them.

Describing this particular pattern, he said: "They did it at the petal stage and if you

brush the petals of oil seed rape you lower the yield.

"Last summer an especially dramatic formation which covered almost five acres, ruined £2,000 of wheat, said Mr Torrens.

"There is nothing magical about them. They are made by people who come into our fields and spoil our crops."

But Dereka Dodson of the Wiltshire Crop Circle Study Group yesterday begged to differ, believing them to be the result of a combination of the Earth's energies and energy "beyond this planet".

She said of the first of 2005's crop: "Yes I've seen it. It looks like a six petalled flower. It's beautiful, isn't it."

She did not for an instant believe it was created by a team of nocturnal field tramplers.

167. Playing with Polo mints to recreate the formation.

168. Ground shot in the centre of the flower.

169. The stones up above Avebury which are linked with Sirius.

170. The thistle by the dolphin stones at Temple Farm.

171. The poppy in Green Street at Avebury.

*172. One of the dolphin stones
with the engraving on it.*

173. The stone which arrived for me to pick up, among the dolphin stones.

174. *The farmer's collection box in the Y formation in barley at Stanton St Bernard, which arrived at the end of May 2005.*

175. *My new stone with Flordemayo's staff in the Y crop circle formation.*

176. The scarab formation which arrived in East Field on August 21, 2005.

177. The light that came into my sitting room on November 3, 2005. Just to its left on the wall is a picture of the heart formation from 2000.

178. The rainbow just above the Angel from the Andes.

The Transcripts

These transcripts are of the readings received through Psychic Counsellor Mavis Meaker, sometimes while I was with her in person, but usually via the telephone. They were all faithfully recorded and transcribed, but in places they were a little repetitious, and these repetitions have been gently edited out. In addition, where an additional word or two has been inserted for the sake of clarity, these appear in square brackets [like this].

February 8 2003

In the experience with this Group [Crop Circle Study Group] you will have realised it is dealing with energy from outside this dimension. In that process you have accepted that there are many galaxies in this universe.

For this connection to occur there is this means of communication and you understand it is a communication. That communication is not only done with the circles in the corn. You have understood how their energy is provided in other ways in your journey. It has opened your consciousness in many new directions. So you joined this Group thinking it would be like a hobby but it is really not a hobby at all. It is something that has changed the direction of your life. The intent that you had has now become communication. So in which way do you wish to communicate?

I wish to communicate with those who are putting the information in the fields, to help them, and know what my relationship with them is.

We have explained to you that they have a great deal to gain from connections with this dimension, because in this dimension, where everything is allowed, they can manifest information that will assist the development of this dimension.

It has been impacting on you in the way you perceive reality. You can observe what they manifest and you can analytically understand. It is not something that impacts only on one level of consciousness so it is very much about an experience. Many people do not understand that it is to impact on you if you participate in the experience. So you have been able to experience these pictures in the corn and equally you have experienced the energy that those formations offer.

Now that was not your intent when you began the process. For you it was simply to understand that this was of value to find out about, and now you know it is important for you to tell others what you are learning. So you become an educator in this process. At this point what do you want from the energies that communicate?

I want to know what else I can do to help them.

And how can they help you? In what you are trying to do?

They can help me by being better able to protect myself from the energies that are trying to deter us from what we are trying to do.

Now as a minority in this dimension – and you have always been a minority in this dimension – you can see that there is an illusion that there is good and bad and right and wrong. And you know that in this dimension everything is allowed and that means there cannot be good or bad or right or wrong. There is what has value for you as an individual, and what does not have value for you as an individual.

Now that energy that communicates with you is from another galaxy, and they can energetically produce the energy in the corn [crop circle]. You have observed enough of these phenomena to understand that they are not made by man. [There are] people who feel threatened by believing that there are other civilisations outside of this dimension. So then they want to dismiss what you are telling them. Now it does not matter what other people say. You know that these are not made by man. Now that is the truth.

Then the question is, but how can this be created? And you understand that it is created to manifest a message. And the message has to be – you use the word 'de-coded'. So it's like you get a letter in a foreign language and you have to interpret what it is telling you. So you have taken on this challenge to decode the information that is presented.

The first way to express the information is to feel it, you then feel how it impacts on your energy. Some are positive, some are uncomfortable, and you are able to assess very quickly whether it is something that Dereka is added by or something that she is made uncomfortable by. That is the first experience you register.

Then you begin to look at what that is offering to this dimension. Sometimes it impacts on one level of your energy, sometimes two levels, sometimes three, even four levels of your energy. For you that is what you keep records of. That is all they are trying to give to you – support. And as you experience what they manufacture, they realise they are supporting what this dimension requires. So you realise that you live in an experience where many people have difficulty in knowing their own emotions without judgement. Sometimes that is the gift of the energy of the circle. Sometimes it is to offer some spiritual input and we do what we do by symbols. And you are interested in the symbols that are provided because you know there is an energy in the symbols.

So for you it is to look at the way the energy is presented, and to understand how that impacts on your body. Your energy is impacted by the light. The light is geometry, so as you let the light shine on the geometry, and come into contact with that pattern, it can make a difference to your energetic understanding. So we are not trying to manipulate anything, we are offering different energies for people to utilise. And you are prepared to do the research, and to share what you are learning with anyone who is wanting to take this information from you.

Now in our galaxy we do not have experience like you where everything is allowed. So we have the ability to observe what this experience does to your energy. We do not come with agenda to control the outcome. We come to offer you the tools we work with. And we do not work like you in simple understanding of energy. We have technology. And you want to understand our technology. And for you it has been to realise that the formations that have been manifest are not made with physical tools and for you that is the first understanding, that it is not made from human energy.

So then the question is, but what do you want from us? Your question is what do they want with our energy? We are simply offering you our technology. So you have sat in these formations and have asked for input from us. And you have been given pictures. And then sometimes you do not understand the pictures you have been given. So it is important that you learn to communicate the way we communicate and you can interpret the understanding of the pictures, the messages. Because that is how we communicate. You communicate in writing, we communicate in formations. You understand?

In symbols?

Yes, that is our form of communication. And sometimes it is something you would recognise. Sometimes it is a formation you would not recognise. But whatever is presented is a communication. And you find it frustrating because you have not the ability to comprehend. You are a very impatient lady! So you sit and you look at what we have created, then sometimes you see that it represents a chemical symbol. Sometimes it represents some energetic symbols. And sometimes you just enjoy what you see. It is a joy for you just to look at what we have created. Maybe that is all you need to understand, that you enjoy what you are doing. It does not need to be classified in research. We enjoy giving that experience to you, because you never know what the next communication will be. It is that anticipation of what the next communication will bring.

And then when it is presented you think, 'Ah, now where does this one come from?' You can see eventually that they are different styles of communication. You have kept records of where each one is presented and in which order they arrive. Then you begin to understand how that is development of a complex picture. So then you begin to realise that we can just enjoy with you.

But sometimes it becomes complicated in your head. What [do] you think we can achieve in this communication? You have sat and you have said to us, 'I want to understand what this is about.' You have asked that of us. And we have replied – we are giving you ways to change your patterns. Now when you understand the patterns for yourself you can begin to understand that we show patterns of balance and patterns of imbalance. And each pattern we show is either pattern of harmony or pattern of disharmony. You begin to understand that as those patterns manifest in physical form, they are helping this dimension to heal the patterns. And each person that goes into that experience has some impact from [it].

For you it is to be highly sensitive so you do not need to spend much time in that energy. But you are very much the researcher where you notate what you experienced of each pattern. That is not the work of the Group in general, that is the work of Dereka in particular.

So it helps us to experience what you experience. And we do not have understanding of emotion, and that is the only way back to the Divine. So when you do not understand how to feel, you cannot understand how to own the Divine in yourself.

It's like when you meditate. You can take out of your mental body all disharmony and you can sit and experience 'being'. And that is the place of your core essence. And the challenge is to bring that harmony of your core essence into every level of your life.

Now that is not an easy challenge because each time you react to something around you, you are stepping out of your core essence. So when you are living in harmony you are able to experience what goes on around you, without the need to change that experience to what others want, or something you think they should want. So you stop manipulating – we are not manipulating anything. We are simply utilising the lines of energy to manifest patterns. And its something that for you is fascinating because you cannot achieve this yourself. It is outside of your scope. But we cannot experience emotion which is outside of our scope – you understand?

So we are simply observing each other. You want to understand our technology and we are saying we work with energy in the earth. Now you can stand on that line of energy and you can utilise it in any way you choose. That was known by ancient man, how to utilise the energy of the earth.

You have visited many stone circles. And those stones were put into the energy lines to enhance the energy to tap into that energetic source. And then those stones become transmitters of the energy. And you have done much research of stone patterns and you can see that they are where the energy lines are in the earth and they are what you call doorways – portals, yes? And each of those portals has been impacted by what has occurred at that place.

What you have been doing is finding your Group and gathering that energy at a portal and working with that portal energy, to take away anything that does not allow the energy to flow. And then you see that what we provide is opportunities to clear the portals in your body so that all the parts of your body that are not flowing in harmony can be allowed to do that.

We are giving you the assistance to do what you are doing for the earth, because what you are doing in yourself you can add to the earth's energy. So although you are saying, 'I want to clear this portal', you have first to deal with yourself. And many people just want to do the work outside of themselves.

So our input of those patterns allows human people to clear their own centres. And then you can utilise your own energy to help the earth to clear its centres. And there are many known patterns of energy in the earth. You have spent much of your life working on energy portals so it depends on who is gathered, and what is their intent [as to] what can be achieved.

You ask our input when you are doing that work because you know we have the technology to work with the energy. So then it becomes an exercise of earth and you and us in co-creation. And you as the humans are the link between heaven and earth. But if your energy is not flowing freely then that connection is not as powerful as it might be. So you are the bridge between our dimension and the earth. And that is what you are trying to achieve, so that everything can become in harmony.

What if you only understand 'harmony' intellectually? What if you have never done the work to clear the discomfort from your life, Dereka? That bridge is not a strong connection. And as you clear away anything that is not the Divine which is all your emotions of sadness or anger or fear, all the negative patterning of your mental body, and all the physical impact that those emotions and mental patterns have, then you can become [a] very strong connection between our dimension and the earth.

And then you are showing others how to live as heaven on earth. But that is quite a challenging process and most people don't want that responsibility, to change their patterns or their emotions. But you have realised that in the work you have been doing, many of your emotional patterns come up. And many people want this harmony without understanding what disharmony represents. Disharmony represents that there is good and bad and right and wrong. There is not acceptance of the way it is.

In our dimension there is not only the light, there is also the dark. So you have clearly set the intent for your Group to work with the light. You have said you want to allow truth and integrity to be part of the experience for everyone. But you have to equally understand that there are many people who do not know how to deal with the truth, and even think they are being kind by speaking polite energy to others. And when you do not speak the truth and tell someone what they want to hear. you are not a clear channel for truth, are you?

So we are not only here to give you our technology, we are also here to experience what you offer as a bridge between our understanding and earth understanding. We cannot present this technology without the earth's energy. And you understand that. So we cannot utilise *any* energy, it has to be specific energy. And as that energy in those ley lines fluctuates, we have to be able to utilise the energy when it is appropriate to use it.

That is why sometimes you wonder why they come in the random patterns that they arrive [in]. Because the energy fluctuates according to the moon and the seasons. So it's like you have utilised the energy of the [waxing] moon – because you know at that point the energies are different to a waning moon.

So it is with the way we utilise the ley lines. So depending on what we want to manifest, we have to wait until appropriate energy is in that place. Sometimes you say it is confusing for you, because you like chase around from place to place, and you think why does it occur in this way? Because there is a need for resonance in the earth and our energy before we can do what we can do.

Everyone in your organisation has realised that the work has changed everyone. It is very important that you understand the bridges that you are, and you do the work on yourselves.

You have worked with the energy since you were seventeen or eighteen years old, not always consciously – but you have understood energy. And for you it is almost a mission and you need to know that you have to enjoy what you are doing, it does not have to be something that drives you, it has to be something that is part of your life.

You know the difference between truth and illusion; you do not need to make others accept what you know. And what others do with the information you provide is none of your business.

What would you like to achieve from this point forward? You want to connect more closely with us?

Yes.

Well we cannot connect with sadness, anger or fear, Dereka. So as you release those experiences of those emotions and transmute the sadness to joy, the anger to boundaries, and the fear to love, it will be easier to connect to our energy. It is called raising your consciousness.

You have any other specific questions you want to ask us?

I've got a list.

Right, we are waiting . . .

The first question I asked was about an incident with my car at the end of April 2002. It was a Sunday evening and I was driving to meet up with Isabelle's group. I was travelling on the A361 between Devizes and Beckhampton just by North Down. As I drove I was wondering where one gets the first sighting of Silbury Hill along that stretch of road.

As that thought came into my head, my car's engine cut out and came to a halt. The car was only a year old and had just had its first service, so I didn't blame the car for stopping – I looked for a UFO! Several lights on the dashboard lit up as it stopped, and I heard a bleeping sound. I failed to spot a UFO and nothing seemed to be happening, so I gingerly tried to start the car again. All was well and I continued on my way.

A week after this incident a formation appeared at North Down in the field beside which my car had been stopped. It was in oilseed rape and the design put me in mind of an acorn with three smaller circles below it. The largest of the three had a standing centre with the flowers arranged as if in a beautiful bouquet.

When I visited this formation, on one of my photographs there was a light anomaly. An area of pink and green energy, with an eye at the centre, could be clearly seen.

Several formations in 2002 featured a left eye in their design. One of these was the ET formation at Sparsholt in Hampshire, discovered on August 15.

At our 2002 Conference at Devizes School, I had not only my first reading with Mavis, but also a healing session. The healer told me that, like him, I was part E.T. He also said that after seeing me, he had booked a reading with Mavis!

After the Conference I started thinking about the film ET when he says, "ET phone home." I decided to reverse this and put out the thought for 'home' to phone ET. Imagine my surprise a week later when the Sparsholt formation arrived directly below some telephone masts!

When I first saw a picture it looked like the rear view of a cat sitting down with a large CD above it, to its left. This picture, however, had the formation upside down. The right way up it shows what looks like ET holding out a CD in his left hand. There was a message in the disc, laid down in the wheat in binary code. The message ended with the sound of a bell. It spiralled round the disc for some two miles, as walked by TC and LJ.

When decoded the binary message said, 'Beware the bearers of FALSE gifts and their BROKEN PROMISES. Much PAIN but still time. Believe. There is GOOD out there. We OPpose DECEPTION. Conduit CLOSING – (BELL SOUND).' ET had his left eye wide open and his right eye closed, as if he was winking.

We flew over it to film and photograph it and then spent hours on the ground inside the formation.

So during my February 2003 reading through Mavis, my first question was about the incident with my car.

It was experience of energy impacting on your vehicle and you were not afraid, you just understood that this was something to give you a message. And at the end you were not damaged, the car was not damaged but it had moved. Is that enough information?

Was that anything to do with the formation that went down a week later?

It was to show that the energy was being manipulated, it was being moved. And for you it was very unusual experience and you were not afraid.

No, I was excited.

So it was our way of connecting with you – you understand? You registered that energy in your crown chakra; that was what that energy was impacting on, the crown chakra. That is where you experienced that energy. Is enough answer? It was like your hair stood on end. It was working on your crown chakra because that is how we lay down the patterns to have a certain vibration that resonates with other people's energy. It's enough understanding?

Can I ask about the eye on the photograph?

It was not on the ground, it was just in the photograph and it was as though there was other energy at work. It was not like the eye of a person, it was pattern of eye and for you it was added experience to what you photographed. It's like when your eye perceives, that energy can be absorbed. So that particular experience of the eye on your picture was in one corner of [it].

Fairly near to the centre.

But it was not all over the picture, it was in one part of the pattern. So, for you it was to understand that was the way to look at that pattern. For us the eye was to represent the Divine but eye is also self. So it's important that you understand what that eye represented to you. You could not understand how it has appeared on the photograph and for you it was also validation there was other energy at work, But you know that, just like when in your car, you know that was not what *you* were doing. It was what *we* were doing, and that eye was what we were doing. And again for you it was important validation. So it is all experience, yes? It was not in physicality.

No, but would it represent your eye if you were to present in physicality?

Yes. It was not like your eye, it was like a different eye. So you understood it was not a human representation.

Was it a similar eye to the open eye in the formation at Sparsholt?

Yes.

Was that 'home' phoning ET?

Yes, it was communication, yes? It was to say we not have the same physicality as you. We have different, you call it DNA. So what your DNA represents is not the same physicality as our physicality. So our structure is not like your structure. Our eye formation is not like your eye formation. We do not have the same energy in our galaxy as in your galaxy. So it's important that you accept that signature. It's a signature. We [do] not always have that signature, but that makes you understand where that energy originates. It's enough answer?

Yes. The message, have we decoded that in its entirety?

There's one small piece still missing. You had to add your emotion. You had to feel that experience, and you did. And then you could understand what that message said. That message said 'Love'. But love is [a] word, it is not an experience. You had to have the experience, and each person that took on that information was shifted in some way. And you all discussed what had occurred, and everyone had the same experience, you understand? It's enough answer?

Can I just ask about the 'bell sound' at the end of the message? What sort of bell was that?

It was like [a] Tibetan bell. Bell is vibration, it clears energy. It was to clear anything not appropriate in anything that got that information.

Will we ever get to see you in physicality?

It would take a great deal of energy for us to manifest in physicality. If it was necessary it would be presented. At this point it is more important we build a relationship of trust. You do not need to see to understand. It would take a great deal of energy to physically manifest. We can use earth energy to manifest the pictures. It would take more energy to manifest in physicality. It's enough answers?

I had more questions and the next one was about a formation that went down on Sunday July 28 2002. It was the second day of our Conference. The last speaker of the morning started his talk in the school hall and got us all very willingly to sing 'Jerusalem'. He then suggested that we should all go out into the quad on the grass to continue. He asked us to form two concentric circles. There were so many of us that he changed it to three circles. He directed us to focus our thoughts towards the centre and then, as a group, we harmonised to send up sound.

As this was happening, a huge flock of seagulls gathered above us and flew round in circles. They only dispersed when we finished.

During the weekend a helicopter was taking people from the school on a circuit of local crop circles. The pilot had been amazed to find a new crop circle just before lunch time. It consisted of three concentric circles with fine lines running towards the centre. It was situated at the Gallops at Cherhill. The pilot was so impressed that he joined the Group! He had made several flights over that field before the formation appeared.

I asked Mavis if this corresponded to our formation in the quad and the energies replied:

Of course. It was for you to set an intent and in that intent we showed that intent in physical form in the same format. And when you set that intent you are asking for harmony in your intent. And we simply made our signature to show that we were in line with your intent – you understand?

Did it go down at the same time as the sound?

Yes, we used that energy. You put up that energy as a group. We can utilise that energy.

My next question was about Jupiter. One of the speakers at the Conference was Jay Goldner, an Austrian researcher. His work had lead him to believe that there was a connection between the energies responsible for some of the formations, and Jupiter. On the morning of his talk he saw a formation at Coate that was a quintuplet, five circles. He thought it could represent the moons of Jupiter. He told us that February 1 2003 was to be a significant date and suggested we should all try to link in with the energies on that date.

At the end of January the field with the formation had not been ploughed. It was clearly visible in green where wheat from the circles had germinated and grown like grass. I visited the formation and tried to link in with the energies. I decided to send up three OMs. It was an extraordinary experience because sound came back to me. It got louder with each OM, the third one being so loud that my whole body vibrated.

February 1 was a Saturday; our Group was due to have its monthly meeting. We all duly attempted to link in with the energies.

My question to Mavis a week later when I had my reading was:

Can I ask if there is a connection with Jupiter?
Jupiter is a place that magnifies energy. It can be utilised by many different energies.
So did the formation that came down on the day of Jay's talk – was that for him?
He was talking of Jupiter, yes? It was just our message to you. What he said was innovative knowledge. It was for us to accept that what he was giving was his truth, it was the way it is. It was simply our way of acknowledging that he is to be encouraged.
Did you receive our message on the Saturday?
You constantly communicate with us, yes? There is no time that we are not in exchange of communication. For you it was to say we are willing to continue this journey. We understand. You were to lay down specific parameters for us to connect, yes? We have understood what you have said.
When I stood in that formation which is still there, and sent up a sound, what was that sound I heard?
You first of all thought it was echo. It was not echo, it was a different sound. It was for you to know we can operate in the same parameters. You understand? It was not echo. It's for us to show we can, if that is what you want to connect with, we can show that we can connect also. For you it was release noise. It was unwinding for you, a release experience. And we simply make noise for you to understand we can do same as you.
Not half! I'm still in shock!
Why? You not think that we can do what you can do?
You did it so much better.
No, we not think it's better, it's different. We are different.
Vive la différence!

That's what we say, vive la difference. You learn from us, we learn from you. We all become more of who we really are. So we trust what we offer to you will help you keep taking the steps forward. We have answered all your questions?

What are the little rainbows above some of the formations?

(On several occasions while lying in a formation there has been a tiny rainbow in a clear sky above.)

It's refraction of light, yes? So it's important to know that that energy, manifest[ing] physically, is manifesting the rainbows. There is no rain. Rainbows normally appear when there is rain, but there is no rain, so it's not a rainbow from rain. It's simply refraction of light. It's a signature also, you understand? What does a rainbow signify for you? Joy?

Beauty, love, joy.

So then you know it's a signature you understand?

We thank you for the work you are doing. You did not know this path would take you down this avenue of research. But it continues to fascinate all of us. So we give much love to you, Dereka. We will give you the answers to your questions as it is appropriate for you to receive them. You shout at us, we will shout at you!

Thank you.

Til next we meet.

November 4 2003

The energies asked if I had any questions. My first was about birds. They seemed to have started interacting with us. In 2002 a robin befriended me and used to come to me every time I went out of the door. It would land on my hand, and come into the house.

On one occasion I took a photograph of it on the kitchen window sill. On the picture were light anomalies, five white circles like thought bubbles seemed to be coming out of its beak. It seemed to be a visual representation of telepathy.

Can I ask about birds, seagulls, hawks and swallows? What is our connection? We seem to be interacting with seagulls or they seem to be interacting with us.

When you understand everything is energy, in many ways your journey of growth is to balance the heaven and the earth. And the energy of birds has a very different intent to the intent of man who walks the earth. So in this process with these birds, you are finding that they are being attracted to you. You are finding you can communicate with them by thought. And that is because your energy is very different to much of the energy on this earth. When you begin to understand all is one, you understand that everything plays a part in the whole experience.

Now these birds are coming to you and you are beginning to work with that. You have worked with birds before, you have worked with the robin. So you have developed this understanding where you realise that they can read your thoughts. So that is now happening with these seagulls. And you are finding that they are coming and understanding how to trust people.

It is important that there is this foundation of integrity between energies. There has to be trust, and these birds trust you. They do not come with the emotion of fear. They come with the understanding of trust. So when that happens it helps other birds to understand that not everyone is going to harm them. There are people who shoot birds; there are people who destroy birds. But you are trying to build a relationship of trust with these birds. They are trusting you and then they can show others how to trust people.

They have brought more – yes? So they are bringing other birds to say, 'Look, this is how you can interact with people.' You are not harming any of them, you are not saying it has to be one or ten because more and more are coming. What do you want from the connection with them?

More communication.

So if you understand telepathy, which you do, you began the process with the robin. You are able to say, well we want to share our journey with your energy. And then you begin to understand that they are simply another part of the whole. So you just want more communication, what do you want to communicate? That you are trustworthy? They know you are trustworthy. You are standing and they are coming to you.

Yes, they seem to be interacting with the formation of the crop circles.

You understand you are coming to a time of shift in energy in this dimension. Now everything has to shift in this process. So they have to understand that the energy that creates the formations is energy outside of material world. That is just an energetic experience. Now they can experience some of that energy. They are coming to you when you are interacting in that energy. So they can find from you how to utilise that energy just as you have learned to utilise [it].

When you go into crop circle you find that it has impact on you. So they are also realising that it can have impact on them. You have found that initially animals will not go into that energy, because it is different to what is [outside] that circle. So many people fear what that will do to them, including the animals who do not speak, but they have the understanding of how to read energy. And the birds are the same, they can read the energy.

You interact with the energy that makes the crop circles, and you have communication with that energy just like you have communication with the birds. So you are developing this understanding of how to communicate without words. [If] you stand next to someone, and you do not feel comfortable with them, you would know that without one word being spoken.

When you look back at the robin, the robin was not afraid of you. The seagulls are not afraid of you. You are not going to harm them, you have sent out that thought pattern and you are trying to help them understand that people are not all the same.

You have accepted that people are not all operating within the same values and principles. You are happy to let the birds into your life. In fact you are much more comfortable with nature and its beings than you are with people . . .

You have other questions?

My next question was about my recent trip to Peru. I had left the main group in Cusco and caught a bus to Puno and Lake Titicaca. I spent two nights there. On the first night I was awakened at 3 a.m. by a violent storm directly above, and on the second night, after I had put a crystal in the lake, there was another amazing storm which seemed to be interactive.

It was a fascinating experience for you to observe. You just observed it and for you it was realising the energy was doing battle. And when you understand that when there is storm there is some kind of energetic clash. And for you it was simply to be an observer. You were partly involved because you were walking. It was part of your journey, and this was one stage of your journey. You were staying at that place for a few days and this occurred while you were [there].

Yes, I was there for just two nights.

And you observed what occurred it was fascinating to watch – it was electrical. And there was light and there was energy. And you were not afraid – you were just fascinated. And for you it is to understand how energy works within the whole. There was great amount of rainfall and that is the extremes of that place. They get extremes of heat, extremes of rain, extremes of everything. So when you go to somewhere like that where the climate is very different from your much more gentle climate, you understand the energy is very different. But you were just fascinated to watch, yes? What was your question about? You just observed that, you were not caught in that.

The first one woke me and was directly above but I wondered if putting the crystal in the lake had any effect on the second storm, which seemed very interactive.

When you placed that crystal in the lake you placed it with the intent of healing. That was your intent, yes? You didn't just put it without intent. You asked that the crystal could anchor some understanding of healing. So what then occurred is this interaction of energy. It was for you to simply add your intent to that place.

When you take your energy to a place, you are impacting on that place and it impacts on you. It is an interaction and you added the [extra] dimension of the crystal. You had taken the crystal with you because you wanted to take that energy and impact on where you were going. And the storm was an interaction of those energies. And you were not afraid, you did not react, you responded. So what did the storm say to you?

It seemed to me to say that my intent was . . .

Honoured, it was honoured. So that is your answer – yes? Anything that is no longer appropriate can be released from this place. That is how you do work on the energy of this planet. But like attracts like, so with your energy in that place we could work to anchor something that was conscious in that place. And you were not afraid of the storm – many people would be afraid of the storm. To you it was just something to stand and watch and you said, "Ah, my intent has been honoured."

I hoped.

It had. It had been honoured. You asked for consciousness to be anchored there. That is what you ask for wherever you go. That is what you will ask for when you go on your next journey [to Sedona in the U.S.] You will do the same thing.

You will go and take something [to] place in the earth with intent. And you understand crystal can hold intent. So, if you put the intent into the crystal, the crystal can give out the intent that you have put into it. So that is [why] you are going and placing that intent, and allowing that crystal to hold that intent. It's enough answer?

You have put crystals in some of your crop circles and asked that somehow the energy that has been brought to that crop circle can be anchored in the earth. It's the same process and certain crystals can hold that energy; quartz can hold that energy easily, you understand?

Yes, so quartz would be a good one to take to America?

Yes. But it is more important that you set the intent because then the crystal can hold that intent. And you are a very powerful lady. You are beginning to understand that. You have done much of your own work within yourself. You have transmuted much of your sadness to joy. You have transmuted much of your anger to boundaries. You have transmuted much of your fear to love which is the Divine.

That is what each person comes to achieve. So that crystal was the way to anchor that consciousness and the storm was part of that experience. And you simply learned to say, "Ah, I am being given the answers to my questions." You will take a crystal with you on your next journey, yes?

I will.

Crystals come from the earth. You gave one back to the earth. You have other questions?

Can I ask what connection I have with Venus?

The planet Venus?

Yes.

Not the goddess Venus?

The planet.

337

Venus is always shown as the energy of love. And you now understand that love is the Divine in everything. So you are trying to work with that understanding of unconditional love. And you thought that unconditional love was to give care to everyone else without including Dereka in the equation.

Venus is the energy of unconditional love. So you cannot give it out to someone until you have first given it to yourself. It is very important that you accept that whatever that planet's energy is, you have to incorporate that unconditional acceptance of yourself. You are attracted to understand that energy, yes? What do you understand the energy of Venus to be?

Well, I remember just seeing it as the red and the green when flying and I wonder if that was the red and the green energy that came on my photographs when all the pictures were turned upside down. (My camera appeared to malfunction one night at Cherhill at sunset).

You understood that that was interference in what you had done. And you began to realise that you were photographing some of the energy that was in that place. You understood that, because it has happened more than once. So whatever that energy was, does it matter where it originated?

No.

You understand you were photographing energy. It has happened more than once.

Oh yes. But I'm never aware of it until I see it on the pictures.

So why is it you can't register the energy before you see it in physical form? You can understand that every place you go to, you can be impacted by, and it can be impacted by you. And you are beginning to realise that you are more and more stable as time passes. You do not *react* to things around you, you *respond*.

It does not matter what that colour means – colour is energy. So red is the energy of the earth and green is the energy of emotion. It is the energy of your heart centre, your feelings about yourself. So it is about anchoring in this earth that love for yourself. That is what Venus is about. Bringing love for yourself which is green in your heart centre, where the child in you lives, into the earth's energy which is red energy, the base centre.

So that was your challenge in this lifetime. In that picture there was a balance of the two energies. Colour is just another way of observing energy.

Red and green are the opposites on the colour wheel. So it is also saying you are in a world of polarity.

Sometimes you have had just light in your photographs, not colours, just light. And you have understood the energy that makes these patterns in the earth is light. You understand that and for you, having understood it is not made by people like you, it is made by energy, you begin to understand it is simply explaining to you that there are more things in this dimension than you can see and touch.

How many people have understood that experience? There will be those who make all the intellectual explanations. But then there are those like you who just understand the energetic experience. So when you see it on your photograph it says to you, 'Ah, there is something more than I can see and touch.' You have always known that. Here is your proof. There it is for someone else to see. There is something going on that is not physically there. You don't need that proof, but other people might.

So that's the purpose of it appearing on the film, it's for other people to see?

Yes. You don't need the proof. You are teacher to a great number of people. You never set out to be a teacher but you have become a teacher. But in the process of what you teach, you are not having to do it because *they* want you to teach them. You are having to do it because *you* want to learn yourself. And if other people want to learn from the things you can show them, that is for them to decide, not for Dereka to decide.

January 28 2004

*A*m *I being very impatient or is it now coming time to put some of the information that I've been given into book form?*

Yes, most definitely.

Right. Have I now got all the photographs I need?

You've got enough to give the evidence you want to give. There may be [more] that will be presented at some point, but they said you have enough to begin.

Now for you the format is difficult because you don't need to prove yourself to anybody. You have to write this from your perspective. You didn't go into this journey understanding that this would be the [result]. But you have found that things have been given to you, and shown to you, and you have been able to work with [that] to put together the full picture.

Now you might need other pieces of that jigsaw puzzle, but you've got enough to start. Your hesitancy is what if other people don't understand and don't accept? It doesn't matter because you understand and you accept.

It's their problem really.

Exactly. That's their problem. Now you can do this in your head as you've done for most of your life, or you can do this book with a balance between your head and your heart. What was your feeling about what happened? When you put the balance between your head and your heart you are including yourself in it. There are many books written from the head alone, and this one won't be written from the head alone because there is no explanation for a lot of the experiences. So you have to be able to put in what you felt emotionally, so that aspect of it is included. What is the problem with starting doing that now? The book?

It just feels such a responsibility.

To whom?

To the people I want to understand.

[But] you understand. So if *you* understand, you can only give it from the perspective you understand. How other people understand is for them to decide. You don't go into this with a need to prove yourself to others, you are just explaining your experiences. Some of those were with other people, so you might include other people's experiences that were with you at the same time.

Do I give people's names?

Not unless they are happy for you to do that. You might need to change their names. If they don't want that involvement then you can say, 'These people were with me' but you can explain that the name has been changed for their protection. You are quite prepared to put your name to what you are doing. So other people will need to be asked are they happy for their name to be included. If not, maybe you can give them another name but that is their decision, not yours. That will validate some of the experiences because some you had on your own, but some experiences you had with [other] people. So you can include all of those experiences.

What is your intent in writing the book? Just to help others to understand?

Yes.

Or to be able to say these are the experiences I've had and I would like to be able to share them with you so that it might open your understanding more. How much people's understanding opens is not your decision to make. You've got to be very clear about that before you begin. Is that enough information?

342

You've already got the scribblings and all you've got to do is look at [the] order you put them in. Do you put them in chronological order? Do you start at the end? Do you go back to the beginning? Do you take out certain aspects or do you do it in a haphazard way. But you've got the scribblings. So you've now got to decide the structure of what you are going to present.

You need any other information about that?

If I do it chronologically, starting from when I was nineteen and had my first premonition, am I supposed to include my experiences in the ocean in this?

Yes, you are simply saying these are the connections I've had with the next dimension. When you began that journey, with those premonitions, you had no understanding of that energy you were working with. As you have developed, and you had other experiences, you have begun to ask what is this energy I am connecting with? And you understand that there are many different energies you have connected with.

That is important because when you began you were naïve. So you can go back to that point and you can say I didn't understand what I was dealing with, but as time passed, I began to ask what I was dealing with, and these are the answers I was given. It is quite important that you are able to help people who might be at the beginning of their journey, to understand how to listen to the voice within.

You didn't know how to listen to the voice within, you had not been taught that in your childhood. You had not been made to understand that everything is energy, but now you *do* know, and you are dealing with energies that are not at the same level of vibration as you. So, yes, go back to that point. Bring up the emotions you experienced by listening to the voice within.

That is your beginning point, [where you] grew up in a family that only believed in what they could see or touch. [And say] when I began hearing voices in my head, I wondered why. Their first explanation was there is something crazy about Dereka. And now you know there's nothing crazy about Dereka.

Dereka knows the difference between truth and illusion. So that is the book, yes? That is what you will be showing people. You have had these experiences. What they accept of what you tell them is irrelevant. They cannot take away those experiences.

And you continue to have those experiences. You still understand we get information to you and you listen. You understand we will not provide you with anything unless you ask for it.

When you ask, you receive. And you have learned that now, so when you have decided how you want to structure this book, where you put the information is not important. You might start at where you are now. You might then go back to the beginning and bring everything back to the point you are at now.

Should I start with my latest car crash?

That was an awakening right? That was a situation where you began to realise that you were protected.

Oh yes.

And you wondered what was happening in your life that you were protected and something was taking the knocks for you. You were not afraid, you were angry.

I was relieved, having dreamt it without knowing the ending several times. I was very relieved that it was such a soft landing (a hedge).

And what did that bring up in the way of emotion? Gratitude?

Yes, you took the word straight from me.

Gratitude.

Gratitude.

And you have learned that your life is what you choose it to be. So you could see the picture in your head, but you then realised you were protected. You have always been protected, you invite protection, ask for protection. It can be from material situations, it can be from energetic situations and it can be from intellectual situations – it doesn't matter. If someone tells you everything you cannot see or touch does not exist, you can tell them, 'Well that isn't my experience'.

They might not want to accept what you tell them, but that's irrelevant. You need to constantly protect yourself because you understand not everything functions in the same values and principles as Dereka. So it is important to realise that the protection is there when you ask for it. We will always provide the protection you ask for.

Thank you.

And next question?

The three cards on my pillow, (Dolphin Divination cards were Synergy, Entering New Dimensions and Abundance) *was that you guys?*

Well you did not put them there!

No.

There was a message in the cards and you understood the message, you listened. You need to ask about the message?

Well if I listened to it and if I got it right, I'm going to get help in entering these new dimensions, and hopefully the book will reach people and enrich them.

It is about what you experienced and then you realise not everyone is interested in what is truth and what is illusion. So if you are going to invite support you have to be specific about what kind of support you want. You are going to do the writing right? You already understand that we exist. You have worked with us for the last ten or eleven years. So those experiences have taught you that you are not a crazy lady. And it is important that you ask for the help you specifically need at any given point in time. We can get the information to you, [but] cannot decide what you will do with the information we give you. It is for you to work with the information and let other people decide if they want to do that work themselves. You have simply to provide your experience. You are amused when we give you the information in that way. Yes?

Yes.

You think. Ah! This is a new way of doing something. And you are prepared to look at what we have given, and work out the message, which you did, [and you were] right. You will receive the support you ask for. You did not put the cards there.

No. Was it significant that it was on the Chinese New Year and it's the year of the Monkey?

What did that signify to you? A new beginning?

Yes, my Chinese birth year.

So the cycle is complete. It is a new beginning. You have done the work to complete the past. You have got your energy out of the past. You are now focusing very clearly on your intent from this point forward. So it is a new beginning, a new birth.

You have gathered the information, [you] have done the work on [your]self. [You are] now taking these steps forward, to simply talk of what [you] have experienced so others can become enriched. You are not stuck in the past anymore. You are not looking back and thinking I should have done it differently. You are simply accepting that each of the experiences was something to learn from, even if it was only not to repeat it. You do not wish to repeat your car incident again?

No.

No, you have said that.

I'll try and make sure I stay awake.

You have to get the lesson from the experience. You cannot beat the law of cause and effect, Dereka. And your next question?

Can I talk about the Winter Solstice? (On December 21, 2003 a group of us had gathered for a sunrise ceremony at Adam's Grave, the Neolithic long barrow above Alton Barnes. As we started to leave, Lisa spotted a tiny rainbow in the sky in front of us. I took lots of photographs as this tiny rainbow developed into an incredible light. At one point it divided into two halves. It stayed for over an hour.) *What was that wonderful light?*

In the sky?

Yes.

What did you imagine the light in the sky was? It was light being brought into this dimension. And you understood [that]. It is a time of different energy when the planets are in a certain situation and we can bring that light into this dimension. Light is truth, light is information, it is wisdom. It is what you bring into the world yourself.

And you just stood and observed it. And you were grateful also for that experience. Because it is a privilege to watch that kind of energy. It impacts on you. You were also with a group, yes? So that group also witnessed some of that light. It was not only you, it was others too.

You were simply able to observe and understand that this was an opening of another portal. There is a constant change and rise in consciousness in this dimension right now. It is not static, it continues to change. At every opportunity we are able to bring more understanding into this experience for you. If people do not shift as that energy shifts, they will dysfunction. And you understand that now. You realise many people are not taking the steps forward. You can watch that light and understand that it is accessible [to] everyone if they understand energy. You all invited the light into yourselves. Is that enough answer?

On the last two photographs I took it looks as if that light is in a bubble. Is that just an illusion on the photo or was the camera picking up?

That was not how you observed it with your eyes.

No.

So what you saw with your eyes and what the camera saw were not the same thing.

No.

So it was just the camera's way of describing what was there. It was not what you picked up with your eyes. The light was not contained, it was pervading into everything. What you saw on the camera was contained. It is important that you understand it was not as you observed it. Sometimes the camera can deflect the light, [it] can be reflected or refracted by the camera. So you have to be able to understand what you observed.

Sometimes you have taken photographs and had on your camera things that you have not seen with your eye. That might have been one aspect of the light. But you imagined it would portray what you had seen with your eye, and it didn't. So you just have to understand it could have been refracted. At the time you took the photograph you were looking at the light and not seeing what the camera showed you. Is that enough answer?

So in actual fact that light did not have any boundaries, it was not contained?

No. The light was was able to illuminate a great area. And in the photograph it did not show that.

No, it appeared to have a limit.

And light does not have any limit.

What was the ray of light going down into the field? The single beam in the corner of the picture that came from a higher elevation than the sun was? Was that single beam from that light?

Yes, it was not something you saw with your eyes.

No.

No, but it was something you saw only on the picture. It was one single area of a different kind of light. It showed as different, it was very straight. When you see something like that you realise we are able to have different aspects of light. But that was very focused on one place and you had not seen that with your eyes. So yes, it was a specific aspect of light.

Was there an element of preparation for a formation in the summer in that location?

That could be. We are told that was not the intent. It was just something that was focused energy.

How about the picture I took of the formation from last summer (in East Field on August 2, 2003, which could still be seen in green in the field) that was completely out of focus? They didn't even print it.

And everything else was fine?

All the other pictures, yes.

But that one was not fine. So it was something about the energy that was not clear. You understand that different energies make those formations. They are not all made by the same energy. So that particular energy was disturbing something in the earth. What you saw was not clear. Therefore it is important that you understand the energies of each formation are different. And it just showed on your picture in a way that was a blur. So it tells you something about the energy of that space. Nothing else was like that and you had not moved your camera. So it makes you understand those formations change the energy. Therefore you need to be discerning which of those energies you interact with and which you don't.

That's the one I put the heart shaped stone in. Is that working there?

Yes. You anchored something there, you set an intent. You wanted to anchor some emotion in that place because you were not comfortable with the energy when you went into [it]. You need to ask more?

I wasn't sure because that's the one I hoped would depict a firewalk (we were due to have a firewalk at our Conference on that day) so it seemed to come in response to that.

And what docs a firewalk represent to you?

Opening the heart.

It is a passage of rite. It is walking through a fear. So every time you walk through a fear you transmute that fear to the Divine, which is love. And love represents that heart, not human love, but the love of the Divine in you. So you were asking to anchor the Divine.

If you understand that each fear you walk through transmutes the fear to the Divine, you were anchoring the Divine love. So it was more about the experience while you were in that energy than it was to depict it in a photograph.

That is what your challenge is, not to do this in your head alone but to do it in balance between your head and your heart. What do you feel? It is like when you have any experience, you can deal with it intellectually, you can deal with it emotionally or you can deal with it with a balance between the two. You will learn how to deal with it as a balance between the two. You anchored that heart as your understanding of the Divine.

You wanted the picture to depict a firewalk or you believed it was the energy of the firewalk?

Both.

Earlier in the summer, on several occasions, I had walked first up Knapp Hill and then up to Adam's Grave. From both I had looked down on to East Field and asked the energies for a formation to celebrate the firewalk. The formation was found on the Saturday morning. The firewalk was in the evening.

So you have experienced the firewalk, yes? To you that was about trusting the Divine in you, an important intent to set. Now at that present time you were going through quite a lot of chaos, a lot of decision-making processes and for you to be able to walk through that fear was quite a challenge. But you did [it] and you were given the protection you asked for. So it was a rite of passage for you. It was, 'I have to walk through my fears. I have to be able to transmute my fears because no one can do it for me.' And we have pushed you through a great number of fears from that point forward.

So your photograph was not that important. You were going through some of that chaos, the energy was disturbed. So at this point you need to be able to look at how far you have come since that rite of passage. It was a new phase of your life.

It's like the newborn child, it cannot see, it cannot focus. It doesn't mean that things aren't there, but the child doesn't have the ability to focus on anything, everything is a blur. But as time passes, things become clear.

At that point you had not clarified your intent, but now you have. You are not the people pleaser. You are not carrying anyone on your shoulders. You are not the mother to any organisation. You are learning what fulfils you and what doesn't, and let the things that fulfil you in and keep out the things that don't. So it was a time of decision making for you. And were you anchoring that Divine in you, or were you trying to do it for others as well?

I think I've been trying to do it for me.

Good, so that was your rite of passage. You now understand that the Divine in you can only create for Dereka what Dereka believes Dereka deserves.

And Dereka doesn't need the struggle and effort any longer. The world can manage to create that without any example from Dereka. You are now trying to teach the world something more constructive. And what the world learns from your example is not your decision to make, is it?

No.

Is [it] enough about that?

Yes, can I ask about alterations on my computer, on people's records, telephone numbers, house names?

It has been three different [times]?

Oh, I've only noticed two I think. Maybe three.

Have you found three?

If Stephen Mulhearn is one of them.

And you didn't change it yourself?

No.

And it brought attention to that person?

Yes.

And then you began to [wonder] why you were being brought to look at that person. And that was the intent – for you simply to look at that person. What was happening between you and that person. And you have let that person go. You don't understand that.

No, I wasn't sure if the third one is correct, but I do need to contact that person. But the two alterations to somebody else – I think we had a shared memory of fire. Was that why my attention was drawn to her?

Yes. It was just to focus your attention. And you get the message, you observe what you need to focus on.

Is there any benefit in trying to get help from somebody to go back and re-experience that or not?

What, with the person to do with the firewalk?

No, with the lady who had a shared memory of fire with me in a previous life.

If there is any unfinished business from the past it will be presented to you in the present, as and when it is appropriate. What the connection was between you then may not be the connection between you now. So what you learned from the experience, may not be what they learned from the experience. It is not to have your energy in the past, it is to have your energy in the present.

The present is the only point you can make a decision. If there has been something in the past, if there is unfinished business, it will be presented to you in this lifetime so you can deal with it in the present. And it hasn't been presented so far. So for you it is simply to understand there has been some connection. She has not understood the connection. You do not need to do anything because if it is presented it will be presented in the now. And you will ask why has this been presented to me? And what is my agenda in this situation?

And it was clearing that fear?

Yes, it was clearing that fear. That was what your firewalk did. Because many people have in the past died in fire.

During a workshop at Coronation Hall at Alton Barnes, a group of us were working with the four elements, earth, air, fire and water. Working with a lighted candle as the fire I had a sudden memory of being surrounded by fire. It seemed to me to be a memory of burning at the stake.

So it was an old pattern that has been resolved for you both. Is that enough answer?

Yes, yes thank you.

The rainbow that came outside my surgery on my last day of work, and the photograph of it that I received last week, was that the first time the pink energy had come in on the rainbow?

Yes.

Right.

It was also ending one era of your life and at that point you had no understanding what your next step would be.

No.

To you it was almost like you had to close one door before another could open. And it was our way of celebrating with you.

Oh! Thank you.

It was a big step for you, much fear attached to that step. Your work in many ways had been an escape from dealing with the empty space of your life. You needed a life of your own, but you had no idea what that life would bring. So it was our way of celebrating the closing of the door with you.

It was great, thank you.

You have another question?

I've asked before and it wasn't appropriate to ask at the time, but I wonder now if it's still inappropriate to ask who is providing this help for me?

Who is providing the support to you?

Mmm.

Many different energies. You are not supported by one particular energy, you are supported by many. And we will always bring the kind of input that you ask for. It cannot all be provided by one kind of energy.

Is that why sometimes if I ask a question about the formations, sometimes I hear you say 'we' and sometimes you say 'they'?

That's right, because there are different levels of understanding. Just like in your world there are different levels of consciousness, in our world it is the same. Now we may not have the answer to your question, but we will try to access that information for you. And then you will find that you are working with many different levels of understanding.

You have always accepted that about the formations, that they are not all formed by the same energies. Some are much more complex than others. Sometimes you try to work them out in your head. Sometimes you have to just be able to understand the feeling of the experience. But it is not one energy you are working with. You work with some very high levels of energy, Dereka. So, yes, when they say 'we' or 'they' it means it is not necessarily the person you are talking to.

And we don't have bodies like you, we don't often have names like you, we are just energy. Sometimes we show ourselves as colour, [sometimes] as light. So that is how we can represent ourselves. You understand? And when you realise that the universe is infinite there are many different levels of understanding. It's enough answer?

Yes. Was it after that convergence of the planets in November, the green colour that I see — did that start then to come through?

What is green? Green is the heart centre, green is the balance. It was the beginning of the balance between the head and the heart. And it was a merging of those two levels of understanding. Those who do not operate like that will find their bodies become imbalanced. It will help people to open their heart centre.

But most people don't invite that energy in. You do. You understand that if you invite something, it is provided. And you are able to see that as well as feel it. Most people might feel it, but they wouldn't see it. You see and hear and feel, so you are able to understand in many different aspects. You understand? You have the sixth sense. The voices you can hear, and yet you still like to talk to us like this.

I know.

You need to trust what you hear. You are getting more able to do that. But then you realise all we do is validate what you know. It is sometimes comforting to have validation of what you know.

Very, very. I should have more confidence, I suppose.

Well, it will come with time. But as you take this journey that very few people take, there are very few that understand what you are trying to achieve. Because many people would think you were one wacky woman, but you're not. We have answered all of your questions?

How are my crystals in America?

The ones you planted? They are fine. You wanted to anchor the love and the light there. We heard what you asked for. You set that intent and they will give out that intent. If you set an intent, we have to work in that intent with you, Dereka. You wanted to give out the love and the light to those places where you anchored that energy. It is happening. People might not understand what is happening energetically but that intent will be respected, Dereka. Enough answer?

Yes, yes.

You can do it by simply setting an intent. Just ask for anything inappropriate to be cleared from any place at which you stand, ask that love and light be anchored at that place. And that intent will be honoured. The crystal simply enhances what you asked for. Crystals just amplify your intent.

Thank you for the butterfly that came too.

What in America? That was just you learning to spread your wings.

(The quartz crystal that the energies had asked me to take to America, I had placed in a medicine wheel not far from Thunder Mountain. I later worried because I had been asked to put it *in* the earth, not *on* the earth. I decided to get another crystal and bury it elsewhere. When I told the lady from whom I was buying the crystal what I wanted it for, she gave it to me. My time was limited and somehow I had to try to find somewhere to bury it at Houston Airport! I was very aware of all the security there as I ventured down a ramp to where I had seen some trees. As I went nervously down the ramp I became aware of a butterfly flying beside me.)

That was your confirmation. 'I am prepared to spread my wings and fly'. So we trust what we have given will be of value.

Thank you.

We will continue to support what you are doing. And as you take those steps forward, there will always be more that you will be able to take, and you will do [so] when *you* are ready, not when we are ready. We are not the masters of your destiny. You are always the master of your own destiny. We are always the support structure. We will not abandon you, Dereka.

Thank you.

You do not ever take one step of your journey alone. So we give much love to you.

Thank you.

And encourage you in the work you are doing. You are teaching truth to many people. What they do with it is none of your business. Much love.

June 17 2004

*T*here *was a series of events when everything was reversed.
I got a final bill before the first one, my photographs –
the first one came out as the last one on the prints. What
was the message with that reversal of the first with the last?*

What did *you* get from that? That time is beginning to have a
different way of functioning in this dimension? You have heard
about Zero Point, and how things are slowing down until we
reach the point where everything is in the now. That was a
message for you to understand time is not the factor that drives
your life. It isn't [a matter of] did this happen before that, it is
[about] what the value was of each of the experiences? Learning
that the order [things] happen in is not the important issue.
What did you learn from each of the experiences?

*I do have trouble remembering the sequence of events but it's not
important.*

No, it is not important. It is what is the end result? What is
the effect? [That's what is important.]

In the now.

In the now. And you have worked with our dimension long
enough to understand that whatever information you invite, you
will receive. So when you get the last bill before the first bill, and
the photographs are [out of sequence], it didn't really matter. It
was just an experience where you recognised time, and the order
[in which they occurred] is not important. What does it matter

357

who you took your power back from first? It is the fact that you have taken back your power from anyone who creates discomfort in your life. You have learned how to confront situations but you still have difficulty in respecting the child in you. Is that enough answer?

Yes. The number on my number plate that I took as a guide to a reference in a book, was that correct? (The book was entitled *The Standing Stones Speak* by Natasha Hoffman.)

It was. You were to connect the dots and you made sure you read that piece of information. It was very relevant to something you were dealing with. They are what you call signposts. You have spent your life working with that kind of synchronicity.

And in that connection between the number on your car and this particular piece of information, you recognised why we had drawn your attention to that. But you have learned to get messages from what is presented to you. You understand?

Yes – like the clouds.

Like the clouds, yes. You see pictures in the clouds and you just say, 'I've got it.'

When I was told in Peru that I would have contact, was that contact in the cloud?

Yes, initially.

Initially, and then on my birthday was that contact again?

Yes.

(June 10, 2004 was my sixtieth birthday. Although I did not remember them, I decided to go up to Adam's Grave and repeat the promises I had made when I incarnated into this current lifetime. When I awoke at dawn my vision was very blurred and it was a very misty day. Up by the long barrow two beings appeared out of the mist. I had heard voices and then there they were, standing about fifteen feet from me. Nothing was said. After a short while they turned to their right and disappeared. I didn't see any hands or faces, they seemed to be wearing hooded cloaks.)

It was noise?

Shapes in the mist.

But there was noise also?

Yes.

You hear the voice in your ear. So it is a connection between what you see and what you hear. You hear the information. [What you then see is] connected with the intent of showing you this picture.

Although it took me about two days to realise what I saw.

But you then registered what that message was about.

Is that why my eyes were so painful that day? (after seeing the beings.)

Yes, because you need to have your eyes out of focus. And when you don't have your eyes out of focus, you can't see the next dimension.

So that's why everything was out of focus all the way I was driving there?

Yes, in preparation. Then you begin to understand the bigger picture. You have come a long way on your journey, and you have said 'I want to make direct connection.'

Yes.

You will make your direct connections. But you have to learn it is a process. We have to learn to give you the information in ways you [can] understand it. So it is a two way learning curve, Dereka. Not only do *you* have to learn, *we* have to learn also. We have to know if we give it to you this way, will you understand? If we give it to you another way, will that be easier to understand? But you are learning to connect all the things you are given. It's enough answer?

Yes.

And it is a process that never ends. And for you it is just to be impatient, Miss Impatience! The perfectionist. If I start today, surely I can have it finished by this time tomorrow. That's you, yes? And that isn't balancing work and play. It isn't balancing giving and receiving, it isn't balancing giving to yourself and giving to others. But you are getting better.

Good.

And we really like the opportunity to say 'Well done' to you.

Thank you.

Because if you look back three years, your life was chaos. You always [felt] the odd one out. Now you are not the odd one out because you have recognised that your way doesn't have to be anyone else's way. And no one else has to do things like you [do], just as you don't have to do things like them. So we have answered all your questions?

My next question was about a friend who was not comfortable with the depiction of what I took to be E.T. in the formation at Sparsholt in 2002.

When you understand that everything is energy, what does that represent to the person that has been shown it? There is fear involved. It is not a [frightening] picture for you. You have seen all different kinds of energies and you understand it is what [that] energy represents to you. [But] what does that energy represent to the person who has been looking at it?

It seems like a mixture of a lot of love, but the formation I took to be E.T. holding the disc with the message, she saw as a praying mantis and didn't see it as holding a disc at all. But maybe different people have their own interpretations.

And that is what is important, how each individual [perceives] the energy. To you it was not uncomfortable.

No.

To her it *was* uncomfortable. That says she did not resonate with that energy. You are shown this face, and to you it wasn't an insect, it was an energy from another dimension. To her the only way she could interpret what she saw was within the parameters [of what] she understood. Now if you accept that everyone will find their own perspective, it is like is the glass half full or half empty? Each individual has to make that assessment for themselves. To you it was not [frightening], it was a welcome offering and you appreciated that.

It seemed to appear in response to my request for home to phone E.T.

Yes. And then you understood the energy was something that was the Divine energy of home. Now if this other person did not understand that energy, they would translate it into something understandable [to] them.

You can see a circle as eternity; you can see a circle as the sun; you can see a circle as anything you wish to interpret [it to be]. So it depends on what *you* perceive. It is like when you have seen the shapes in the mist and the shapes in the cloud. You just watch the shapes change. And you are fascinated, it is almost like a meditation. You take your energy from everywhere else and focus it in the now. It is a very re-charging experience for you.

Yes.

And you are really grateful for the opportunities when they are presented. There are others who wouldn't have the patience or the interest to do that themselves. Is that enough answer about that picture?

Yes. I couldn't understand the lightness that I felt when I walked down that hill (from Adam's Grave). I didn't even think I'd got my . . .

Feet on the ground.

No, or the crystal night light holder in my pocket. It was sort of weightless.

That is that feeling of home. It is the feeling of light. And then you come into this dimension where there is light and dark, you learn not to [be] impacted by the energy of the dark. It is simply the absence of light. You can explain that in your head or you can explain it in your heart, and you were light in your heart as you walked down that hill.

It was a great birthday.

And this was your gift to you. It was not a gift from anyone else, it was your gift for you. So we have answered all of your questions?

Yes thank you.

Well we trust that you will keep taking those steps forward, Dereka. And we will continue to provide you with the support you invite.

Thank you.

You do not walk any step of your journey alone.

No.

You know that now.

I do.

So, however much you think you are alone, you know that there are always beings walking your path with you, understanding how hard it can be to be a spirit having a human experience. We give our love to you.

Thank you.

August 4 2004

After an initial introduction . . .
So what are your questions you want to ask us today?
As if we didn't already know!
I asked a question about the security of the phone at Coate,
in the house I shared with my mother. I was concerned that the
house might be bugged. I had been told there was some very
sophisticated equipment in the loft.

During the answer there was suddenly an ear-splitting noise
down the phone and we were cut off.

I had gone round to my friend Lisa's house to make the call.
I re-dialled Mavis's number and found that she had had another
incoming call before I got through again.

*It's really weird because I've come to a friend's house and I wanted
to ask about coming here. When I had that thought the other day this
huge gust of wind blew through the house slamming all the doors.
Was that a confirmation that it was a good idea to come here?*

Absolutely.

*I'm advised not to spoon-feed information to people, but how does
that tie in with writing a book?*

That is going to be some exchange for you. Writing the book
it is going to help you process what has happened. It is going to
help you understand [if your readers] can recognise your
experiences. [It] is going to be about what you have experienced,
not someone else's experience.

What is important for you to take from the experiences is how it changed you. When you began this journey of exploration you had no concept of where the path would lead. It was just something you had [an] interest in and you imagined it would be a nice hobby to explore.

But you now realise it has been much more than a hobby to explore. It has become for you a recognition that the phenomena that occur are simply gifts to this dimension. And you recognise that the gifts they offer can impact on people at different levels. You have recognised that by looking at the phenomena, you get one level of change. If you walk into that experience physically, you get another level of change. [And] if you go into the connection with the energy that formed the phenomena, you get an even different level of change.

So you have explored all of those experiences for yourself and you have realised that understanding each level of change is important to you because you wanted to explore it to its fullest potential.

Some people do it academically, they will look at something [and] talk about geometry, they will talk about mandalas, they will talk about what they can see and touch. There will be others who talk about the phenomena in an energetic way. By going in, you experience the energy and [they] can be very different. You can then go on to say how do they occur? What is the energy behind the experience? What do they want to experience these phenomena for? Why are they bringing these phenomena into this dimension?

You have explored all of those elements and you would write your book based on what you have experienced. When you began you were as green as grass. You did not recognise that there could be interaction between you and the energy that forms these phenomena.

And now you have come to recognise that not all the energy that created the phenomena is of the light. You understand there are different galaxies of energy involved. So you have learned to ask where does this energy originate? Is it appropriate for me to experience this energy physically? Do I need to experience this energy intellectually?

For you it has been a journey of exploration and growth, and that is how your book [should] be written. It would be like a diary. 'This is how I began. I had an interest in these things because they were presented on my doorstep. And I wanted to understand why *my* doorstep? Why not other people's doorsteps?'

And then as you realise they are laid down on powerful ley lines, you begin to explore what the land contains, and how it is a combination of the energy of the sky and the earth, and how that combination of the sky and earth [enables] the phenomena to be produced. You realise there is some change in the earth as these energies of geometry are impacted on the earth. And it creates a shift in consciousness for that particular area.

So your book would be your journey of growth. People may read the book and not do anything with what you have told them. There will be others who will be able to identify with some of the experiences you have had. Writing the book would be your way of presenting and understanding what has [happened] to you. What other people do with it is none of your business.

If you write the book, you [will] know the value of what you have experienced, [as it is] summarised in the book. And it will be an ongoing process of development for Dereka. You are not going to stop exploring the phenomena. You are not going to abandon any of the intent you have set. But your intent has probably changed from the intent you set at the beginning. It has developed.

Initially, it was simply to recognise that these were not man-made phenomena. That was your [original] intent, to recognise that these were not things people had produced. So then the question became who does produce these phenomena? So then you go and talk to others, and you ask [about] their experiences, and gather the information and make your own decisions. So you are going to continue in what you are doing, but not necessarily in the way you have done in the past. Offering this kind of knowledge to others is not something you are doing to prove it to yourself. You have an understanding of what you are discussing, but you have never stood up and given the talk yourself.

No.

Why not?

I didn't think I knew enough.

You have had the experiences.

Yes.

You may not have understood some of these experiences, but you are learning to understand them. One day you will believe that what you have experienced has great value. [You are] still putting yourself down.

It is why we want to push you from behind, give you the shove! Go and shine your light in the world, Dereka, we want to say.

Writing your book is simply providing information. What is important is [that] you do not decide how other people will understand it. There will be those who say, 'Well that is not what I understand about these things.' It doesn't matter does it?

No, that's their problem.

You have got way beyond other people's need to validate what you know. It's enough information?

Yes. Why do people always rubbish the Dolphin formations?

When you say 'rubbish', [do] you mean they did not understand why it was produced, or [that] they did not like the energy? What do you mean by 'rubbish'?

Well...

There were three of them, yes?

There's a beautiful one with dolphins and whales that has just appeared, and already somebody has written on the Internet that he saw people coming down [the hill] who had obviously been making it. People don't get the joy because they've been told it's not real.

But they have not experienced it. You understand that the dolphins and the whales carry the energy of joy. And if there is that symbol, then that energy contains the energy of joy. There are many people who do not want to enjoy their lives.

For you, dolphins mean freedom, and joy, travelling through life without the baggage. They are holding the energy of consciousness. Now when that appears in any form, it is simply for you to recognise it.

Now what if people are for example religious? They do not want others to be empowered or conscious. They want to control. There are many people in politics who do not want to empower, they want to control [too]. They have ego, and they want to make decisions for other people's lives. Just because other people say the [crop circles meant nothing] to them, does not mean you cannot enjoy the picture or that energy of that phenomenon. You understand?

The farmer has now got his gun out to stop people going in there because of what's been written about it being man-made.

And you know that is not the energy you experienced. Surely if it was man-made, he would have seen the men?

Well, the farmers get paranoid about it. They lose money when their crops have been damaged, they almost feel their fields have been vandalised (by humans).

Well, the farmers do not always understand the phenomena [either]. They do not like people who come and sometimes do not respect their land. You have to recognise that they have experienced people who did not respect their land. So for them it is almost a pat on the back when they think there is something that is conscious energy in their land. If there is something they think they have been made to look a fool about, they are going to be very protective. Now you know [to create a crop circle] would be very difficult [for a man to achieve.]

It's huge.

And the farmers don't really want to explore the truth about these phenomena. They see it as a business hazard, and if some of their corn is lost because of these phenomena, and then people come and trample [what's left], they are not pleased. So there are always going to be different opinions about [it]. And the farmer has every right to say, 'This is my land and I do not want people on my land.' And you would go and talk and ask permission, yes?

I don't know that I'd be that brave if he's got a gun by his side!

Well, maybe you need to discuss what you want to experience that for. Maybe that is his way of protecting his land. They do not always want to attract people onto their land.

Oh no. I understand that.

They normally have not got that kind of experience. Is enough answer?

Yes. In the three star formation at Coate, there appears to be an arrow in it, pointing. Is that directing me to go back to the place where I photographed the energy at Cherhill last year? Or to be in there and looking in that direction? Or am I misreading it altogether?

It is pointing in the direction of the energy line. And you had the experience on another part of the energy line. It wasn't on that part, it was in another part. It is just pointing in the direction the line flows. And when you photographed that energy, you did not know it was there. So for you it was only to see the picture. And it is for [you] to understand what you are dealing with. [The arrow] points in the direction of the line.

It was there in a formation a couple of years ago when, as you say, I shouted at you, you shouted at me. Is that a good place to go in the hope of a meeting? Or am I being mega mega impatient?

No, it is a very positive place to make the connections, that was when you recognised you *had* a connection. It was an opportunity for us to use that energy. You need to understand that is simply one of the places of energy. There are vortices of energy. And sometimes we use those vortices to put down the information. You understand? Is that enough answer?

Yes, yes thank you.

You have spent a great deal of time checking where the energy lines lie. And this is another way of helping you to understand the flow of energy. When you stand on that flow of energy, you are either in the flow or against the flow. You will stand in a place and say I need to experience what this energy is telling me and where this energy will be expanded along these lines. Because it isn't only at that point that the energy is, it is expanded along the lines. So sometimes you need to look at where that line lies. Then you can go and work constructively with the energy of that line.

Each of those symbols has different kinds of energy. So yes, if you want to make a connection, that is quite a likely place to begin. You are trusting more and more the information you are given. You simply recognise it is a place where there is an energy vortex where you can tap into the energy of the earth and the energy of the sky. And you will be the bridge between the two. Enough answer?

Yes, yes thank you.

Going back to the dolphin formation in East Field a couple of years ago, when did the peacock feathers appear in that?

What, the physical peacock feathers?

Yes.

On the third day. You found the feathers, yes?

Yes.

And they were not there before.

I don't know.

They were not there. You went in after the third day.

They weren't put there by people, were they?

No.

Was my hand actually put on that formation – or another one?

(I had recently undergone Kinesiology and my hand was placed on a picture of the Dolphin formation for muscle testing and my arm had been very weak. I asked about this.)

No, on that formation. You have changed your energy from that point a great deal [in 2002]. Do you not understand that as you take the energy from those experiences, your [own] energy changes and shifts? It was put on that pattern, but that energy would no longer improve *your* energy. It would make you realise where you were at that point. And it will help you understand that you have moved on beyond that. You are not resonating at that level of energy any longer, so [it] would not improve or strengthen you, because you have shifted beyond that.

What was the [muscle tester's] fear of this particular creation? Why did they have to have your validation of their perception [that it was sharks]? Your perception was very different from theirs. Each individual's energy is unique. So whatever they perceive does not have to be what you perceive. If they were looking for some kind of validation, they did not get it from you. Why did they need to make you consider things in the same way as them? You were not trying to change their belief. You told them you had an affinity with the dolphin energy, and they said they wanted you to know that this energy was not dolphin energy. But you had been into that experience. You had been into that creation, yes?

Not when I was first told that it was sharks, no. I hadn't been into it.

But we are talking about this picture that you have just discussed. There was some need for them to change your perception.

Yes.

But it didn't.

No, I looked on it positively, even if it was sharks, and it took me a long time to realise it was dolphins.

People may not resonate with the same energies as you. It is why some people collect frogs and other people collect fairies. You need a sense of humour, Dereka.

(This reading was three days before our Conference at Alton Barnes. The energies gave me instructions to rest after the Conference and not to go into formations.)

You will put up your feet and do nothing, and you will give your body and feelings 'time out', you understand? Because you know going into formations impacts on you, and you need somehow to gather all your energy back together, because at this point it is scattered far and wide. You are just trusting that everything will unfold as you have planned. You have invited us to offer our input, [and] we will add our input to what you have planned.

Good, thank you.

We have answered all your questions?

Yes, you'll be very welcome at the Conference.

We will recognise that the intent has been set to educate, to inform, to inspire, and that is what will occur. You will educate, inform and inspire. And what people do with what you have given is nothing to do with you.

We give our love to you Dereka. One day at a time is enough. Much love.

(The energies then showed Mavis a five-pointed gold star for me to use as protection during the Conference.)

September 22 2004

I n your particular work with your crop circles you have begun to work with our dimension. And you understand now that you have the ability to hear what we tell you, and all we have done is validate what you already know. You will eventually get to the point where you don't need the validation [in] this way. But you [must] realise how much you understand our dimension, and how much you understand what we tell you.

You are just seeking to enjoy the exploration of our dimension, and you have a very powerful connection with it. You understand the messages you get. You have questions you wish us to deal with.

Yes, I want to ask about some of the formations this year. When I went into the one with the dolphins and whales, when I finally got there it just seemed like heaven on earth to me.

It was wonderful energy. It was the energy of integrity. That is what the whales and the dolphins carry, love and light. They don't go through life with baggage on their back. They go through life simply being themselves. They have the oceans to swim in, and they have the freedom to choose what they want for themselves. They have group energy around them, they do not walk their journeys alone. They have support and that feeling was for you – being supported. [Because] when you come into this world of illusion with the kind of knowledge you have, you realise how isolated you are. For you, going into that formation was just the feeling of coming home. So it was a feeling we want you to hold on to.

Is that why you gave me the stone?

(A stone was lying on the downed wheat, about six by five inches. It reminded me of the stones at Avebury.)

Yes, so that you can have that energy with you. Because there is so little support for people on this journey of growth from the world of illusion. So that was the feeling of being home, yes?

Yes.

So you could close your eyes and imagine that feeling again.

Yes I do.

So that is something for you to be able to sustain the feeling. Imagine you are back in that, and remember what it gave you. It was the feeling of being home. Is enough?

On the first photograph I took as I stepped into it, that rainbow that looks as if it's lying down, does that signify the Rainbow Bridge?

Yes. It signifies light. And for you, your light carries all the vibrations of the colours. So some of that light was coming from you, and some was coming from the energy around the circle. The circle was about light and love. Your photograph just captured some of the light.

Sometimes you have had large areas of the photograph filled with light and you have thought, 'Why is this not what I want to see? Why is it just this light?' Because that is the energy of what you have taken the picture of. And then you see that the dark is simply the absence of the light. Lots of people who talk about the light do not live that way.

So when you took that photograph and you saw the light, then you go into your head and say what does that mean? All you have to remember is the experience. It is learning to be. And that has to include the head and the heart. So for you the feeling was of being home.

The picture, the intellect, was showing you the light. So then you begin to understand that is how light and love feel. There are many people who would have gone into that and not been able to feel anything. Whatever those photographs showed did not take away the energy you felt. So then you see the light in the rainbow. Sometimes you see the light on the photograph. But then, when you balance the two, you understand what you are dealing with. There have been some circles that you have not enjoyed, yes?

Some I just chose not to go into.

Exactly, that you have not enjoyed. And then you understood it was not appropriate for you to experience that energy. So you have learned the art of discernment. And there are others who are like junkies, yes? Who rush from one [crop circle] to the next, and the next, without understanding anything, except they think it gives them some kind of ego to have done everything. And that is when you need a sense of humour.

It is a way of giving energy to people. And sometimes it is not something that resonates with *your* energy, so it is not appropriate to get into that situation, and you know that. At the end of it all, you sit down and you try to assess, 'Well, what was all that about?'

Is that enough about the photograph?

Yes. How would you describe what came on the other photograph, number 21? (The UFO). (See photo 151 in colour plate section).

How would we describe that?

Yes.

You understand energy shows in different ways. It was like light, yes? But it was not like large light, it was smaller light, yes?

It looked like a vehicle.

But it was like light, yes? It was shown as different levels of light, yes? And shape. [It was] not a vehicle that you would know with wheels. It was a vehicle of different form, not something you could see physically. So that is what you have found with your photographs, you see the energy. And when you look you think, 'Well, that was not what I saw when I [took the photograph].' What did you perceive it as, a flying saucer?

That was my first thought.

Yes, and then you [realize] you could not see it with [your] eyes. But it has that shape, that light. And that is what those things are, energy. Then you begin to understand, we *want* you to see the energy.

I felt it, I felt it come in.

But that makes you realise how sensitive you are. When you took the photograph, all you were aware of was the feeling. You couldn't see it.

No.

And that is what you need to understand. That you don't always see energy.

When I was looking through the viewfinder on my video camera, before I took the still photograph, I saw the pink energy coming in and I thought there'd be something on the video film, but . . .

But there wasn't.

There wasn't, no, it came on the still photograph.

So you trust what you know, [yet] if you explained that to someone, they would say, 'But we didn't have that experience.' You are learning to trust what you read [from your experiences], not what other people tell you they have experienced.

So we will give you the feeling and then we will show you the energy. When you saw it you said, 'But I understood the energy because I felt [it.'] Even if you didn't see it on the photograph – as you say, if you had watched [only] the video – you would say there is nothing [there]. But on the other photograph there was something. When you take your photographs, sometimes they are just a simple photograph, other times they have things on them. You have very aware energy. So when you saw that and you thought, 'Ah, it looks like a flying saucer,' it was just the energy you felt. It is like when you have sat in the circles and you have felt their energy.

There will be others who feel nothing; it doesn't take away what you experienced. So you don't always need to have the confirmation with the picture. It is like us talking to you, we validate what you know. But it has helped you to trust what you know. Because we know how lonely the path [to] enlightenment is.

You have other questions?

When I flew over the formation at Coate (the triple star below Etchilhampton Hill), I didn't like the look of that man in black who was striding in there. Was he up to no good?

He was doing it in a way that was aggressive. He was not doing it with respect. He was going at it like a bull in a china shop. And you thought, 'I wonder what his agenda is?' He was trying to work with the energy in a way that suited him. That is what many people do. They do not want other people to have the energy of the circle and they try to change the energy. It is like every person that goes into a room, will change the energy of the room. And for him it was this very determined way he was going to do it. He didn't look like a casual visitor.

No.

There are always those who will try to manipulate the outcome. It was by your home, yes? And for you it was interesting that it had come as close as it did. It had not come as close before.

Er, once I think (recently), the Jupiter moons were on the same spot.

So all you need to understand is what you do when you go into that energy. What you need to understand is [that] they are on the energy lines. If you go and ask for that love and light to be anchored on those energy lines, you will be offering something constructive to the whole area. And you know where the energy lines pass. So even if there was no circle, you could go and anchor some kind of love and light on those energy lines. It is like when you do a meditation in a formation, and you will set the intent in that meditation. You will then send out on the line the energy of that meditation. And that becomes entwined with the energy of the circle.

I tried to undo what he had done when I went there later.

Yes, you just asked that love and light be brought back into the circle. Simply do that wherever you go. Going back to the man in the circle, they say you did undo what he had done.

Good.

You didn't have to know what he had done, you just simply said, 'I would like to bring this energy back to its original form.'
Good.
And you did achieve that.
Good, thank you.
Why did Flordemayo (a Mayan Elder and Priestess who had spoken at our Conference) want to go to Glastonbury on her last day? Or why was she told to go?

It is a place of much spiritual history. She needed to gather some of the energy from that place. She thought [it] appropriate for her. She didn't do anything specific, she just went and enjoyed the experience. For her it has much spiritual history, where they say the Christ Consciousness was brought by Joseph of Arimathea, and much understanding with long history of King Arthur, the Knights Templar and lots of spiritual connection. So she wanted to experience the energy of that place.

Also very powerful ley lines go through that place. And for her it was a pilgrimage. There are certain places that you would enjoy in that place, like the Chalice Garden, it's a place of peace. A lot of the hype is nothing to do with the Divine. Enough?
Yes, thank you.
Can I ask about that formation just by West Kennet Long Barrow? Am I right in thinking there's a hidden Venus transit, like under a mushroom, or have I got that all wrong?

Is the one with the mazes?
The one above that, which looks like a sun.
And you believe there was the Venus transit energy anchored in that circle. We are told not.
Right.
There was some experience of transit at the beginning of August (the Venus transit was on June 8). You begin to understand that there is much energy shifting right now. What is occurring in the earth is equally occurring in the heavens. So the heavens are simply monitoring back as a mirror what is going on in the earth.

The Venus transit was balancing the male and female energies. It was about making people understand that their thoughts and feelings are equally valid. But at the beginning of August was a different transit, whereby people are beginning to understand that they have to have every level of their energy in balance. It has to be physical, emotional, mental and spiritual.

So in that formation there was something of the sky and something of the earth. And then you begin to realise it is simply showing you what is happening energetically. Because near that there was also a star of balance. And then you realise everything was in balance on both sides, making you understand what is now happening between the heaven and the earth. So things change in the heavens, but it is just to show you the energy of that particular place.

They want you to understand you have now balanced the male and the female within you. You are not only being driven by your feelings, you are now being driven by intellect as well. It is to make you understand that there is the need for balance at all levels. That formation had the heaven and the earth. It was the balance between those two.

Was it supposed to look like a mushroom – or was that just my interpretation?

It was something you understood as the earth. It was what grows on the earth, something growing. There was something of the sky as well. How you interpret it does not really matter. Some people might see one form and some will see another.

It just seemed as if there was something hidden there, as if keeping a mushroom in the dark.

You understand it was simply something growing on the earth. People who live on this earth can live without understanding what light really means. They may live in the sunshine, but they may not understand the light within themselves. So it is the same as the mushroom. It can grow in the light but it can equally grow in the dark. But it is seeking the light. And the mushroom depicts [that].

And then you realise most people who live on this planet are not seeking the light, they are not realising what the challenges were that were given to them at the beginning of their lives. They are just repeating patterns that they have repeated lifetime after lifetime after lifetime.

How you interpret what is laid down is personal to you. [And] how you experience the energy is also personal to you. There will be some people who will go into the whole intellectual experience. They will describe the geometric energy of the formation, then when there is something that is *not* geometric, they will put some other interpretation on it. And the one you just discussed was not geometric, it was like a picture. So then you begin to think, what does that picture tell me?

The whales and the dolphins told you that was about enlightenment. It is like those that see the picture of the alien, yes? They do not ask what does this denote? What is the information?

Have you ever considered that in our dimension there is the light and the dark? You are not naïve enough to assume that everything changes from dark to light in passing from your dimension to our dimension. There is dark in our dimension [too]. The dark is the absence of the light. Those that have no understanding of their own light, want to take other people's light. Those that have the light do not have to carry the people who have no light. That is why you begin to understand. You are only given the responsibility of your own physical, emotional, mental and spiritual journey. You cannot take that journey for someone else.

So what did you perceive was hidden, the energy under the mushroom?

I thought it was a second Venus transit simply because the position of the small light within that central sun was very similar to my photograph of the projection of the Venus transit on June 8.

So that was about balancing the male and female, and that particular formation was balancing the physical and the spiritual, [assuming] that the head and the heart were already balanced. So it was a pictorial explanation [showing] if you have balanced the head and the heart, then you can balance the physical and the spiritual.

And it was directly in line with the heart and the head formations of the year 2000.

That's right. Then you begin to understand, yes? And the whole challenge is to continue to work towards balance. So when that transit occurs, anything that is not in balance between the head and the heart would become more evident after the Venus transit. Anything that was not balanced between the physical and the spiritual would become more apparent after that other transit. Then all the issues will come up for healing. And you might go and ask ten different people how will you heal this? And you will get ten different answers, yet the answer is within you.

Was that other transit recorded here on earth?

No, because most people do not understand what the spirit would be denoted by. Many of the planets are not measurable in this dimension. But when there are planets that *are* measurable they put the interpretations on [it] that *they* understand. But the Venus/sun transit was the male energy and the female energy coming into balance. And it is an opportunity for each individual to bring their own male and female energy into balance.

For you it was learning to trust what you feel. You had to balance your intellect with your emotions. And now you do not deny your discomfort emotionally. Because your emotions are simply information that tells you what is going on in your life, and when you learn to observe them without judgment, you can deal with them constructively. You have other questions?

The formation in the Savernake Forest, with the nine squares within the square that was all out of sync. When I cut out a picture of it, by turning four of them anti-clockwise it came into sync. Did that imply going backwards in time from 2012 or did I just make that up?

It is where you are now. And it shows how much has to be achieved for that synchronicity to occur. So that ideal will be when everything is formed. But where you are now was what you were shown. So things are not yet in sync. And it is coming to the last phase of being in sync.

So it indicated nine years from 2003, the 21st of December.
Yes.
Right.

It shows that some things are in balance, but there are many that are yet to come into balance. The more people become in balance, [the more they can] help others. For you, looking at something out of sync was uncomfortable, and you wanted to put it in sync. You realised it was possible to put it in sync.

By utilising the four directions.

Yes. And then you realise everyone has the same challenge to get themselves in sync, but most of them don't want to.

So you are all on the final leg. Those who do not achieve what they have come to achieve, will find their bodies will dysfunction. Look around you. More and more people are becoming uncomfortable, and rather than beginning their healing process, they just ignore the discomfort. You have other questions?

The dragon formation at West Overton. Is that pointing towards the place known as the Seeding Place? Do I need to go there?

It was on another of the ley lines and if you [continued] on the ley line it would take you to this place. So what would you go to that place with the intent to achieve?

To put love and light in the line.

That's good. Fine, please do it. You will be given the tools, you will be given the information. And, as you add that love and light, it will begin to change the balance in the ley lines. You understand that these lines were recognised many centuries ago. But a lot of the people at that time were not what we would call conscious people. They gave their power to cults, to organisations. They did not understand 'the Divine' in themselves. As each person understands the Divine in themselves they can anchor love and light on those lines. You are recognising that everyone has the same power, if they [would] only recognise it. So yes, please go to that place and do what you have said.

Wherever you go just ask, that anything that is no longer appropriate be released from that place, returned to its point of origin and transmuted in the process so that love and light are anchored there. And then we can work in that intent with you. We will always work in co-creation with you, Dereka. You do not do any of this work alone. You do not walk one step of your journey alone.

You recognise that more and more. You realise that once you have dealt with your own anger, sadness and fear, you are simply learning to live in harmony, balance and peace. People cannot take that harmony or balance or peace unless you allow it. And if you respect yourself, you will not allow it. You learn to *respond* not react, to what happens around you. We have answered all your questions?

Yes. I'm hoping to contact Flordemayo in Phoenix in November.

She will be happy to spend time with you. So we trust what we have given will be of value.

Yes, thank you very much.

And as you take that journey we will come with you. You will not take the journey alone. You have done it before with others, but this time you will do it for yourself. And you will do the things that you enjoy. Anything else you wish to clarify?

I don't think so. Thank you for your input at the Conference.

We enjoyed the experience.

Good.

It was very different from before. And for you, you did not get involved in all the agitation. You were able to step back from those issues. You were able to say, 'Well, we have done what we can do – we do not have to create instant perfection.' And it was enjoyed by many people, so we enjoyed it also.

Good.

Much love to you.

January 18 2005

So what are the questions you want to ask of us today? *I want to clarify this business of writing which seems to have come to a halt recently. Am I right in thinking I really should be trying to get this finished in the time I've given myself?*

Where you stand now, you are at a crossroads, because it is as though you have come to the end of processing the past. [It is] now about the present, how [to] tie up all the loose ends to come to some kind of conclusion. And right now you cannot see how to do that.

Please understand [if] you cannot do it, it is not an appropriate time. There are pieces of the puzzle [still] missing and you must wait for them [to fit].

So accept that what you have done so far is deal with the past. We do not see that there is anything of the past left to resolve. You have this understanding that there may be more writing for you [in] the future. Maybe what you have to do is not complete something, but come to the point where you are willing to take it forwards. It may not be possible to do everything in the time frame you have allotted yourself. You are a very impatient lady sometimes.

When you have sat down to write in the past, you have invited us to assist. And sometimes you have had no idea what would come on the page, but what has been given to you, you have trusted as appropriate. So it has been necessary to know that while you are sitting down saying I am willing to write what is appropriate, [but] nothing is being given, you trust it is not the appropriate time to do it. So just trust that you need to be doing other things instead of sitting down and writing.

It is pointless sitting there saying, 'Right, I want you to write with me now', and nothing is happening. It is not an appropriate time when nothing comes to mind. We can see that there will be a continuation. Your experiences will continue. For you, working with us has not been something you take as flattery, [or as] your ego. You have just said, 'I am willing to work with your dimension to anchor some kind of stability of empowerment in this dimension.' You have to do that in your own life. And you have taken the necessary steps, and you understand that like attracts like, so as you take those steps to develop yourself, you will invite in higher levels of consciousness to work with you.

You have to understand that our dimension is the same as your dimension, [with] lots of different levels of consciousness. Nothing changes in the transition from your dimension to our dimension. There are levels of consciousness in our dimension that are very basic, [and] extremely refined, and everything in between. There are energies in our dimension that have lived no lives in yours. You have not utilised this connection to fulfil your ego's needs. You have simply used it to access information. You can access what information you want and apply some of that knowledge to your own life. That is how you function. So when you set yourself a time frame, and it does not unfold in that time, just trust that it is not appropriate. If you did try to complete it, you would really struggle. You have tried, and you cannot see how it will come to completion. Look at the title and bring it back to what the title says. So is that enough answer to the question about the writing?

Yes. Can I ask a question about Moldavite?

It is a stone from outside of this dimension. It is a very powerful stone you have been working with, a stone of transformation. What do you want to ask?

The piece of Moldavite I picked up at Giza in Egypt, was it Angus who led me to find that?

Yes, and you have worked with that stone, yes?

Not that particular one, I left it there.

What did you leave it there with the intent of doing?

At the time I didn't realise what it was. When I asked about it, you told me it was probably too soon for me to possess it.

But you now have a piece?

Oh yes, yes.

So you understand that the energy is appropriate for you to work with now. It is energy from outside of this dimension that has been brought back, and it is a very powerful energy to work with. It changes things around it. It is attracted to people who are willing to do the work of being in power. At the time you went to Egypt, you were not even on the first step of your journey.

Is that why I broke my leg before I went? Should I not have gone?

That leg was an indication of what was happening in your life. You were stuck at every level, but you had booked this trip so you decided to go. And it was quite a difficult challenge for you just to do that trip. When something happens, if you have a clear intent of what you want to achieve, you will take those steps into the unknown. You were always a very determined lady, you were determined to go. Basically you thought, 'Well, I'm not going to let this stop me.' It did not really impact on the visit except it made you realise you had to learn something from this. At that time you had not really begun your journey of growth at all.

No I hadn't.

You were marking time, putting your energy into staying stuck. And you somehow imagined that by going there you were going to learn something new. You didn't learn anything new – you simply realised what you needed to remember. You understand you have lived in that culture before, and that there was some of your energy left at that place that needed you to go there to collect [it]. And then it became a catalyst on your journey of growth.

You didn't know any of that when you went. But it is always wise to look back with hindsight. Looking back you can see it was the beginning of your growth process. So gathering the energy you had left there, and observing the stone that was there, was telling you you had worked with these things before. But you had worked with them for other people's gain not for your [own] gain. So in this lifetime, by respecting yourself, you could work with this knowledge for your [own] gain as well.

That has been your journey since then. That was your life in Egypt, to serve others. And that was what you had done lifetime after lifetime, serve others, never validating your own power, your own knowledge, never using that knowledge for your own gain. Because you had been taught it was holier to give than to receive with grace. Now you have let go of that illusion, you have understood this knowledge has to be utilised to improve the quality of your life.

And Moldavite is simply going to support what you are doing. It is an energy like lots of other stones, but it is an energy from outside this dimension. So it carries with it a different kind of charge. You understand it is not a stone everyone would be able to work with. And it was simply for you to remember what you had done in previous lifetimes, so you went there to observe some of those experiences. You had an experience while you were there?

A hand on my shoulder.

Yes, and for you that was not scary, it was just, 'I need to understand [this].' We always walk beside you but we cannot support you unless you invite that support from us. That hand on your shoulder was the beginning.

Now you do not need the hand on your shoulder to understand that we participate in your journey. Sometimes we have to say 'We are waiting!' Sometimes we have to say, 'Why are you not asking for support?' You didn't consider yourself worthy to receive the support, a belief that first needs observation and then some kind of attention.

You have let go of the belief that you are not worthy. You are not someone who assumes you are better than others because you have developed a connection with our dimension. You simply understand it is available to everyone if they are prepared to do the work themselves. Do you want to know anything else about your Moldavite, or is that enough?

Was it after acquiring the Moldavite owl in particular that there was the manifestation of the slug, (which one day mysteriously appeared between the taps while I was having a bath).

Yes. And you understood what those messages were. You always ask, 'What is the purpose of this experience?' And it may not come to you immediately, but you do get the information.

Sometimes it takes a very long time.

That's fine. Maybe you need to have grown to be able to understand that experience. And when you can have an experience without making it good or bad or right or wrong, your life is a very different journey.

You have learned to talk to all kinds of energy. You have learned you can talk to the birds, to the animals, to the trees. They may not talk back in the language you talk, but it is a communication.

Can I ask about the blue lotus?

In your meditation?

Not in my meditation, in physicality, the car and then the link to what I heard in the talk at the Conference in November, about the use of the blue lotus in Egypt.

And it was a remembering.

Yes.

It was a realisation that these things had been part of your past. They resonated with you. You listen to any talk, and there will be parts of the talk that you resonate with, and there will be parts [that] you do not. So this was presenting you with an energy, and then you observed it is an energy you are familiar with. It is a [memory] of something you have worked with before. And this person was communicating what they had perceived of the blue lotus. There were parts of it you accepted, and parts you did not resonate with. That is where you learn the art of discernment, Dereka. And for you it is to ask the questions and understand that the answers will be given in Divine right order. This person was saying how they had worked with the blue lotus, yes?

Or how he had observed it in drawings.

And how had he worked with it?

I don't know.

That needs to be the question. He has gone back and looked at the past. You are only going to understand the value of something when you work with it in the present. So he had done the intellectual research. He had gathered how that culture had worked with certain symbols. And what is important is that you are then able to say, 'How can I work with this in my life?' We would suggest you take that symbol into your meditation.

Is that why I was so determined to buy that car although everybody advised me not to, all those years ago?

Yes, because it was something you understood the energy of. And you enjoyed it, yes?

Yes.

And for you it was a pleasure. So you learned that other people may have advised you to do it differently, [but that] was something [on] their agenda. And you never regretted the decision?

No, no.

So it was something that was an energetic symbol for you, you understand?

Right, although I didn't understand it.

No, [but] did you need to understand it? You enjoyed it.

When they talked about it, the man did not tell you how he had worked with it himself. So it doesn't bring the energy back to present time. It is just, 'Well, I have learned how people have behaved in the past.' Until you have had the experience yourself you cannot know if it will enhance your life or not. So that is part of why you cannot complete what you are writing. Take your blue lotus into meditation.

The car or the flower?

The flower. Not your car, it would be difficult to take your car! Sit in the middle of it. And understand it will enhance your meditation. It is a protective symbol. It has been used by many different cultures. It is the symbol that says there are many parts to the whole.

Like your book. There are many books written, but this is about *your* experiences. You are not offering these experiences to people [to] have themselves, these were experiences that were unique to you. Some you shared with others, some you shared with no one, some you shared with us.

In the talk you were listening to, he had done the intellectual research. He did not say how anyone could utilise that in their lives. That is the step most people do not take. They look at what has been done before, what has been done by others, but they do not say, 'I need to understand if this can be of value in my life, in my journey.'

That is what you have been doing. You have been letting go of everything that does not enhance your life. You have been open to letting in things that may enhance your life. You are taking the steps one by one by one. When people say, 'I do not want to heal myself, I want someone else to heal me,' they are not taking any responsibility at all. Hence your medical profession is based on the victim consciousness. They do not want to understand their own bodies. They go to someone who equally does not understand their body, who simply gives them some panacea but does not deal with the healing process.

So yes, by all means observe what other people tell you about their experiences, but then ask, 'How did this impact on your life?' Most people are just doing the intellectual exploration, they are not walking any of the talk. So maybe that could have been a question, 'How has this helped you in your life?' And if they say, 'Well I have not worked with this,' then maybe you can ask, 'Is it appropriate for you to go and work with it?' It will simply get you back to remembering what you may have forgotten.

Am I right that the lotus crop circle that looked as if it had been made by car tyres (West Overton May 2003), was that to help me connect?

Yes, most definitely. That was your circle you are discussing, yes?

Yes.

It was for you to go and experience how those interconnecting energies can assist you to interconnect with all of your energy.

Was it you who gave the information to the website, where that formation was? (The Crop Circle Connector website received the co-ordinates of the position of the formation anonymously).

Yes.

And do you do that with many?

Not often. Usually they are discovered.

Yes.

This one could not be discovered.

No.

And it was provided for those who needed to access that energy and you found the site, yes?

Yes.

And you are quite discerning about the sites you visit. You do not visit them all. Because you know it is not necessary.

But they actually asked me to go there, so that was your idea?

Yes.

Got it!

You trust it unfolds in Divine right order?

Yes.

It was a challenge for you.

Yes.

Dereka likes a challenge. Dereka does not like hum drum. If it is easy, Dereka isn't interested. If it is a challenge, Dereka gets going. We know Dereka!

I know. Oh dear!

We find you have really taken [great] leaps during these last two to three years. You have any other questions or have we answered them all?

No, I've got lots.

Come on then.

When that flying saucer landed on the whale in the whale and dolphins crop circle, did I see occupants in there on the photo?

You saw patterns, shapes, yes?

Yes.

You begin to realise we are not people like you. We are energy. There were shapes in it. We blend with the energy of everything around us. Sometimes you would not see any form. It does not mean we do not exist. It is like your wind. You cannot see it but you understand it exists. It is the same. You will see the wind in the trees [because they] move. But you will not necessarily see us as people.

You understand we are a support structure that provides information as energy. It is the same with everything. It does not always need a form. You saw it as a shape of light, yes?

That is what your photographs show you, form. You might not see the wind, but you might take the photograph with the wind moving the trees. So you don't see the wind, you see [its] effect.

You understand the effect of our energy. You want to work with the light to enhance your life. You would not work with anything that tries to control your life. There are energies that will control your life. You would not work with those energies. You understand you have to be discerning what you work with, and what you don't. Your photographs sometimes show you what you did not see with your eyes.

Back in 1999, when I walked out of that serpent formation (East Field), was that a hawk flying with me?

We are told it was.

Right, and that was indicating to me to go to the field next door?

Yes, to the other formation?

391

To where these other formations have come.
What did the hawk signify to you?
Communication.
And you then went to look at the formations when they came.
Yes, but they didn't come that year.
No, but when they came.
Yes.
It is like the stepping stones, the pieces of the jigsaw. You understand that each formation carries an energetic note. And you see it can enhance your energetic note.
So was it a hawk's eye that came as the eye in the formation there? (Golden Ball Hill, in 2000)
Yes.
Right.
And what is the eye for?
Seeing.
But it is not only seeing, it is recognising you. It is learning to see yourself. That is the journey you are now on, Dereka, learning who you are, and learning to present who you are to others without any judgment of yourself, or involving yourself in judgement from them.
That formation had a corresponding one at Honey Street, which I never saw as whales before because it was called a propeller (in 2000). These two formations seem to have swapped over this year.
What do you mean? In the same places but opposite energy?
Well, the whales have gone from one field to the other (Honey Street to Golden Ball Hill) and the tongues of flame have swapped places with them.
That creates a balance. You begin to understand that we are balancing the earth as well. It has an impact on the earth. It is bringing balance to the earth.
The six circles (Honey Street 2004) that seem to be released from the 'flames', is that the release of information?
Yes.
Or does it signify the six planets?

It does not signify the six planets. It signifies that things are becoming more and more connected.

When I photographed the little grape shots in the first whales one at Honey Street, and the portal above (in the cloud) let down that little pentagon, (a light anomaly in my photograph), were they a mirror image of Orion, those three little circles?

Yes. It was the same geometric equation. And what does that equation equal?

As above, so below.

Yes. But there is also something of the mathematics that is important to understand. You understand sacred geometry? You understand that geometry has energy in it. And you understand that each of the circles has some kind of geometry. So sometimes we will add an element that brings a certain kind of geometry to that experience. You understand we do not come from your solar system, but we are part of the whole. And we come to add our knowledge to your journeys.

Yes. How should I describe from where you come?

We give you the words, 'Over the hills and far away'

Right!

Is enough?

Yes. The bee I found trapped in a spider's web that lead me to a page in a book, did I deduce the right thing from that? The natural selection?

Yes. You understand that all is in Divine right order. It helps you to see there is no wrong or bad, that energy may change its form, but it doesn't disappear. That was what the page informed you, yes? So even when something changes form, its spirit does not disappear.

That is part of what you are explaining in your book. you will explain to people, 'I have changed form. I have had lots of experiences, and taken steps on my journey into all kinds of new experiences. It does not change me, it does not change my spirit. It allows me to make my own choices without being impacted upon by other people.'

You use those situations as opportunities. You ask 'What is [there] for me to understand?' And you listen. For you it is simply saying, 'In the past I would have seen this as something to be distressed about.'

But there is no way the bee has lost its spirit, there's no way, the spider [was] wrong. It is just that everything is part of the whole, and most of the food chain understands that. Yet when you become human, you seem to have all kinds of limitations about understanding being part of the whole. You seem to consider you are greater than everything else. You start creating imbalance in the world in which you find yourselves. You lose respect for things that are different. Then you begin to accept that, as one part of the whole, you cannot control anyone else's behaviour. We really honour you for coming into this dimension because it is not going to be a comfortable experience for people with consciousness. That doesn't mean you can do the work in our dimension, so you have to come into this dimension and be in the world, but not of it.

Was the bee and the spider crop circle accentuating what I found?
What did the circle teach you?
That I have my freedom.
Exactly. That you didn't have to be in the spider's web.
Right.
That you still had your wings and you could still fly.
With the horse. (The bee crop circle in 2004 was below the white horse at Milk Hill.) *I took the crop circle of the left eye crying very personally, was I right?*

It is to get people in touch with their emotion of sadness. It is to understand, yes it may be necessary to grieve for your losses. You had never grieved for your losses, but you are learning. We want people to understand their emotions. That is a gift of this dimension, that you can feel. And you don't judge your feelings. You accept that if you do not put joy into your life, you will continue to feel sadness. Yes, it helped you to grieve some of your losses. Enough answer?

Yes.

So we have given you enough answers?

Golly, you have given me loads.

You are learning to understand the messages.

Yes. When I took out two matches in one, [joined by one head], when I was thinking about two lights in one [body], was I right about the cat?

No.

No?

No. What do two lights make?

One flame.

One flame. Why would the cat be one flame? The cat is part of your journey, yes? There is only one flame, one Divine flame.

Yes. Did she lose her flame and another one come in?

Yes.

Right. And was that a cat I know?

Yes.

My previous cat?

Yes.

Right, great!

You understand? There is one flame. So when you understand spirit is in everything, but it is limited by your feelings and your thoughts, you learn to let go of all the limitations. You learn not to judge yourself, not to judge others. You learn to observe what you are dealing with and you learn to invite exchange in relationships. If people cannot or will not provide what you have invited, you learn to put those things into your own life and stop providing anything to other people. We thank you for this opportunity.

Thank you.

Til next we speak, much love to you.

And you, thank you.

May 24 2005

You have other questions?
Yes. The formation at Golden Ball Hill . . .?
The new one?

The new one. Am I right in thinking that is your way of putting your stamp of authenticity on last year's formation? (The whales and the dolphins).

We continue a process. Where we leave off, we start again. So it is a path of continuation. Then you begin to understand, those who have taken the steps of growth and development can take the benefit of the continuation. But those who have not done any of the work would find some of the energy of the new formations quite challenging.

Many people only deal with them intellectually; 'Ah, how interesting.' But for you, it was to have something in it that was what you connected with last time, last year, yes? And there is going to be a pattern of continuation.

You understand that there are different elements that are at work. There are some elements that are not wanting to empower the world in which you live. There are some elements at work that are wanting to feed off the energy of your world. You begin to recognise that some, how can we say, some universes do not have understanding of emotion, and emotion is the only way when balanced with the intellect, that you can connect to the Divine spark. You understand they put down what will beguile.

You are quite discerning about the energies you will connect with. You understand that how you utilise the energy of those experiences depends on each individual. You do not go into something with the intent to control an outcome do you?

No.

So when you went into that formation what did you feel?

Protected.

Right, but you had invited protection. So if there was energy in that formation that wanted to control you, it could not do so because you would not allow it. You have understood that your protection of Dereka is Dereka's responsibility. So you have learned about protection. What else did you feel in that experience?

I felt the same energy I felt when that UFO landed.

Which was joy?

Yes. That came on the whale, and this formation looks to me as if it's on the dolphin next to the whale. (A shadow of the 2004 formation could be seen in the oilseed rape.)

So that was joy, right? Can you sit now and experience that joy? Just close your eyes and experience that joy. That is the gift of the formation. We want everyone to understand joy, a personal expression of joy. You cannot sit in that circle all of your life.

No.

But you can go and have the experience, then you can take that experience and you can say, 'Ah, I can create joy in my life in many different ways.' That joy has been given to you as a gift, you understand?

Yes, that's why I still have the stone you gave me from the dolphin last year.

But in the process of understanding joy, how could you describe that to someone else? To put that in words is very difficult.

Yes.

So if you wrote in your book, 'I can sit in this physical experience and I can experience joy', they might think, 'Well, that sounds an interesting experience.' But they may not go and experience the joy, because for them joy might be something completely different.

To you it was an energetic experience. Now most people are not energetically aware. It is like they might sit in the sun and only be worried about the colour of their skin. They might not feel comforted by its warmth, [or] safe in its energy. They may not feel recharged, they may simply be there intellectually, considering they have to go brown. And you realise that everyone is at a different level of consciousness. So for you the experience was something you enjoyed.

Very much.

So if you were to go into another formation and experience something that was uncomfortable, you would not recommend anyone to create discomfort. So you begin to understand that everyone is impacted differently by those formations.

Some of them will just say, 'What a pretty picture.' Some will say, 'Well, I don't believe they are made by energy, they are made by man.' They don't think, 'Well, why would people do that and not claim the credit for it?' It would seem somewhat ridiculous to spend time making formations and not want some kind of credit.

I think [the] farmer must be much in fear to be so cross about them.

Yes, but that means they are challenged by them. It means they have this belief that the world is out to get them. That is their issue, that is where they are in life. 'The world is out to get me. So I have to be one step ahead of the world.'

They cannot see anything to be gained from recognising these formations. As far as they are concerned, they have more important things to address than pictures in the corn. Those who become obsessed with them are equally unconscious. If all they are considering is where is the next picture in the corn, that is not living your life, that is not having a life.

You [can] see the ones who become obsessed. It is almost as though they have to prove something to the world. They have to get some kind of acknowledgement for what they know. That is arrogant. You have never behaved in an arrogant way.

I hope not.

No, if people become obsessed with anything it becomes an addiction which controls their life. They want to prove how geometrically balanced it is. Does that change the feelings? You might walk in that formation and never see what it looks like. But that isn't going to change what you have felt. You have to do it in both ways, Dereka, intellectually and emotionally. And you can only experience the feeling if you are physically in it. So yes, it was simply to give you another experience of joy.

Thank you.

And that is what we want your life to be, something you enjoy. Not an experience where you are looking over your shoulder waiting for the next judgement or criticism. That's how most of the world seems to function. They think they have to prove themselves to someone. They have to do things in a way that other people will accept or understand. We do things in ways that people do not always accept [or] understand. And those [who] *want* to have the experience, it is there for them to do so. All it needs is their interest and their wish to spend time experiencing the joy. And if they do not want to do that, so what? We do not have an agenda, we do not judge, they are free to live their lives in any way they wish.

At first I called it a yellow lotus, but then when I looked at the aerial shot it made me think of a yellow Polo (mint). Was I entitled to think that?

You can think whatever you wish. What you feel, that is more important than what you think. You can intellectually put any kind of title you want on it. That is not what we are providing. We are providing people with an opportunity to get in touch with their feelings and to enjoy the feeling.

Joy.

You understand? There is peace, there is harmony. That is why they are in the places they are in. They are away from the hustle and bustle of life. They are not in the middle of housing estates. They are where there is space, open energy, no ground pollution. And if people are interested [in having] the experience, they have to make the effort.

We do not do it because we want some kind of glory. We do not put a signature on the bottom; we want you to pay to experience this. We want people to understand joy is theirs for the taking. And that is what your book will eventually teach people. Not 'Look this is something I need to prove to you.' It will simply explain, 'These are the things I have enjoyed. If I didn't enjoy them, I didn't do them, because I have learned to respect myself.'

You are not going to rush round like a headless chicken making sure you have done the whole thing, which is what many of them do. Then they intellectualise on what it means and how it has impacted on their life. They do it with an ego, [their] ego is what needs to control the outcome. And it is mysterious because they cannot control it. You have invited formations, yes?

Yes.

Yet when they have been provided, you have been surprised.

Thrilled.

But then you realise it is something others can enjoy. You do not claim it for yourself.

No.

You have learned to be honest about what you have experienced, but it is not your life. You cannot make this into your life.

No. It was for a while.

Yes. But then people get pulled in, they make it into some kind of addiction. You understand?

Yes. When it was said that the watchers or the makers of some of the formations would use men to help them, did they mean physically or telepathically?

Telepathically.

Yes, I just wanted to confirm that.

400

Then it becomes co-creation. Then people begin to understand they have a right to make part of the experience themselves. You have any other questions?

About that formation?

No, about anything else.

Can I ask, go back to Egypt, we talked about it last time I spoke with you. The energy I left behind there and collected when I went in 2001. Did that have anything to do with canopic jars and Canopus, the ship that rescued me?

Yes.

Right.

It was to help you understand some of your issues in this life. And often the patterns from previous lives become repeated in this life. Sometimes the fears those experiences have left behind need to be addressed. You might gather all the intellectual information, [but] ultimately the challenge is to deal with the fear; that is the understanding you come to walk through, to change the fears back to the Divine. And if you have the intellectual understanding, it just gives another dimension to the situation. You are learning not to go down the path of the intellectual explanation only. You understood it was about that experience in another lifetime. But you [also] have to relate it to now, Dereka.

Yes. Does that tie in with my opinion on organ transplants now?

Yes. Because they take someone else's energy and they put it into another body. And that can impact on the other person in many other ways. When you see that in the Egyptian period, there was genetic engineering as well. Then you begin to understand that man interferes with Divine understanding. And yes, they are given free will, but they do not [use] it with integrity. For example, if someone has not cared for their own body, and part of their body has dysfunctioned, and they simply take a part of someone else's body, and continue to be self destructive, what have they learned?

Nothing.

Right. If they [are here and] only needed to live for a short amount of time to have a specific short experience in this world, and modern medicine decides No – they must live this life of survival, where is the quality in that life? It is very different [once] you understand your spirit does not die. Some of that person's spirit would be in that organ, but that keeps part of the spirit locked in the physical world. It makes it difficult for both the person who has the organ transplant and the person who has returned to our dimension and left a part of their body behind. You understand?

Yes, so that's what I did in that lifetime.

Yes. And now you would not choose that experience.

No.

So you can see how much you have grown and developed. It is like those who believe love is traded. They go looking for someone to love them rather than learn to love themselves, and they may go into all kinds of abusive relationships and get into, 'Well, they are wrong, they have to change to fulfil my expectations.'

We observe this and think the world's gone mad. And at the end we say to each individual, 'What did you learn of responsibility for your own life? What did you teach by the example of your life to other people?' And you'd be amazed at the fairy stories we listen to. When we tell them what we watched, they say, 'Well, how could you possibly have known all these things about my life?' And we say, 'Because we can observe, but we cannot judge and we cannot interfere.'

And we don't ever interfere. When you become aware, it is so useful to be able to offer that example of your life to other people. But if no one follows, at least you've laid down the example.

Yes, so I should link in the friend who had the car crash and my experiences when I was working in the hospital?

Yes.

All under the same flag.

402

Yes.

Do I need to remember who I was in that Egyptian lifetime?

No, you have remembered enough of what you needed to remember.

Right.

It does not really matter who you were. You had enough understanding that you were doing what everyone else was doing at that time. And you were made to feel that because everyone else was doing it, you would be wrong if you did it differently. But at least in this lifetime you have learned you don't have to live like everyone else. It's enough answer?

Yes. I asked you about the dragon formation that was pointing towards the seeding place. When I looked at it I saw one green circle, yet the photo I've seen had several. Were there several?

Yes, there were several. The dragon is the energy of passion. The dragon brings the enthusiasm, the light. And it is always portrayed as being slain because people are afraid of passion. The dragon breathes fire, because fire is passion. And you understand that what people do not understand, they fear. So they go down the old path of the intellect.

It doesn't matter how many circles there were. What mattered was you understood the energy of passion. The circle is the circle of life. That is why most of the formations have circles. It is about life. They often have circles that are interconnected because all life is interconnected. There is our planet, your planet, other planets, all connected because it is all part of the creation. And your next question?

Can I ask which is your planet?

We have been through many planets. We do not have a specific planet of our own.

No. You just said 'our planet' so I took you up on that.

Yes. Whatever planet we are working with at a particular time is our planet. We have learned to live in [the] now, we do not call any particular planet 'home', just as [your planet] is not your natural home, but it is the only place you can develop and grow.

And your next question?

The piece of native copper that I got in the market, with the two faces that I detect on it, did I interpret that correctly?

You did.

Right, the face with the third eye is shown either receiving or radiating, is it doing both?

It can do both, yes, it is doing both. You can receive information there, you can give out energy there.

Yes and that's reminiscent of the Egyptian symbol?

Yes.

Rainbows. Have all the colours come into the rainbow now or will there be more?

There will be more. There will be more defined shades, but there will [also] be subtle in-between shades, light has all colour in it, and it is becoming iridescent light. As that occurs, then it can present a wider selection of colour. You start with the primary colours of blue and red and yellow. And from that you can make any colour you wish.

When we saw the aquamarine colour coming in above the river (Thames), was that the first time that colour had come in?

Yes.

It was, right. You told me I needed to review the title of my book. The title that I'm looking at now, is that...

It is appropriate.

That's appropriate.

It is about rainbows?

Yes. Well as I've got it written now its 'The New Rainbow Bridge, Heaven on Earth'.

That's fine.

Good.

One last question, in Peru that lion rock at Sillustani with what looks like the Milky Way and a comet on it, was that to indicate the date of the place?

No.

No?

No.

It's just a lion?

It was just something that ... it was a symbol that meant something to the people of that culture. It is often related to what they could see in the heavens. For them it was a physical manifestation of what they could see in the heavens.

Of Leo or of the comet?

The comet and of Leo. To them it was just something that symbolised power and strength. So it was imbued with the energy of power and strength. If you put your hands on it, you would be able to feel some of that energy, which you did.

Yes.

It's enough?

Was it significant that my life raft was a hexagonal shape?

What does hexagonal represent?

The six-sided.

It represents balance.

I was thinking of it in terms of the beehive and the bee crop circle and so on.

It had a significance energetically. It represents balance. If you look at the way the bee makes the comb, it is a strong shape. When the bee makes the honey they put it into a hexagonal shape. The bees hatch in those shapes, they store their food in those shapes, they build those shapes because they are strong. They connect together, it is a connecting shape. You can put them all together and make a whole. Whereas with circles there are spaces.

It has much more strength than other shapes and you needed the strength. It is one of the natural shapes of nature. We have now answered all of your questions?

Yes, yes. Thank you.

You have recognised that your intent must be clearly defined [as] an ongoing process. And we will continue to support what you are trying to achieve and we give you our love, as always.

Thank you, and mine to you, thank you.

We will be only too pleased to continue to work with you in co-creation.

Thank you.

In 1968 I was working as resident dental house surgeon at King's College Hospital. One patient we saw with facial fractures had multiple injuries and became an organ donor. One of the theatre sisters was a friend of mine and she invited me in to observe the liver transplant operation.

When the recipient was ready I watched as the life support was switched off on the donor. Shortly afterwards the door flew open, someone had come to collect the kidneys for another hospital. I felt as if I was in a butcher's shop and I didn't like it at all. Little did I know at the time that a past life memory had been triggered.

The car crash I mentioned in the reading with Mavis happened in 1985. I heard the crash and went to help. I ended up giving mouth to mouth resuscitation to the lady passenger. The next day I found out that the passenger was my friend Margaret's sister, Jackie.

Amongst other injuries, Jackie had a head injury and was unconscious. She carried a donor card and, to cut a long story short, the hospital wanted her kidneys. Margaret had numerous battles with the hospital staff, trying to save her sister's life.

I talked to Jackie after she came home and she said she had heard what was going on, and had been very frightened. Hearing is the last sense to be lost. When someone is unconscious it is worth remembering they may be able to hear everything that's said.

In the early 1980s my uncle, Charles Dodson, had a motorcycle crash at Brands Hatch. He was in hospital unconscious. I used to visit him every night after work. One night I held his hand and asked him to squeeze my hand if he could hear me. He squeezed my hand and I was able to talk to him knowing that he could hear me. I was also able to tell his other visitors that they could talk to him and he would hear them.

One night I told him I was going to see a medium the next evening to try and see if he was expected on the other side. While I was with the medium my uncle regained consciousness!

September 6, 2005

In your book you have simply written down your experiences. Most people will read what you have written and think, 'Why have I not had these experiences?' But you have invited those experiences from us. You have said [you] really want to make a difference to this world, but [you] want to allow input from the next dimension as well.

When you work in co-creation with our dimension, you are simply allowing the information and energy that we can provide to support your intent. Because it is never *our* intent, we are not entitled to make a decision for anyone on this earth plane.

If anyone tries to make decisions for your life, Dereka, they are not working with the light. They are working with the absence of the light, which is the dark. They want to take your energy, your power, your knowledge, whatever they want, using their need to control, because they do not want to access their own understanding and knowledge.

Now your book simply describes your experiences, and in that process you have recognised that we have always been a part of your journey. It took many years for you to recognise that we were adding something to your journey. We are never going to judge you, [or try] to control you, [or] decide your journey for you. You [are] now learning the only person you can ever trust is yourself. You cannot naively trust us, [or] anyone in your world, you can really only trust yourself.

So what is your question, Dereka?

Do I need to do anything to fix my knee?

Your knee is a result of not wanting to walk forwards through your life in the last thirty-five years. And now you have stopped marking time, you have decided to move forwards. Your knee will resolve, it needs some manipulation. There is some kind of misalignment. (Soon afterwards it was cured by a lady using an Egyptian Isis healing pendulum.)

So what are your other questions?

I've got some thank yous. Thank you for the stone that I found on my birthday.

On my birthday I had driven to Avebury very early in the morning and walked up on to the Ridgeway. I went to where there is a collection of stones that represents a pod of dolphins. I asked for a small stone that I might have, turned round and saw one lying on the grass. When I picked it up the grass sprang back up and was the same colour as the rest of the grass. The stone had obviously only just been put there.

Can I ask a question about one of the rocks in that Dolphin Formation? The carving on one of the stones, how did that come about?

This was a stone in the ground, yes?

On the ground, yes.

For you the energy of the dolphin signifies the freedom of the spirit. That is what you understand about the dolphin energy. That they enjoy the experience of their life and that they carry the understanding of their spirits.

Now in that formation, for you it was the energy of the freedom of your spirit. But [you] have to understand that the earth is also developing the freedom of her spirit. You will have observed that there have been changes in the world, and how the physical world is growing. As that occurs, there are changes in the environment. In this world where you have land and water, there are dolphins that can carry the energy of the spirit in the water, and there are people who can carry the energy of the spirit on the land. Then the land itself needs to carry the understanding of the spirit.

And that was what that engraving was about. It was anchoring the spirit in the land. When you work in those formations you work with the land as well.

You ask for the energy of the Divine to be anchored in those places. So you are anchoring the understanding of the spirit in that earth as well. And you understand you are a bridge between the earth and the sky. And because you work with your intellect and your heart, you can anchor that balance in the earth. And that is what that engraving was about. It was anchoring something physical.

You see the circles that come and go change something of that energy, but only for a period of time. As you go into the circle when it is first created, the energy [is] quite powerful. If you [go] into it [a] month or two months later, the energy would have dissipated. So in some ways the stone was holding that energy because the stone would not disappear. It is like [when] you have taken crystals and put them in the circles, and you have left them there. But you have [also] left in it some kind of message that you want to implant in the earth. Now crystals hold the energy of the earth, so they can be taken from one place to another, [and] continue to hold the energy. You cannot stand in the circle all the time. So you have anchored the crystal in the circle because you wanted there to be some kind of understanding in the ground. You have always worked with the energy of the earth. So when you were given that stone on your birthday, you asked what is this for in my life, and what answer did you come up with, Dereka?

That it held information.

Right. And how do you retrieve the information? Not all at once. You know it will not come all at once. You will sit with the stone, you will invite the energy, the information to be released to you. And that is what the stone in that circle was for. It was holding some information that was necessary for the earth.

You can draw a triangle, you can visualise a triangle, you can read about a triangle. They are different levels of understanding a triangle and a triangle is about balance. You can make it three dimensional and make it a pyramid.

You have worked with energy at all of these levels. You understand the intellectual element of crop circles. Just looking at the picture, that is the intellectual, the mental level. You can walk into the circle and feel the energy. That is the emotional level. You understand that it can impact upon your body, so that is the physical level. And then you realise that in all of [this] is the understanding of the spirit.

You have taken this understanding and you have written about it in your book. So you have described how you felt, how you have changed, how you even talked to our dimension because you have involved that element of spirit.

So then you realise that some people would be very challenged by what you have done. You have learned that we can communicate with you in your head, in your heart, in a physical way. So if you are given [a] stone you look at the stone and you don't just see it as a stone. You understand that it can release information into your life. Just as you can use a stone to put information into different situations. You learn how to deal with yourself [and] the earth [at] every level.

So this stone on the ground was simply a stone with a message. Now you couldn't read the message, and for you, that is where you always begin, in your head. You want to be able to read [it], but it is like another language. You understand the language of light, and light contains geometry. So then you understand that there is a message of light in everything. Many of the crop circles contain the geometry of the language of light. And that light is either going to be accessible or inaccessible because people are closed to the information. If they stood in the circle, they might in some way be impacted, but they would never attribute that change to what occurred in the circle. You know the ground itself is changed by the experience, so then you ask how does this experience improve or not improve my life? In many ways people get focussed on the intellectual element.

Your understanding of our dimension has been there since you were a child, but you [did] not realise most people do not have the same connection. And you are probably more comfortable with us than you are with most of the world in which you find yourself. You have learned how to be 'in the world' but not of it. But you have to have your feet on the ground. You cannot have one toe on the ground and the rest of your energy in our dimension, Dereka.

Your stone was given to you because you understood it was a gift of knowledge, and the stone in the circle was a message for the earth, which you did not need to understand. You did invite the knowledge from your stone to be given to you. It will be given as it is appropriate for you to receive it. You have at least learned to trust the process now, and you know it doesn't all happen at the same time. You are given the information as it is appropriate for you to receive [it]. Is that enough answer?

Yes, yes. I took it with me into a formation that day on my birthday and I started getting the information about Peru. And then I started looking in books, am I putting two and two together and getting the right answer in that book about the pyramids in Peru?

Yes. And again it is geometry. It was made into physical form, to represent the light they saw in the sky. It is pointless assuming that [all] the information is relevant to your life. You have visited Peru physically, and you went because [of] an experience you had [there] in another lifetime. But much of what you experienced in that previous lifetime is no longer there. You begin to understand what was important was that the knowledge you have is either used to control or empower. In the past you had a lifetime in Peru and you understood that when you [went]. And then you say, 'OK, what of that knowledge is still required in my life today?' The stone said you need to understand that a pyramid is a physical manifestation of light. But then people seem to think well, look at that, it is an amazing physical achievement. They forget about the energetics. So what does a pyramid say to you, Dereka?

Shape.

But what does it say? It was a place to enhance energy. It was a place to expand energy, just like all the temples that were built. You went to Machu Picchu, yes?

Yes.

What did that place say to you? It was a temple to the sun. They worshipped the light, and at that point they did not understand why there was light and why there was dark. So they worshipped the sun [because the sun] was what gave everything life.

But then you realise the sun does not disappear just because the dark is there, you learn that everything in this world is in balance. You have time for light, you have time for dark. But at Machu Picchu, they worshipped the sun. To them it was a miracle. And they worshipped it as it came up each day. But they had not learned how to integrate that understanding into themselves. They saw [it] as something greater than themselves. But you understand you carry this light. Because light is knowledge, light is life, light is your spirit. Everything is spirit. That culture did not understand their own power. They worshipped the light outside of them[selves].

In this life, Dereka, you have learned to worship the light within. You have learned that you carry this knowledge, you have come to work with this knowledge, to improve and enrich your life. But the only way that can occur is when you respect yourself and consciously take responsibility for every level of your life. So the hardest part for you was acknowledging and dealing with your emotions. What did you feel at Machu Picchu?

I felt a memory. It seemed familiar.

It did, yes. But you have moved on. You were not in any way believing this light was a god. You were going back, and you were anchoring the knowledge you have since acquired. That was why you physically went there. You were taking back to that place, not the person who worshipped the light, but a person who understands they carried the light. You were giving back to that place the knowledge that you now carry.

Right. That photograph I took in the hotel in Lima?

It shows light, yes?

Instead of the lilies I was photographing, the picture shows a pillar on the left containing what looks like a light being. In the centre of the picture there is a being with arms upraised, wearing a white robe with a black belt, and there is a collection of orbs.

What does that tell you? Many of your photographs contain this light.

Yes but this one's different. It is reminiscent of the drawing of souls in the book about the gods and the pyramids in Peru. And the being in the picture also seems to represent Viracocha or Foam of The Sea.

And there is another message for you. That is what we have done, we have given you the messages. You have taken the messages and worked with that knowledge yourself. You have not just said, 'How interesting,' and left it as a physical experience. You have taken it beyond the physical. You have incorporated that knowledge. So when you can physically see, it is in some way proof of what you already know.

One of the globes of light looks blue. Is that the communication?

Yes, blue is always the will, the communication.

So is that an indication to me to communicate all of this?

Yes, but that is what your book [will do]. You have taken what you experienced yourself. This is not someone else's experience, [it] is *your* experience. You have been willing to open yourself up to other people's ridicule, to their scorn, to their denial, whatever. Because it has been *your* experience, all you can do is say, 'Well, I have utilised this experience [in order] to develop.' You cannot only do it in your head. If you look at that picture you took at Lima, it simply confirms what you know. You did not go on that journey alone. You knew you had support energetically around you. The pictures were simply the validation of that.

Yes, like the angel.

(Two photographs I took up in the Andes on the Inca Trail showed an angel on them.)

Yes.

Was that by water or a landslip, the pictures I took that showed an angel?

It was by water.

It was water, right.

You are more fascinated with what is not physical, but it is for you to understand that there has to be the balance of both. You cannot live with your energy in our dimension. You can bring that support into your life. We can provide you with the energy, we can provide you with the information. It is just your validation [proof] that we exist. You know we exist, there is no doubt in your mind.

No.

Is that enough answer about your photograph?

Yes, yes. And that linked being on the same film as the tree that's seventeen hundred years old. That would link the energies.

Yes. There was light around the tree, yes?

Yes.

And then you realise [it] holds energy. Everything living holds the energy of the Divine, at the same level, depending on how much they are able to enhance their understanding of spirit. You understand each individual that chooses to incarnate will either enrich or enhance or energise or clear the world in which they find themselves, or they will destroy it.

Then you begin to realise that most people take the world around them for granted. And here you are trying to educate, to inform others, and most people [say], 'No, well, that is outside of my understanding, so I do not wish to discuss this with you,' instead of saying, 'How interesting, maybe I should begin to look at what you are telling me.' If you abuse the earth on which you find yourselves, ultimately you will not be able to continue your experience.

It is like your weather traumas. There are people manipulating the weather. There are many people, certainly governments, that know how to manipulate the weather. And their agenda is not for the world's benefit, it is for their own benefit. You realise it is so that they can control the people on the earth. They can only control if people allow it. And then you begin to recognise there are many people who, rather than empower their lives, will continue to play the role of the victim.

That is what the world cannot carry any longer. Each individual will contribute something constructive if they are going to be able to go forward. And there are many who have no interest in contributing anything constructive to the world. Their money becomes their god or they are willing to take everything and give nothing back. You have other questions?

The 1999 formation in which I saw fifteen number nines (Milk Hill in oilseed rape). Does that also link in with the sun gods and all the nines?

Nine is a number of completion. For you it was completion of the past. It was a recognition that there may be elements of the past that have value, but most of the past was how resolved. So this sun god that was worshipped not only in Peru but [also] in Egypt, they worshipped the sky. They did not understand it was in some way relevant to them. They never understood their own spirit and they always gave their power to others. It was a completion of that limitation so when you understand nine is at the end of a cycle, for you it was the end of a specific cycle.

It was the end of playing the game, Dereka. It was the end of being part of the illusion. And from that point forward you have been able to recognise that your life doesn't have to be what other people want it to be. We have watched you move on and take responsibility for your life, and give everyone else back the responsibility for theirs. In that period you have been back to where you worshipped the sun and you have understood it is not something to worship. It is a necessary part of your life, but it is not something you worship.

Ultimately it is about everything working in harmony together. That is what your last six years has been about. It was a completion of one cycle. It was time to move forwards, onwards and upwards. It's enough answer?

Yes, I interpret a lot , especially the oilseed rape formations as being messages from Angus, am I right?

Yes.

Yes.

They come early in the year.

You led me to find a book about Aboriginal art. Did I deduce the right things from that about the Wandjina?

Yes.

Right.

It was their limitation. They had an affinity with the earth and the sky and you can see they did not know how to utilise this knowledge in their life. You always start with the head, but now it is time to get into your heart. It is time to deal with letting go of all the emotions you have carried in your body. That is what this healing journey is about. It is not about what you have understood in your head, it is what you are now understanding in your heart.

Those original bush people were all used and abused by people who came and took away their lands. They did not know how to stand up and fight for themselves. They were told [their lives would] improve, [things] will be better, [but] in fact none of them found that to be the truth. By then it was too late because they [had been] introduced to concepts and understandings that were out of balance, and it was difficult for them to go back and recreate that life of balance. So reading the book gives you some understanding of how they [had] lived that life in balance. They lived off the land but they respected the land. They did not abuse the land. They understood they had to live in harmony with their environment. And that has been lost. So is that enough answer?

Yes, the picture of the Wandjina that I connected with the UFO that landed and the beings in there, was that correct?

(The Wandjina are mythical beings often portrayed in Aboriginal art with large dark eyes and a nose but no mouth.)

It is.

Right.

That was what the picture showed.

Yes.

Was there a lot of energy around in July?

Yes.

Right.

It is the time just after the Summer Solstice, when the light is at its greatest. That brings the energy, so it is a time when energy can be utilised. We have answered all your questions?

Yes, I think so, thank you very much.

Well we want you to understand we will provide the support and the healing on an ongoing basis.

Thank you.

We give our love to you Dereka.

And mine to you, thank you. Thank you for the red velvet heart I found by my car.

Much love.

Much love.

November 9 2010

*Y*ou said once before that I was right to interpret some of the formations (crop circles) as messages from Angus. May I ask what is his role with the formations?

What is important is that those patterns create energy. Now you are either going to understand it intellectually or you're going to understand it emotionally or you're going to understand it physically. His role was to create the emotional connections. And that is why you found them fascinating, because it started to trigger your feelings. You had a passion about [it] and you have found very little in your life to be passionate about. So that was the gift to start to open your heart chakra. And that was the purpose of his connection. Because you started out doing it in your head, and you ended up feeling it in your heart. Is that enough answer?

Would that work the same for everybody?

No, no, not at all. If you had taken your mother somewhere like that and put her in the middle of a crop circle, she would have sat there whinging and whining about the price of bread, without any understanding of what she was feeling. So you have to be willing to make the connections for yourself.

Yes, but for those people who are willing, would they have appreciated what he had put into the formations?

At some level, [but] probably not as deeply as you did. You put in the intellectual part of it first, and then you began to feel the passion. That's how you've always done it. Your head engages before your heart.

We'd like you to try to engage with both at the same time. Some people might do the intellectual bit but not be willing to go beyond that and do the emotional connecting. The opportunity is there but people may not be willing to take the opportunity. So it's important to know that you look at things at a much deeper level than most people, but that's how you want to live your life. Most people simply do it in their heads.

We have explained to the lady we are talking through, not all of those formations are made by energies of light, some are made by energies who want to control. So you have to ask what is the intent of this formation? And you have to be able to work out what you can use to enrich your life. Many people need their heart centres to be opened. Many do not have any understanding of how to observe their emotions without judgement, [but] emotions are not good or bad, right or wrong; they are simply telling you what is going on in your life. So that was the gift of those formations for you. You understand that?

Yes. I didn't go into any this summer. I somehow didn't feel the need.

No. You weren't drawn to do it. But to understand the connections is as important. In the past you have gone in and you have come out more confused than when you went in, because you have often become unsettled by those energies. You understand that? So you weren't prepared to take any [more] risks.

No.

So there is a discernment about how you work with it now.

Yes. Also I feel that the energy in the whales and the dolphins (formation) and the little yellow flower that came the year after was so amazing, I couldn't wish for anything better than that, and I still hold it.

Exactly. So you didn't see the need to take that experience further.

No.

You'd had what you needed to get from it. So it was a closure for you. A closure of the circle, a completion.

Right.

And you can observe how people just get intellectually involved. They don't actually deal with a deeper meaning [but] you got your deeper meaning.

Yes.

It's enough answer?

Yes, yes thank you. Can I ask a question about Avebury?

Yes.

How did ancient man transport the stones there?

As you are aware there have been connections, you call them avatars, on this planet for many, many aeons. And they used skills that are probably not available today.

Right.

And it was to anchor there a place of connection to the earth and the sky. And that is why it has remained. It is to bring a place of connection between the earth and the sky. And that is what people forget. Most people are living in their heads, not grounded in the earth. And you have learned to be grounded in your body. You have learned you have to deal with all aspects of your own life. So they were using energetic skills that are not available today.

Right. Is that the same with the stonework in Peru at Saqsayhuaman and similar places?

Yes. Because those stones were not natural to that environment. So it was not as though they were brought from a local area.

Right.

So it has taken men with many intellectual questions to just deal with the tip of the iceberg. Because underneath the physical there is an energetic message. But what you need to realise is that you have probably outgrown the messages. You have your own connections, so you don't need to have those connections in a physical manner. It was for people who did not have an ability to connect to the energy realms of light. It made it easier to do that.

Right.

And it became a kind of shrine where people would come to invoke energy, whereas now it is not used for that purpose.

No.

It is just shown as an interesting experience. And it can also be manipulated by the dark energies. You have always worked with the light to empower, you do not want to control anything.

No.

But there are energies in our dimension that do want to control your dimension. So they can use those energy portals for that intent if they are allowed to. Does that answer your question?

Yes, yes thank you.

So why [and] how they happened is not relevant. What is important is that at that point it was the easiest way for people to make the connections between the earth and the sky. You understand? So we have answered all of your questions?

Not all my questions, no. Can I ask more?

Yes.

Was it a message from the dolphins in the Atlantic about waiting for four days to be rescued?

It was a cry for help. You sent out a message of support, yes? And you got the message that it was a cry for help. What you have to understand is that, like everything, man has lost the balance between having enough and wanting more. And the dolphins are now utilised as part of business ventures, yes? And that was never their role in the bigger picture. They were to show people that you could go through life without carrying any baggage. That you could live with joy in the now. And that is what they offer and they have been traumatised in certain areas and this was the message for support.

Right.

And you sent some kind of energetic healing, yes?

What I was asking about was when I was shipwrecked.

Yes . . .

And I got the message saying I would be rescued, but I'd got to wait four days.

Yes . . .

Was that from the dolphins?

It was from the high realms. Why would you perceive the dolphins singularly as the high realms?

It was something I read in a book about dolphin telepathic communication with humans, and they did play around the boat the night before the storm and I wondered if it was a message from them.

No, it was a message from the high realms.

Right.

And it came to pass, yes?

Yes.

And the dolphins were affected by the trauma of what happened to the ship.

Yes.

So in some ways they were wanting you to be assured that they had to address their trauma. And they didn't want you to experience any more trauma than you had to.

Aahh!

So it wasn't necessarily just from them, it was a message from the high realms. And for you it was quite a comforting message.

Oh, very.

And you were happy to wait.

Oh yes, in that knowledge.

Yes, because it came to pass, yes?

It did.

You were given the information so that there would be as little trauma as possible for you.

Thank you.

You understand? But the dolphins could feel the trauma. They have the ability to feel what is happening energetically, you understand?

423

Yes, I do.

It's enough.

Yes thank you.

Well we think that perhaps we have answered enough for now.

Right.

So we will now withdraw. Please just give us a minute to withdraw, but first we give you our love.

Thank you and mine to you, thank you very much.

Just please give us a minute and much love.

Thank you . . .

- oOo -

Then Mavis said, 'They said have you completed the book?'

I'm working on it now.

O.K. so it is completed in your head?

Just about.

O.K. that's fine. They said that's been part of your healing.

June 7 2011

Now with this book, you want to explain to others what you know. Now what if they do not understand or want to understand what you know? How will you deal with that?

That's not my problem, it's their problem.

Oh! You have learned well. You have understood well. So why do you need to put the information out there?

I just feel I need to, to try and help other people to understand what I understand.

Okay fine, so you are offering others an opportunity. Whether they take it or not is none of your business. So what are the questions you would like us to answer?

Well, one question is who are you to me?

We are the observers of your life. Every spirit that incarnates is given the responsibility for one physical, one emotional, one mental and one spiritual body. They come into this world and all of that understanding is taken away by people's limitations.

So, at the end of your life, we ask you this question – what did you learn of responsibility for your physical, emotional, mental and spiritual welfare, and what did you teach by the example of your life to others?

Now most people do not even understand that question, [but] you would answer openly and honestly. But you are among what we call the 3% of conscious people on this planet, people who know they are spirits having a human experience, who know they have come through this experience many times, and who know that at the end of the physical journey their spirit comes home.

The challenge during your lifetime is to develop and grow to become more of who you really are. So we are the observers of your life. Each spirit can invite support as they require it. The only things we can provide from our dimension are information and energy because we work with the light. The light empowers, the dark disempowers. The dark takes away people's power. So you can observe that when you invite information or energy [during] these connections (readings), we have never been judgemental, we have never made you [feel] wrong or bad, we simply told you what we have observed. And many people find that too challenging and scary to deal with.

You have never been scared by us. You have always found it comforting to know there is someone observing and supporting your journey. Because [you] did not feel there were many physical people doing that for you. So, in some ways, we were your lifeline to what we would call 'home'. [For you] it was like, 'Well, I know that is home and I know where I am now does not feel like home, but I know by coming into this physical experience I can develop and grow.'

When you come home you cannot change, you cannot grow. There is no polarity, therefore there is no resistance, and therefore no growth. You are simply going to remain at the level you were at when you left [your] earth plane. But what is interesting is that people who have returned while the energy of the earth is rising, would not be able to return. Because as it rises the energy brings up anything that does not resonate with it.

And that is why so many people are leaving the planet, because they are not addressing any of those issues. They could not return because it would simply bring up the same issues and create another dysfunction in their physical form. People have understood that the earth's energy was rising for many years. It started in 1987 [and] will complete in 2012. And during that time if you are incarnated and wanting at some point to reincarnate, you have to do the work to raise your levels of energy to match the earth's energy. And you have been doing that.

Yet you look around you at the people who have not even asked the question, 'What is the purpose of my life?' So you have to look at what you are dealing with, [but] not need to fix it or change it.

Other people's issues are not your issues. Your issues are to inform, like we would inform, you can inform. What people do with that information is their choice, not yours, you understand? And many people on this so-called path carry ego, and we always consider that the spiritual ego is the worst. It is the old religious point of view, we are holier than you, we are the only ones who can connect to the Divine for you! Now that is not the truth, the Divine is within everything, not external to anything. But religion does not want you to know that, so religion says, 'We are going to connect to the Divine for you. We are holier than you, you are less than us.' And that is why you could not *ever* have gone down the road of religion.

We have been a comfort blanket for you, because it gave you the understanding that you were not walking your pathway alone. For much of your life it seemed like you were, there was no partner, there was no understanding, there was no companionship, it felt like you were walking the journey alone. [But] you have not walked one step of your journey alone. We cannot walk your steps for you, we can simply guide and support the steps you make, you understand? Does that answer your question?

Yes . . . observers

We observe.

Could I call you my guides?

You can call us anything you wish. The lady we talk through has asked who we are and we have given her the name 'wisdom'. That is what we bring, wisdom. We are not people like you. You could not describe us as people with forms like you because we are not. We are simply energy. We are knowledge, we are wisdom. How would you describe that in physical form? We do not have physical form. So what you wish to call us is irrelevant.

We know what your questions are, we know what you want to understand. And the more you understand of truth, the more you will look at how different you are to the world in which you find yourself. And you don't want to be like the world in which you find yourself.

So you can call us anything you wish. We don't mind.

Right, I've called you 'the energies'.

You can call us 'the energies', you can call us your friends, you can call us whatever you wish, the support structure of your journey, it does not matter. What matters is you know that if you invite information or energy, it will arrive, not necessarily at the snap of your fingers, but in Divine right order, and you are learning that. You are listening to the voice within more and more. You are trusting the voice within more and more. And you are very careful about what you talk about to others because they want to put you in the 'wacky box', and it isn't the wacky box where you belong. So you are more discerning about what you tell people. That's when you need a sense of humour, Dereka, you understand?

'What? You hear voices?' they say, 'really?' If only they knew that everyone has this intuition, the teaching from within. But most of them don't trust what they are given. They would far rather put you in the wacky box, so your sense of humour is vital. That is what keeps you sane, your sense of humour. What do these people know? How to give you another pill, how to give you another label, how to put you in the wacky box? It's very easy to dismiss what is staring them in the face. So you don't have to justify what you are feeling or what you are being told or what your life contains. Your life is probably more stable than theirs, Dereka. You are not looking for answers outside of yourself.

Your conversations with us have really only been validation of what you have been experiencing, because you needed some kind of comfort to help you understand that you were not crazy. You can 'see' as well as 'hear', and sometimes what you see you do not want to believe, but you have learned to accept it as reality.

We look back at many of the experiences you have had and they were as real when you wrote about them as when you had them. They were not something you could dismiss, because they were real. And yet it only seemed to occur when you were alone.

Yes.

It did not seem to occur when you were with others.

No.

Because when you are with others, their energy contaminates yours. And they were messages for you, not for others. And you often did not understand the messages. We want you to understand most of it was to give you comfort.

Right, thank you.

Because there seemed to be very little comfort in your life. Your life seemed to have been one long struggle, trying to make sense of a world that had very little sense in it. Now you're not looking for sense in this world, you're not trying to fit in, you're not trying to give up being who you are. You're trying to be *more* of who you are, the intuitive sensitive lady who understands she is a spirit having a human experience. And if other people do not understand that, so what? Is that enough answer?

Yes, thank you.

You have other questions?

Yes, the last time we spoke you talked about not all of the formations, the crop circles, being made by energies of light. Then you said some are made by people who want to control. Did you mean human beings or energies?

No, energies.

Right, may I change that?

Yes.

Good, thank you.

It is just we used the word 'people' so that you could understand they were different to the energies of light.

Yes, when I played the tape to a friend of mine she picked up on it straight away and said 'people?', as if you were giving credit to humans.

No, no, no, they were energies who want to control. You understand that?

Yes, but I didn't want to change it without asking.

No, no, no it is fine. What you understand is everything is energy. You understand that, but that energy comes in physical form to be able to function in this physical world. But basically it is energy.

We all know that physical people have tried to fool people by doing these things. But they do not have the precision, and it is the mathematical precision that creates the energy. It is the same with your religious buildings; they have a certain mathematical structure which creates a certain energy. But a church is not built to empower anyone. A church is built to disempower the masses. It is a place where you go to feel less than someone else. So they used the mathematics to control people.

And that's what they do in the crop circles?

Some of them, yes. But you would know the difference in the energy of the different circles you have entered. You have observed how those formations make you feel. You are in touch with how you feel. [You] always [need to be] discerning, [and ask] is this appropriate for me to be part of? Those formations can allow those energies to come on to this planet. It is like a portal, you understand a portal?

Yes.

They create the doorway to allow them[selves] access to the earth's energy. Sometimes the energies are to allow you to connect to our world. Sometimes the energies are for our world to connect with your world. There is a vast difference. So it is necessary that you understand the battle that goes on between the light and the dark.

There have always been polarities, the positives and the negatives. None of them is good or bad, right or wrong, they are just different. Night is not worse than day and day is not worse than night, they are just part of a cycle. The dark is simply the absence of the light, the light is simply the transforming of the dark.

Nothing physically changes, just the energy of the experience changes. You carry the light, Dereka, the light empowers and the light offers knowledge. That's what we offer, knowledge. But most people do not accept our knowledge, it is outside their parameters of understanding. It has taken many lifetimes for you to get this amount of knowledge.

You can't expect someone who has not had those experiences to understand the things you understand. It doesn't make you better than them, it just means you carry more light than them. So if you shine your light into a darkened room, people may not want to look at the reality.

That's what your book will do. Your book is very open and honest and it is very, we are going to use the word *damning* of people who consider themselves light workers, you understand?

Yes.

And they may not want to look at themselves in that mirror of truth, Dereka. Best you don't need to prove yourself to any of them, you understand?

Yes.

Because often the dark is disguised in words of light. But that does not mean they are light workers. And it is when you observe the spiritual ego that you know they are definitely not of the light. It is not, 'We are better than you,' because nobody is any better than anybody else. They may be different to but they're not better than. That is simply their perception. So it's enough answer to that question?

Yes, thank you. Can I ask about that photograph that I took in the hotel in Lima?

Yes.

Is the being in the white robe in the centre, is that Viracocha?

No.

Right. Why do I feel such a strong connection with Viracocha?

That person, that energy is the same as yours. But that being in your photograph was not [him]. Your photographs have often shown figures, and usually you do not know who they are. It was simply for you to understand that there were beings around you. And that again was to bring you comfort.

Right, thank you.

But you got your head involved in it. Your head is always wanting to dot the 'i's and cross the 't's. You do not need to know who the energies are, maybe you just had to know there are beings constantly present. [It] is of interest for you to see what beings you can capture [with your camera].

Well, to my knowledge I've only captured this one.

But you are still hoping you will capture others.

Well, I've given up taking photographs now.

Why did you need to have confirmation? You've had [that]; you've had your confirmation. Perhaps you just needed to see what you knew was there, you understand? You saw on your photograph what you could not physically see [with your eyes]. That was your confirmation that these beings exist. You cannot see them with the physical eye, but sometimes you can capture their energy. You have captured it in light many times.

Yes.

So you have seen it in that form. But this time it was more in human form. That was the difference for you. You knew when you got light in your photographs, that was energy, but this time there was a figure, so that was very exciting for you.

Yes, it was.

Because it was your confirmation that the naked eye cannot always see what is there. So it was for you, that message, not for others. But you can share it with others, you understand?

Yes, but I interpreted it as being Viracocha in the white robe with the belt from what I read in the book, The Lost Tomb of Viracocha.

But why did you need it to be that energy? That energy walks with you, the one you have discussed.

432

Right.

That energy does walk with you. You could understand what you have read about. It resonated with you, with some of your experiences.

Yes.

And you wanted some assurance that this person was with you. Well, that energy is with you. And by reading the history [of] it, it was simply confirming what you already knew. It brought up memories for you.

Yes.

It was like, 'I understand this because I have experienced this.' That is simply for you to have understanding of where you come from. You know you have lived many lifetimes. None of [them] are relevant to understand in detail because all of that knowledge you carry.

It is about trusting what you know. That's what this journey is always about, Dereka, trusting what you know. Not justifying what you know, not proving what you know, just trusting what you know.

If somebody said to you you have to give up your knowledge about the next dimension, there is no such thing, could you give up your knowledge?

No.

It is what you know and that's what's important, trusting what you know. Not trusting what other people tell you, but trusting what you know. If, as we said, ten thousand people said this is not true, it wouldn't make one iota of difference to you. You *know* it is true.

You've had enough experience to know that you are energy, there are other energies, that the whole experience of everything is energy. And if the scientists tell you different, you're not going to accept it. So that is what you're here to do, trust what you know.

That photograph was simply to say, 'The energies are around you.' You may not see them physically, but they are around you. It's enough answer?

Yes. Was the pillar with what looks like a light being in it, was that representing the Mayan Sun Glyph Ben?

Yes, yes. That was something you understood.

Yes.

What did that mean to you?

It was confirmation of who I am.

Okay fine, so that is trusting what you know. You have any other questions?

Can you repeat what you said to me when we first spoke, about your having no emotions, and feeling through me?

We do not have any emotions. The emotion is part of the physical experience. We can experience emotion by observing your journey. When you come home there is no emotion, there is just love, or what we call the Divine.

It is just about being. But if you come into physical human form, you can experience the [whole] gamut of emotion. And each of those emotions is information. It is telling you what is happening. And what most people do is ignore how they feel, the challenge is to get the balance between the head and the heart. And for most of your life you have been driven by your heart, and not had it in balance with your head. Now you have a balance between your head and your heart, you don't dismiss what you feel.

So we can observe emotion by observing your journey, but it is your gift to have those feelings, it is not of value to us. Sadness says there is something missing from or leaving your life. Anger is about betrayal, your expectations have not been fulfilled. So you have to look at why your expectations are not realistic. And fear is the absence of the Divine, fear is believing you might get it wrong. And as you understand with your head that you cannot get it wrong, you start to walk through your fears, one by one by one. And the more you walk through your fears, the less they can control your life. So now you do not allow your fears to limit your life. It's enough answer?

Yes, thank you.

We have answered everything?

Is there anything else you would like to say in the book about crop circles?

You have written those experiences from your perspective. You have put a small introduction about how you got involved in them, which is really what the book is about. It is about your experience of crop circles, so it does not need any further explanations. You explained what drew you to that experience, and what you gained from it, and [the] connection. So it is not about us, Dereka, it is about your experience of them.

This is your journey, and how the crop circles have been part of that experience. Now you are much more discerning about how they could or could not enrich your life. Now you are not drawn to them in the same way.

I don't go into them now.

No, that's what we say, you're not drawn to them in the same way. Because you understand that it is a part of your journey of growth, it is not all of your journey. People seem to become obsessed by them and you are no longer obsessed by them. You are just grateful for the gifts they have given you.

Oh, very.

Is that enough answer?

Is Angus still involved with them?

Slightly.

Right.

It is the obsession that is unhealthy, when you see them as a complete solution. Nothing is a complete solution. The crop circles are information, what you do with that information [can] enrich your life. But there always needs to be questions asked and answers provided. If you ask ten people the same question, you will get ten different answers. People just manipulate the information to suit them[selves].

That's when the spiritual ego becomes involved, 'We have the answer.' And you think, 'Well, it might be your answer, [but] it's not my answer.'

That's when you need your sense of humour. It's all in the interpretation, and they want you to believe their interpretation is the right interpretation, [but] most of it is nonsense. It's enough answer?

Yes, thank you.

Well, we trust this has helped.

Yes, thank you very much.

We are really proud of what you have achieved and as you stop moving side[ways], and take those steps forward, the focus is how to improve and enrich the quality of your life. That is what is important now, not proving yourself to anybody.

Part of the experience has been the cathartic writing of [your] experiences from your point of view, and putting it out there without fear of what people [might] do or say, because you don't care what people do or say, it's what happened. And you don't necessarily have to explain why it happened that way, or what it means for you to have experienced [it]. It is just [your] experience.

So we thank you for this time, Dereka.

Thank you.

We are quite happy to share the journey with those who invite the support.

Oh, good, thank you.

So, much love to you and we will now withdraw. Please just give us a minute to withdraw.

- oOo -

Then Mavis said, "They're showing me this picture of a tree, and they said you've really got roots now on this earth, you're not trying to get off it. You've got roots down into it and you're stable like the tree."

That makes a change!

"I think most of our lives we've wanted to get off it, Dereka," continued Mavis. "What am I doing here and who are these people? I know that, only too well. But I've accepted the 'gift' of being here. Because this is where we can grow, this is where we can do the work, and we can't do it when we go home, so it's no good rushing home. We've got to stay here until the energy stops rising, to just hold that energy for those who may or may not want to work on it.

Index of Photographs